HARPER'S OUTDOOR BOOK
FOR BOYS

BY

JOSEPH H. ADAMS

WITH CONTRIBUTIONS BY
KIRK MUNROE, TAPPAN ADNEY
CAPT. HOWARD PATTERSON
LEROY MILTON YALE
AND OTHERS

WITH MANY ILLUSTRATIONS

HARPER & BROTHERS PUBLISHERS
NEW YORK AND LONDON

CONTENTS

Part I

IN BOUNDS

vii

CONTENTS

viii

CONTENTS

ix

CONTENTS

INTRODUCTION

" HOW to do it," might very well be the title of this new handy-book for American boys. It is first and last a practical guide, based upon the experience of those who have done what they describe. Results are wanted, not theories in a book of this kind, and careful tests have been applied to secure working results and the certainty that everything will come out all right.

Another point, which has had the most careful attention of a board of editors, is that of selection. It would be easy to include a quantity of sports and games, and also plans for elaborate contrivances neither particularly amusing nor necessary when done. But the object of this book is to show boys how to do accurately things which are quite within their powers, and things also which will be a satisfaction when they are done. The plan followed is to develop a boy's ingenuity and mechanical ability along lines which will reward him. In short, the book is intended to help a boy to think and act for himself and to have fun in doing it.

The plan of arrangement which is followed is the natural one—to begin at home. The back yard lies immediately at hand. Let us see what can be done there. The aquarium, pet shelters, windmills, and many other contrivances are identified with the home.

INTRODUCTION

Going farther afield we learn the making of coasters and skees, ice-boats and snow cannon, and all that enters into winter sports. There is the air, also, with its invitation to kites and aeroplanes, and there is water, with all the chances for the use of water-power and sport. Fishing itself is something best learned by experience, but the choice and management of tackle afford a most instructive theme. And water naturally has an importance which requires an entire division of the book wherein boat-building and boat-management of all kinds are thoroughly and practically explained.

Camping out, which appeals to every healthy boy, is treated from every point of view in the fourth division of the book, which includes also trapping, taxidermy, and tree huts and brush houses.

In all these general divisions the aim of the editors and author has been to show in the simplest and most accurate way how to do things which are amusing to do and valuable when done.

The principal contributor to this book is an amateur carpenter, boat-builder, and mechanician as well as an artist and writer. One editor has had a wide practical experience in almost everything that has to do with out-door amusements. Another has camped and fished in the four corners of our country and in Canada. All their experience has been combined to prepare a convenient out-door handy-book free from unnecessary words and details, and filled with the latest and best methods, which will be indispensable to every American boy who likes the fun of doing things for himself.

Part I

IN BOUNDS

OUT-DOOR BOOK FOR BOYS

Chapter I

BACK-YARD PLEASURES

SINCE home is the natural centre of life, it will be most helpful if we find out what we can do just outside the house. In large cities there is usually no front yard, and even where such space exists its use as a play-ground is apt to be undesirable. But the back yard even in cities often affords some chances not only for gardening on a small scale but also for making and using a variety of things which will furnish constant amusement.

A Wigwam

For boys who like to "play Injun" in the back yard, here are some ideas for tepees and wigwams that may easily be followed out at a very small cost for the poles and canvas.

Canvas can be bought at a dry-goods or country store, and poles may be cut in the woods; or one-and-one-half-inch-square spruce sticks may be purchased at a lumber-yard and dressed round with a draw-knife and plane. When

2

cutting poles for a wigwam it is necessary to select very straight ones, preferably of pine, for crooked or knotty poles are unsightly and make an uneven exterior.

The real Indian tepee is made from buckskin or other strong hides lashed together with rawhide thongs; but as this covering is beyond the reach of the average boy, the next best thing to use will be heavy twilled canvas or stout unbleached muslin that can be had for about ten cents a yard. The regulation wigwam is perhaps the most satisfactory kind of a tent, for it is roomy, will shed water, and it is about the only tent in which a fire may be built without smoking out the occupants. The tepee will not blow over if properly set up and stayed with an anchor-rope, and it is easily taken down and moved from place to place.

For a party of three or four boys the wigwam shown in Fig. 1 will afford ample room, and it is not so large as to be unhandy. Select thirteen straight poles, not more than two inches thick at the bottom, and clear them from knots and projecting twigs. They should be ten feet long and pointed at the bottom so as to stick into the ground for a few inches. Tie three of them together eighteen inches from the top, and form a tripod on a circle five feet and six inches in diameter. Place the other poles against this tripod to form a cone, as shown in Fig. 2, and lash them fast at the top with a piece of clothes-line. From unbleached muslin or sail-cloth (light weight) make a cover as shown in the diagram Fig. 3. Lay out a sixteen-foot circle on a barn floor, or the grass, with chalk, and indicate an eighteen-inch circle at the middle. Around the outer circle or periphery measure off nineteen feet and chalk-mark the

4

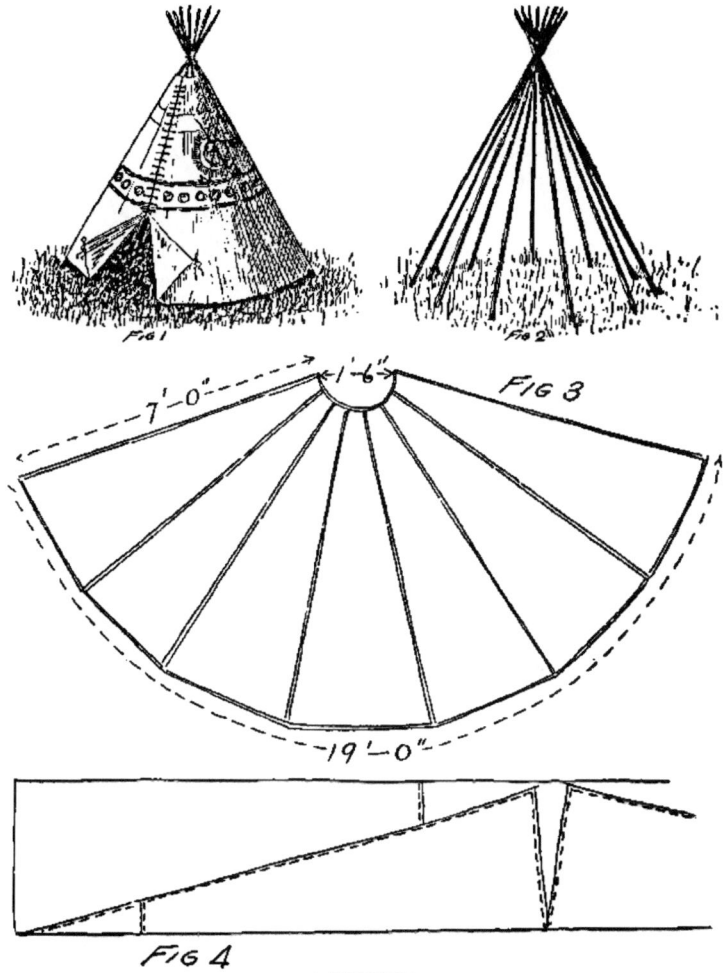

FIG 1

FIG 2

FIG 3

7'-0"   1'-6"

19'-0"

FIG 4

A WIGWAM

space. From these marks to the centre of the circle draw straight lines, and within these limits the area of the wigwam cover will be shown. It should correspond with the plan drawing in Fig. 3. The muslin should be three feet wide and with it this area can be covered in any direction, sewing the strips together to make the large sheet; or the muslin may be cut in strips three feet wide at one end and tapering to a few inches at the other, as shown in Fig. 4, the seams running up and down the canvas instead of across it. The outer edge of the canvas cover should be bound with clothes-line or cotton rope, sewed securely with waxed white string; then thirteen short ropes should be passed over this rope so that the canvas may be lashed fast to the foot of each pole to hold the cover in place. The doorway flaps are formed by stopping the lacings three feet up from the ground. With short ropes and rings sewed to the cover the flaps may be tied back, as shown in Fig. 1.

The real Indian wigwams are decorated with all sorts of emblems, for even the uncivilized red men had their crests and totems, and the boys who make these tepees can easily invent some mark which will distinguish their tent abode from all others. The ornamentation should be done with paint and should be carried out before the canvas covering is stretched over the poles.

A Square Tepee

A square tepee, as shown in the illustration Fig. 5, is another form of rear-yard tent that is easily made. Twelve poles are selected and four of them are lashed fast and spread

6

apart on a square of six feet. Two poles are added to each side and all are lashed together at the head. Four pieces of canvas or heavy unbleached muslin are cut and made on the plan as shown in Fig. 6, the strips being cut from goods a yard wide. These pieces are six feet long, one foot wide

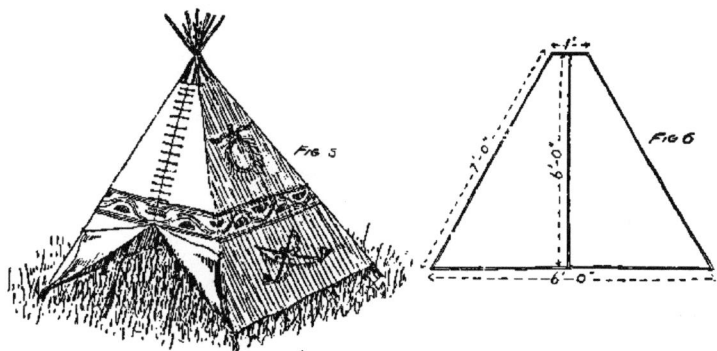

at the head, and six feet at the foot. The seam through the middle of one piece is left open for three feet to form the doorway flaps, then the four sides are securely sewed together with waxed white string. This cover is slipped about the pole frame, tied at the front, and held down by means of short ropes that are lashed fast to the foot of each pole. The cover is decorated with paint to give it the Indian appearance, and when the flaps are tied back it is easy to go into and come out of the tepee.

A Ridge-pole Tepee

A ridge - pole tepee is shown in Fig. 7, and is a very easy and simple one to make, for it is of one piece of canvas with two flaps sewed at each side to form the ends.

One ridge and two upright poles make the framework, and they are held in place by the canvas, which is drawn and lashed fast to stakes driven in the ground, as may be seen in the drawing. The ridge-pole is eight feet long, one and

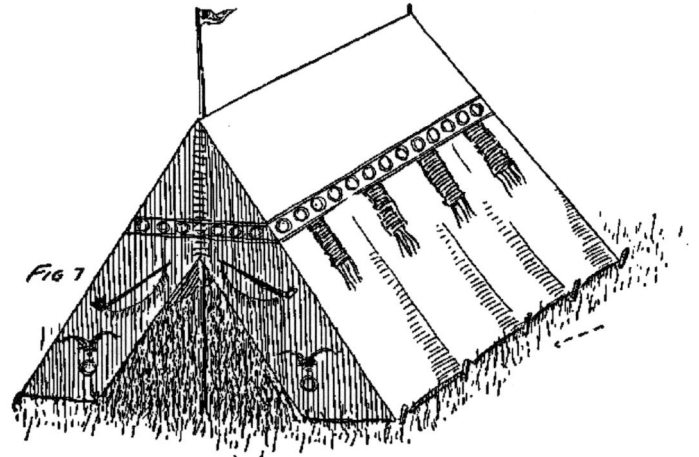

FIG 7

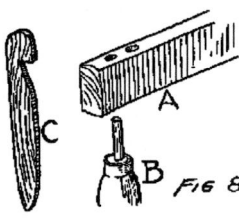

A

C

B FIG 8

a half inches thick, and four inches wide. Two inches from either end a half-inch hole is bored to receive the iron pins that are driven in the ends of the uprights as shown at Fig. 8 A and

B. The upright poles are eight feet long, and when set one foot of the lower end should be embedded in the

8

ground. The sides are in one piece of muslin made by sewing widths of it together. The sheet measures seventeen feet long and eight feet wide; and when stretched over the ridge-pole and fastened down at both sides an inverted shape will be the result. It is ten feet across at the bottom, seven feet high, and eight feet long at each side. For the back it will be necessary to make a triangular piece of canvas the right size to fit the opening, or two flaps may be cut, divided at the middle, and tied back, or laced, to close the tent. The apron or part enclosure at the front is formed from pieces of canvas two feet wide sewed along the edges and caught together at the middle over the opening.

Ten pegs eighteen inches long and two inches wide are cut from hard-wood as shown at Fig. 8 C. These are driven in the ground at an angle and ropes attached to the lower edges of the canvas sidings are lashed fast to them. This tepee is long enough to swing a hammock from pole to pole, and on a warm summer night makes an ideal place for sleeping out-of-doors. The covering, like that of the other wigwams, may be decorated with Indian emblems, and if a party of boys are going to camp in the back yard their tepees can be inscribed with different crests and totems to indicate individual ownership.

A Fountain

A practicable rear-yard fountain may be made with a brick or concrete basin, an underground pipe-line and an overflow, thus insuring a continuous flow and discharge.

In Fig. 9 the basin, pipe, and trap are shown with the inlet·pipe fitted for a hose connection. Three plates of different sizes are used for the traps, and if care is taken in drilling the holes an opening may be made in the bottom of each plate so that it will slip over the stand-pipe. Tin or enamelled iron plates will answer the purpose very well for a while, but the tin plates would soon rust unless frequently painted. The white earthern-ware plates will present the best appearance and will last indefinitely.

Dig a circular hole thirty inches across and twelve inches deep, and with cement and sand make a hard bottom or bed. Use a trowel and smooth the cement so that the top surface is smooth. With some bricks form a circle, as shown at Fig. 10. With a cold-chisel and mallet cut away the edges of two bricks so that the overflow pipe will pass between them, as shown at A in Fig. 10.

The pipe should be half or three-quarter inch galvanized water-pipe, and it may be purchased at a plumber's shop for a few cents a foot.

The supply-pipe is three-eighths-inch galvanized water-pipe, and should be set in place under the concrete bottom of the basin before the cement is poured in. The upright, or stand-pipe, is thirty-six inches high from the elbow, B (Fig. 10), in the ground. The cross-pipe leading out is eighteen or twenty inches long, and the short upright that comes to the surface outside the basin is fifteen inches long and is to be provided with a hose connection so that a garden hose may be attached to it. The stand-pipe in the basin and the cross-piece should be embedded in the cement concrete, and when it is dry and hardens around the pipes

10

it will hold them securely in place. When the circle of bricks is complete, fill in the crevices with equal parts of cement and sand mixed into a mortar. This will lock the bricks together; then plaster the cement all around the inside of the circle and some at the outside so as to make a water-tight basin.

Earth is to be put back into the hole outside the circle of bricks and the sod replaced, so that grass will grow right

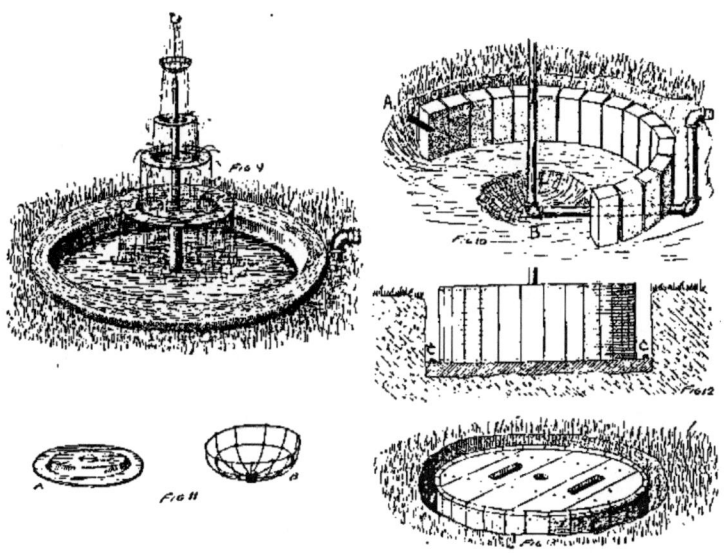

up to the edge of the basin rim, which should project an inch or two above the surface of the ground.

From a plumber or gas-fitter obtain some old pieces of brass tubing an inch in diameter, cut one of them fourteen inches long, and slip it down over the stand-pipe. The lowest and largest plate rests on this. Next cut a piece of tubing nine inches long and slip it over the pipe. The second plate rests on this and the top plate is supported by a piece of the tubing cut six inches in length and slipped over the pipe. If porcelain dishes are used, make the first hole in them as follows:

Obtain a stout, three-inch steel wire nail, a block of wood about three inches square, having an inch hole bored at one end, and a small hard-wood mallet. Place a plate on the block of wood, inverted so that its centre will be exactly over the hole. Place the point of the nail on the plate, taking care to get it in the centre; then give it a sharp, quick blow with the mallet. If this is properly done a small piece of the porcelain will be driven out, but remember that if the blow is not properly centred it will break the plate. For this reason it is best to practise first on a broken plate; or if the porcelain seems to be impossible, the painted tin or enamelled plates will have to answer. A perforated porcelain plate is shown in Fig. 11 A. The ragged hole can be smoothed out or chafed away with an old rat-tail or half-round file. A brass reducer and a gas pillar should be screwed fast to the top of the stand-pipe so that a jet of water about a quarter of an inch in diameter will shoot above the pipe.

If a little wooden ball is to dance at the top of the jet, a half-circular basket will be necessary to catch the ball when it falls, so that the stream of water can pick it up again. This is made from brass or galvanized wire, and where the wires cross bind the joint with fine copper wire and solder the joints so as to make them rigid. A small brass ferrule or short piece of pipe should be soldered to the bottom of this basket, so as to hold it in place when slipped over the pillar or nozzle. This basket and its shape is more clearly shown in Fig. 11 B. It should be six or eight inches in diameter and three inches deep, with the wires close enough together to prevent the ball from falling through.

If it is not possible to get the bricks of which to form the basin, a concrete wall can be made instead. Dig the hole as before described; then construct a cylinder of wood twenty-four inches in diameter and eight inches thick. Floor over the bottom of the hole with concrete, after the stand-pipe is in place, and around the edge of the concrete floor and outside the cylinder embed some small stones so that the filling will hold fast. This is shown at c c in Fig. 12. Slip the wooden cylinder over the stand-pipe so that it will occupy the position as shown in Fig. 12. Make a mixture of coarse sand or gravel and cement, half and half, and add a shovel or two of small stones, preferably cracked, such as are used for the under-dressing to macadam roads. Tamp this down in the opening in the ground so as to fill up the ditch or moat as shown at Fig. 13. The outside of the cylinder should be thoroughly coated with lard or some heavy grease before the concrete is poured in, so that the wood will not absorb the moisture from the concrete and cause it to bind in the hole. As a precaution it would be well to make the bottom of the cylinder an inch smaller in diameter than the top, so that it may draw out easily after the concrete has set. The two slots shown in the top of the cylinder are hand holes to grasp it by.

With nearly clear cement, having but a small portion of sand added, finish the inside of the basin and the rim with a trowel so as to give it a smooth and even surface. The force of water may be regulated with a faucet.

An Aquarium

There is nothing difficult in the construction of a glass-and-wood aquarium like the one shown in Fig. 14, and the boy who is handy with tools and careful in joining wood-

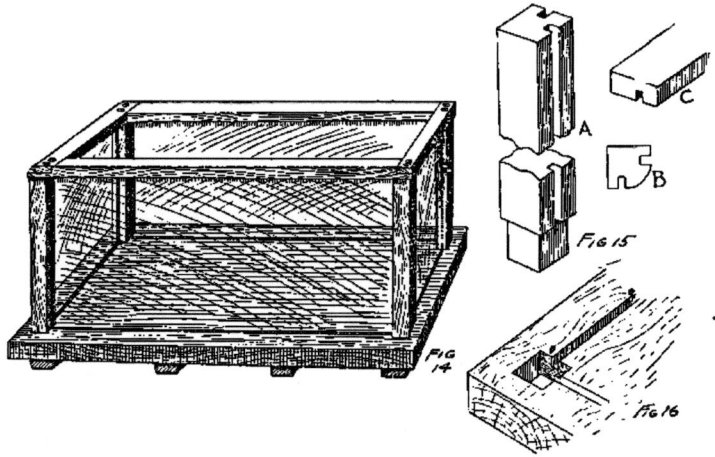

work accurately will be able to knock it together in short order. The best size will be twenty-four inches long, fifteen wide, and ten inches high. This will be generous enough in proportions to accommodate a dozen or so of small fish, some baby eels, crawfish, a turtle or two, and some water-lizards.

14

From a carpenter obtain a piece of white-wood twenty-seven inches long, seventeen inches wide, and one and a half inches in thickness. This must be of selected stock, hard and free from knots or sappy places. Cut four battens of hard-wood two inches wide, an inch thick, and fifteen inches long, and with brass screws attach them securely to the underside of the board to prevent its warping from the action of the water. Obtain a stick one inch and a half square and four feet long; cut this into lengths of eleven inches each and also prepare one eight feet long, two inches wide, and seven-eighths of an inch thick. With a groove-plane having a quarter - inch blade cut into the square stick on two sides as shown in Fig. 15 A. The edge of the stick between the two grooves may then be planed off so that an end view of the stick will appear as shown at Fig. 15 B. A groove should be cut at one side of the long stick three-eighths of an inch from one edge so that when turned groove side down an end will appear as shown at C in Fig. 15. This stick is to be cut in lengths fifteen and twenty-four inches respectively for top rails.

In the four corners of the white-wood board cut a hole with bit and chisel three-quarters of an inch square as shown at Fig. 16. Saw the bottom of each square stick so as to cut away about a quarter of an inch of wood on each side as shown at the lower part of A in Fig. 15. This is made so that the uprights will fit snugly into the holes and the shoulder formed by the saw-cuts will rest on the top of the base board.

With straight rule and pencil mark parallel lines connecting each hole as shown at D D in Fig. 16. These lines should

15

correspond in position with the grooves cut in the posts; then remove the posts and with grooving-plane or chisel and mallet cut the grooves about three-eighths of an inch in depth. The glass sides fit into these grooves, and the top rails made from the long stick cap the upper edges of the glass sides. The ends should be lapped and screwed down to the top of the corner-posts to bind the glass and wood-work in one compact framework.

Before any of the wood-work is put together give it three successive thin coats of black asphaltum varnish, which can be purchased at a paint or hardware store. Each hole and the plug ends of the corner-posts are to be coated with thick asphaltum varnish, and when wet with the varnish the posts are to be driven into the holes. Screws passed in through the sides of the base board will hold them securely in place.

From a glazier or hardware store purchase two panes of double-thick glass ten by fourteen inches, and two measuring ten by twenty-two inches. Give the grooves a thick coat of the asphaltum varnish, slide the glass down into the grooves, and screw the top rails in place. When the glass is in place and before the top rails are put on, the glass should stand a quarter of an inch above the top of the corner-posts. When the rails are laid in place the top edge of the glass should be caught by the groove in the rails, otherwise the glass, having no support at the top, would bow out on account of the pressure of water, and either cause the glass to break or the joints to leak. Press the glass sides against the outer edges of the grooves and lightly insert some wooden wedges into the grooves to hold the glass in place temporarily for a day or two or until the varnish sets.

Then fill the open spaces in the grooves with a putty made from whiting and asphaltum varnish. This you will have to make yourself with a putty-knife on a plate of glass, marble, or slate, for you cannot purchase it. Common putty is not hard enough and will not dry for months, while the special putty will set quickly and dry hard in a few days. When all the work is completed about the aquarium allow it to stand for at least a week, in which time the putty and varnish will harden.

At a paint store purchase some marine paint, also known as "copper paint," and give the wood-work two or three thin successive coats, allowing it to dry for a few days between each coat. Scrape the paint from the glass where it may have been smeared, and the complete aquarium is ready for water and stock.

Another way in which to construct the framework is to take a curtain-pole one and a half inches in diameter, and at a planing-mill have a quarter section sawed out, as shown at Fig. 17, so that an end rim will appear as shown at B. The part of the wood-work the buzz-saw cuts away will correspond with the grooves cut in the square sticks.

Four holes one and a half inches in diameter, or the same size as the stick, are bored half-way-through the bottom-board of the aquarium and V-shaped channels are cut in the board connecting the holes (Fig. 18). The wood-work is treated in a manner similar to that already described, and the corner - posts are held in place by long brass screws driven up through the bottom and into the lower ends of the posts. The top rail is made the same as shown in Fig. 15 C, and the glass is set as described. At the corner-posts

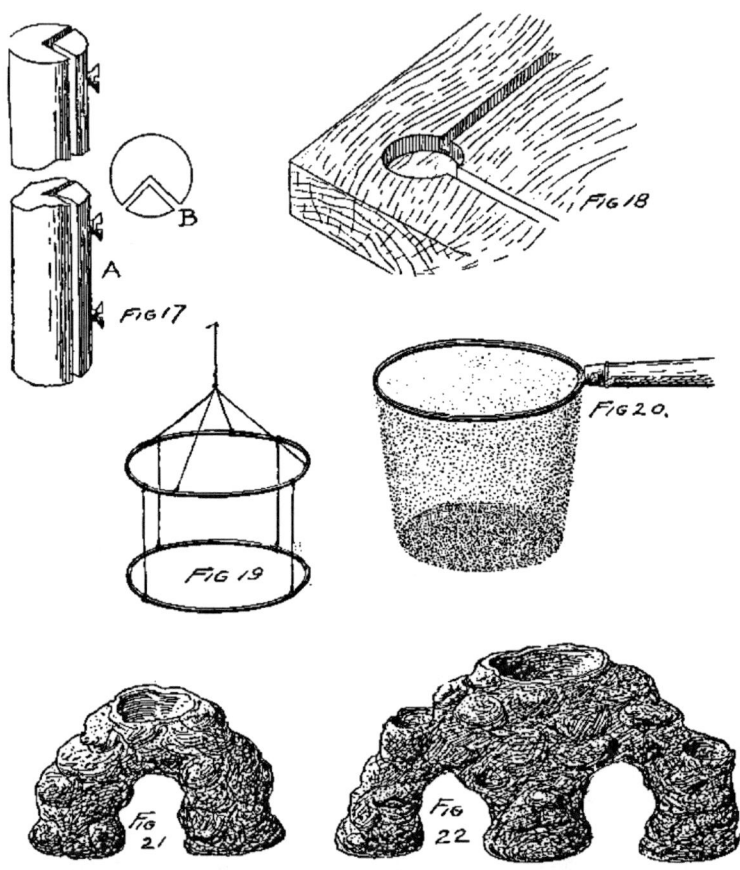

FIG 17

B

A

FIG 18

FIG 19

FIG 20.

FIG 21

FIG 22

the lap is well smeared with asphaltum varnish and putty
and the angle strips are screwed fast to the posts as indicated
at A in Fig. 17. While this is somewhat easier to make it

18

is not quite so substantial for large tanks as the square post and channels.

When catching the stock for the aquarium it is best to use a drop-net. This is made of two iron hoops fifteen or twenty inches in diameter and held one below the other with cord as shown at Fig. 19. Mosquito-netting is drawn across the lower hoop and sewed fast; then a band of it is sewed about both hoops to close in the sides, to form a cylinder open at the top only. Some bait is placed in the bottom of the net, and then it is lowered into the water so that the top hoop drops down and the whole net lies flat on the bottom of a pond. When a number of fish are around the bait a quick haul will raise the upper ring; then pull the net up with the fish captives within the cylinder. You can quickly select the ones you want, and these may be placed in a pail partly filled with water.

For turtles, crawfish, and lizards a scap-net will be necessary. This may be made from stout wire, a broom-handle, and some netting. The ring may be almost any size, from six to twelve inches in diameter, the ends being sharpened with a file and turned so that they may be driven into the end of the stick, which should first be bound with wire to prevent it from splitting. The bag of mosquito-netting is made on the hoop and sewed fast, as shown at Fig. 20. When changing the water in the aquarium it is not necessary to empty it all out. A siphon made of a small rubber tube will answer very well to drain off a portion. The part of the tube in the tank should be held close to the bottom so as to suck up any dirt or sediment that may be there. Good ventilation, light, healthy aquatic plants, clean sand,

and a proper proportion of fish to the volume of water are absolutely necessary to the successful aquarium. A few tadpoles and snails are advantageous in an aquarium, as they consume decaying vegetable matter and help to prevent the formation of algæ on the glass.

For the aquarium large enough to contain them, some artificial rockeries may be made from cement, gravel, and stones, as shown in the illustrations of the concrete rockeries Figs. 21 and 22. They should be made with openings beneath for the fish to swim through, and pockets should be made at the top to hold sand and the roots of aquatic plants. The rockeries should have a good flat base so as to rest securely on the bottom of the aquarium. Always have plenty of pebbles and river-sand at the bottom of the aquarium to make the fishes feel at home.

How to Manage an Aquarium

It is generally supposed that it is necessary to change the water in an aquarium at least once a day; but that is not the case. The true principle on which an aquarium should be conducted is not to change the water at all, but so to aërate and refresh the original supply as to maintain it always in a pure and perfect state. There are several means by which this may be done. The healthy growth of plants is very important, and active and brisk contact with the air of the atmosphere will greatly freshen the water. Motion in the water is absolutely necessary. In large aquaria this is obtained by an arrangement of tanks into which the water is pumped, and from which it flows rapidly, circulating through the tanks where the fish live. In its passage through the air it absorbs considerable oxygen, without which no fish can live. Fish placed in water that has been boiled die in a very few minutes.

The first thing to be done in the formation of a fresh-water aquarium is to start your plants in proper soil at the bottom of your tank, fill the tank with water, and leave it undisturbed until the plants begin to grow and the little bubbles of oxygen are to be seen rising to the surface of the water.

Choose your plants from such as you may collect from rivers or brooks or ponds anywhere in the country. Plant them, and then cover the surface of the soil with pebbles and small bits of rock, or anything that is suitable and in keeping with the rest of your arrangements. Never put sea-shells into a fresh-water aquarium.

Now fill your tank with water poured through a siphon or funnel, being very careful not to disturb the soil or the roots of the plants. You should have some clean river-sand in the bottom of your tank, and your pieces of rock should be so arranged as to form little caves and hiding-places for your fish. It will take perhaps two weeks to get your tank into a proper condition for fish to live in. Every bit of dead or decaying vegetation should be carefully removed. Keep your tank shaded from the heat of the sun, and expose it to the bright light only once in a while.

In order to manage your aquarium properly you will require a few simple tools. A little hand-net that can be bought for a few cents, or made for even less out of a bit of wire and a small piece of mosquito-netting, is useful for catching the fish or shells without putting your hands into the water. A pair of wooden forceps, like a glove-stretcher, will be found most convenient for nipping off bits of decaying plants or for catching objects that may have accidentally fallen into the water. Glass tubes of various sizes are also useful. If you want to catch any small object in the water with the tube, place the tube in the water with your finger over the hole in the top. Until your finger is removed the tube will remain full of air. Place it over the bit of refuse or whatever it is you want to catch, remove your finger, and the water will rush in, carrying the object with it into the tube, which should then be closed at the upper end by placing your finger over it as before. A glass or hard-rubber syringe is necessary with which to aërate the water thoroughly at least once a day, and oftener if possible. Fill the syringe, hold it high above the tank, and then squirt the water back again.

If a green film begins to gather on the side of the tank that is most exposed to the light, it should be cleaned away every day, and the sides of the glass polished carefully. A small piece of clean sponge tied on the end of a stick will answer the purpose very well, and, if used daily, you can keep the glass clear with very little trouble; but if the scum is neglected and left to accumulate, you will find it almost impossible to remove it from the glass even by hard scouring.

It is best to have only small fish in your aquarium, and for this reason trout are not desirable. Although very beautiful and intelligent, they grow so rapidly that they are likely to become in a short time too unwieldy for your

22

tank. Goldfish and minnows are very good, and the common little sunfish or "pumpkin-seed" is excellent.

You must keep careful watch over the fish in your aquarium, and if any one of them appears to be sick he should be removed at once, very gently, with the hand-net, and placed in fresh water, where he will often recover. If, however, the little sufferer is doomed to die, it is better not to run the risk of his doing so among his healthy companions. It is best always to have a hospital for your sickly pets, and as soon as one of them, whether a fish or a bird or any animal, shows signs of ill health, he should be taken away from the others and placed by himself.

Certain varieties of snails live well in fresh water, and will be found useful in clearing away the green film that is almost certain to collect on the side of the glass; but you must be careful or they will devour your plants as well; and if your tank is very small it is hardly worth while to try to keep them.

Water-beetles and water-spiders also thrive well, and their habits are most interesting to watch; but water-beetles fly by night, and unless you are careful to cover your tank you are likely to discover some morning that a number of your tenants have taken French leave.

You must be careful not to overstock your aquarium, for your fish will not thrive if they are overcrowded. Remember, also, that heat and dust are fatal to your pets. The water must be kept clean and cool at all times, and all foreign matter and every particle of decaying vegetation should be removed immediately.

To manage an aquarium successfully, no matter on how

small a scale, requires a good deal of care and time, but you will find it time well spent, and the pleasure and knowledge the study of your pets will give you will be an ample return for the time you spend on them.

A Merry-go-round

A great deal of fun may be had with a merry-go-round in the rear yard, and while it may not be run by an engine or its motion accompanied by an organ, hand power will turn the table and music can be made with an old accordion or concertina. The only difficult thing about the whole affair is the bevelled gear, the shaft and crank; but if an old reaper can be found at a blacksmith-shop the difficulty is solved, for a pair of bevelled gears are on every reaping-machine. Of course a machine-shop or foundry would contain gearing of various sizes, and a five and twelve inch gear wheel will answer the purpose very well.

In the practical back-yard merry-go-round shown in Fig. 23 the revolving post is four inches square and may be of spruce or white-wood planed on all sides and provided with a ferrule at both ends. These may be taken from old buggy-wheels, and will prevent the wood from splitting when the pins are driven in. The lower cross-beams *a a* in Fig. 24 are of spruce, eight feet long and two by three inches. The beams *b b* are six feet and six inches long, and on these four the cross-plates are made fast that hold the top or deck planks. The six cross-timbers are of spruce, one by four inches, and are from two to eight feet in length, according to their location. The beam plan (Fig. 24)

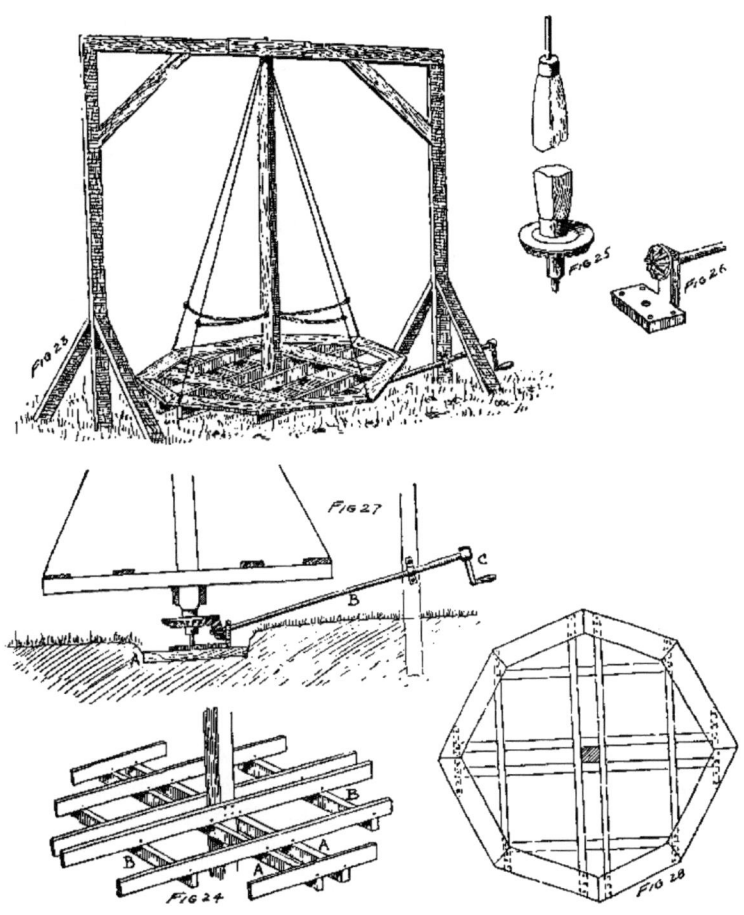

A MERRY-GO-ROUND

shows quite clearly how these supporting beams are arranged. They are held together with steel wire-nails driven down from the upper beams diagonally into the lower ones.

The longest beams are securely spiked to the revolving shaft, and in securing them in place take care to see that they are perfectly true, so that the outer edge of the platform will not dip and rise as it revolves. Drive a three-quarter-inch rod in the top of the shaft and another one in the bottom having a bevelled point as shown at Fig. 25. At the lower end of the shaft arrange the larger gear wheel and pin it fast so that it is fixed to the shaft and will not move.

An iron base-plate with an upright arm welded to it will hold the shaft and the smaller gear, which is to be arranged the right height to lock in with the teeth of the large gear. This plate is shown in Fig. 26; and through the four holes at the corners long screws are passed to bolt the plate securely to a wooden base, which last is set in the ground as shown at A in Fig. 27. The shaft B, to the end of which the small gear wheel is made fast, extends out beyond one of the upright posts, and at the outer end a crank and handle C are made fast, so that by hand-power the platform and shaft may be revolved.

Construct an overhead framework of six by two inch spruce beams twelve feet long, and set them in the ground twelve feet apart, bracing the uprights well, braced at both sides with angle beams as shown in Fig. 23. The top bar should be well braced also with one or two angle brackets, to prevent the frame from rocking. If the ground props are not strong enough to properly brace the frame, attach heavy wires to the corners and carry them out in both directions, making the ends fast to stout pieces of joist embedded in the ground.

At the middle of the top cross-bar arrange a plate of wood eighteen inches long with a groove cut in it in which the pin at the top of the square shaft may revolve. This plate should be attached to the bar with lag screws, so that it can be removed when it is necessary to unstep the shaft and platform. The outer line of deck planking is shown in the deck plan (Fig. 28), and inside of these boards as many others can be laid down as desired; or the entire frame may be all decked over, leaving a small space near the middle so as to reach the gear and lower pin in order to grease them. Where the shaft passes one of the uprights of the supporting frame an iron strap will hold it in place against the wood, and this bearing will require lubrication from time to time.

Four stout wire guys must be drawn from the top of the shaft and fastened at the outer edge of the platform to one of the beam ends. The anchorage should be made with very stout, strong screw-eyes, and to make it easier to draw the wires taut four small turn-buckles should be purchased at a hardware store and made fast to the lower ends of the wires, the hook on the buckle being caught in the large screw-eyes.

Seats may be made from boxes and nailed to the deck, and as a safeguard to prevent falling from the turn-table ropes should be attached to the stanchion wires and to the shaft as shown in Fig. 23.

It would be well to paint all the wood-work in order to

27

give it a good appearance, and all the iron parts should be coated with asphaltum varnish to prevent rusting.

If the gears are properly adjusted and there is no friction at the bearings, it will not be a difficult matter to move the table with several children occupying the seats. The bevelled point bearing at the bottom rests in a drilled depression in the plate, and the friction there is reduced to a minimum, while at the top the friction will be slight if the weight is properly distributed on the turn-table.

Chapter II

PET SHELTERS

MOST boys are interested in pet animals, and at one time or another possess them. Cats and dogs are domesticated and will always stay about the house if they are properly cared for and treated kindly, but rabbits, guinea-pigs, squirrels, monkeys, and reptiles often forget where they belong and will wander away and neglect to come back.

For this reason it will be necessary to build houses and hutches for them, and so safeguard the doorways .and screenings that they cannot escape.

It is not possible, of course, to give a lengthy description of pet shelters, since there are so many different kinds in use by boys all over the world; but the illustrations on these pages will give some ideas for the American and English boys to follow in making houses, hutches, and retreats to shelter their pet animals, birds, and reptiles.

In speaking of reptiles, that does not necessarily mean snakes, for under this classification come the horned-toads, lizards, turtles, and many of the beautiful tropical creeping and crawling things that in warm countries take the place of the white mice, rabbits, guinea-pigs, and canary-birds of our northern climes.

Some boys have a natural aptitude for carpenter-work.

but there may be ideas in these illustrations and the accompanying descriptions that will be helpful both to them, and to the boy who has as yet to make his first kennel or pigeon-cote.

Martin Boxes

In the early spring, when the birds return to the north, the martins are among the first to appear, and long before the swallows, whom they closely resemble, begin to nest they have hatched their young and have taken their departure from the southland.

They are cold-weather birds, fly rapidly, and do not stay long in one place. They seldom build their nests in the branches of trees, but prefer to find a hole in a tree-trunk, and there build a nest safe from the wind and storm. The sand-martin burrows a hole in the side of a bank, but never builds a nest in the chimneys as do his brother and sister swallows. The martin, when sitting on her eggs, likes a dark and sheltered place, and for that reason she takes kindly to a martin box in which a hole is made sufficiently large for her to fly in and out of.

In Fig. 1 a small keg is supported at the top of a post and braced at the bottom with two bracket pieces. A hole two inches and a half in diameter is made at each end of the keg, through which the martins can enter, and the post to which the keg is fastened is cut away at the upper end as shown in Fig. 2.

In one side of the bilge of the keg a hole is cut as large as the post is square or round, and at the other side a corresponding hole is cut the size of the upper part of the post.

The keg is then dropped down over the post so that the shoulder, formed by cutting away the wood, will rest under the upper side of the keg, in which the smaller square hole has been cut.

If a round post is employed, the upper part should be cut square so as to prevent the wind from blowing the keg round the post. A cross-stick fastened at the top of the post will form a perch on which the birds may alight.

A box with a peaked roof and three divisions, intended to accommodate three families of the birds, is shown in Fig. 3.

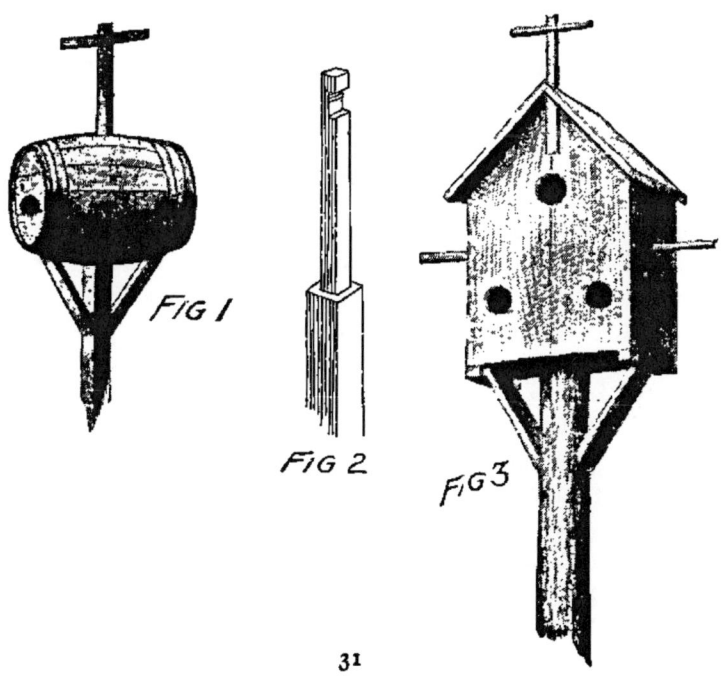

FIG 1

FIG 2

FIG 3

31

An ordinary box may be cut and rearranged with a pitched roof, an inner floor, and the three divisions. A small hole is bored at each side of the box and a round stick passed through it, so that six or eight inches of the wood will project at either side to serve as perches. Another perch can be arranged at the top of the box, and this bird-house is then securely fastened to the upper end of a post and braced there with bracket-pieces nailed both to the bottom of the box and to the post.

The divisions in the box should be not less than six inches square and six or eight inches high. If the box used be square it will probably be an easier job to divide it into four divisions for as many families. Each compartment, of course, must be provided with its separate hole for ingress and egress.

Bird Shelters

Birds do not always seek the shelter of trees in a storm; they will often gather about the house and under barn eaves and piazza sheds, where they are protected from the rain and the drippings from wet leaves. They like a dry shelter, and structures suitable for their needs can be knocked together from very simple material. In the illustration of a bird shelter (Fig. 4), a canvas or heavy muslin roof is supported on two uprights, and under it five perches are arranged from side to side, upon which a great many birds can rest.

The uprights are one and a half by three inches, and the strips forming the Y braces are two inches wide and seven-eighths of an inch thick.

The perches are three-quarter-inch dowels three feet long. If they cannot be had at a carpenter's shop or a hardware store, some small scantling may be planed nearly round to answer the same purpose. Where the perches are attached to the uprights and Y pieces, holes are bored half-way through the wood. Into these the ends of the perches are driven and nailed fast.

In Fig. 5 the canvas is left off from one side so that the constructional parts of the upright, braces, and roof strips

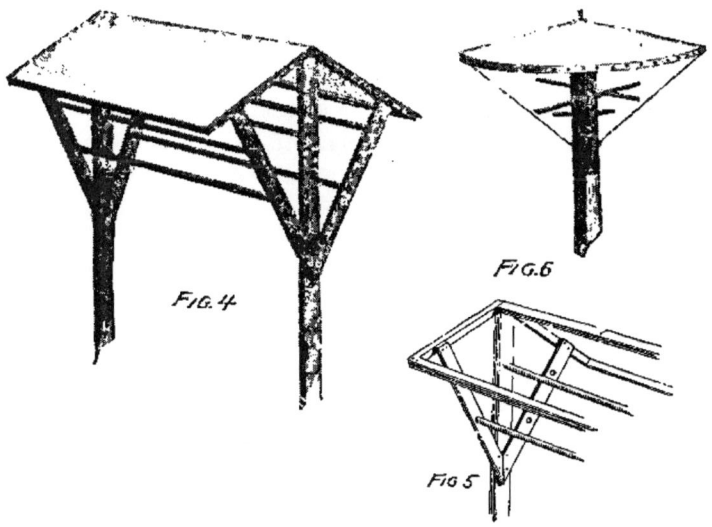

may be seen. When the wood-work is put together the roof should be covered with canvas, heavy unbleached muslin, or a piece of oil-cloth, and tacked all around the edges.

To make the barrel - hoop shelter, shown in Fig. 6, a

flat barrel-hoop is loosely covered with canvas or muslin tacked all around the edge. In the top of a post a wooden peg is driven, and over this the middle of the canvas disk is slipped, having first made a hole in the fabric through which the peg can pass. Four wires are attached to the hoop at equal distances apart, and the lower ends caught through staples or screw-eyes driven in the post a foot or two from the top. Two or three holes should be made through the post in which round perches may be driven.

A shelter for the side of a house or barn can be made from a piece of board, two bracket strips, and three dowels' or round sticks to act as perches.

The board should be three feet long and fifteen inches wide. Where it is attached to the house or barn a strip is first attached, and the inner edge of the board is then nailed fast to the strip. The two bracket strips that support the roof at the outer edge should be twenty-four inches long, one inch thick, and two inches wide. Three or four sets of holes are bored in the strips to receive the ends of the dowels or perches.

Pigeon-cotes

For the ordinary pigeons that fly about the house and barn some open cotes are shown in Fig. 7 and Fig. 8, but for the more valuable pigeons a large wire enclosure should be made and the lodges placed within them, unless the birds are very tame and will not leave the premises.

In Fig. 7 A, a cote with three holes is shown that is easily made from thin boards. It should measure thirty inches long, nine inches wide, and twelve inches high at the back, while at the front the board with the holes cut in it should be nine inches wide, with the holes five inches high and four inches wide.

The wood is put together as shown in Fig. 9, and the roof boards overhang the ends and front for an inch or two. The upper ends of the two divisions need not extend beyond the height of the front board, and this open space will in-

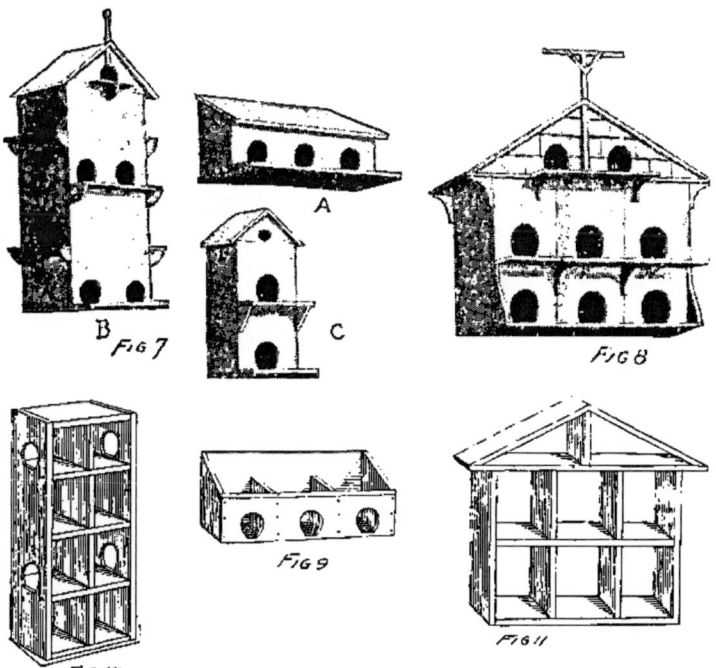

sure good ventilation. Sticks an inch square are made fast under the ends of the cote, and on the projecting ends a ledge three inches wide is fastened upon which the pigeons may alight.

The cote shown in Fig. 7 B is made from a shoe - case divided as shown in Fig. 10; on each floor the entrances are alternated from front to sides. Outside each entrance a ledge three inches wide is supported on brackets, and under the pitched roof the ninth compartment is arranged.

The large pigeon-cote (Fig. 8) is a more pretentious affair to make and will tax the young carpenter's skill. This cote can be made a very attractive pigeon shelter if it is carefully put together and nicely painted.

It is thirty-two inches long, twenty-four high to the eaves or thirty-four to the peak, and twelve inches deep. It is divided as shown in Fig. 11, and the ledges are supported with brackets cut from half-inch wood with a compass saw. From the eaves to the peak the front of the cote may be shingled, and above the peak a perch is erected.

This cote may be attached to the side of a barn or supported on stout uprights embedded securely in the ground.

Dog-kennels

When building a dog - kennel the important features to bear in mind are to make it strong, weather-proof, and large enough for a good-sized dog to turn around in comfortably. A poorly built kennel soon falls apart, and if it is not weather-proof rain will get in on the dog, and dogs do not like to get wet while sleeping any more than boys. Moreover, if the kennel is not large enough it is cramped and stuffy, and, while the dog cannot say so, he resents it, and in his own dog way of reasoning feels that he is imposed upon in being housed in such small quarters. The dimensions of a kennel must be naturally governed by the size of the dog who is to inhabit it; but for one of medium size, such as a setter or collie, a kennel with a peaked roof, similar to the one shown in Fig. 12, should be three feet long, two feet wide, two feet high at the sides, and three feet high from the ground to the peak or ridge-pole.

The floor frame is the first thing in constructing a kennel, and it should be made of two by three inch spruce, thirty-four inches long and twenty-two inches wide, with lap joints at the corners as shown in Fig. 13. On this the flooring of tongue and grooved boards is laid and nailed down.

From three matched boards eight inches wide make the front and back to the kennel as shown in Fig. 14. The lower ends of the boards are nailed to the floor frame, and where they are sawed off to form the peak a batten is placed at the inside and made fast with clinch nails driven into it from the outside through the boards.

The nail heads in the front of Fig. 14 will show the location of one batten, and the other can clearly be seen at the inside of the back, where the clinched nail ends are shown.

Beginning at the bottom and working up, the sides are laid on. Always place the tongue up and the groove down when using matched boards in a horizontal position, as otherwise the rain and moisture will work into the groove and cause the wood to decay.

A ridge-pole is nailed between the front and back at the peak, and to this the upper ends of the roof boards are fastened.

37

In the front a hole large enough for a dog to pass through is cut with a compass saw, and above it, near the peak, one large and three smaller holes are bored, as shown in Fig. 14, and the wood cut away between the holes, as shown in Fig. 12. This is for ventilation, for dogs as well as human

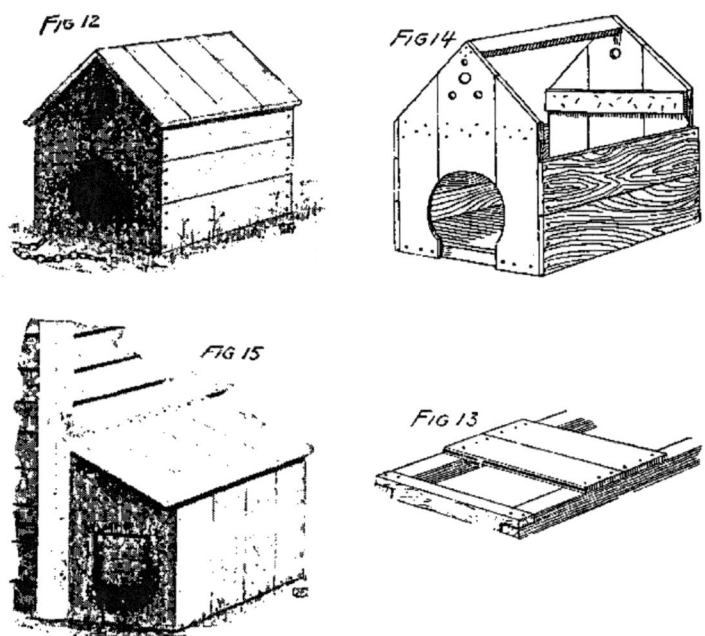

FIG 12

FIG 14

FIG 15

FIG 13

beings require plenty of fresh air. Another hole at the top of the back board will allow free circulation of air across the top of the kennel.

Two or three good coats of paint will finish the wood·

work, and with the addition of a chain fastened to a staple-plate this dog-kennel will be ready for occupancy.

This dog-hut in Fig 15 is built against the side of a house or barn, and is forty inches long, twenty-four wide, and twenty-eight inches high at the outer side, and thirty-six inches high next the house or barn. The floor frame is thirty-eight inches long, twenty-two inches wide, and made like Fig. 13. Stakes are driven in the ground, one under each corner, and to these the floor frame is spiked fast.

When constructed against a building a strip is fastened to the siding of the building on which to nail the roof boards and to the upper edges of the front, back, and side boards battens are made fast to strengthen the hut.

The wall or side of the building may, in such a "lean-to," be used as a fourth side of the dog-hut. A ventilator is cut in the upper corner of the back and at the front a swinging door can be hung in the doorway or opening. This is a weather-door and is made an inch narrower on each side than the width of the doorway. It is hung on screw-eyes and staples so that it will act as a flap and can be pushed in or out by the dog when entering or leaving the hut. In the winter-time, and when it is raining, this door will keep out snow and water and also protect a dog from strong winds.

Guinea-pig Houses

When making houses or huts for guinea-pigs it will be necessary to make at least one-third of the coop dark, or nearly so, as the little pigs like darkened places in which to spend a portion of their time.

39

The illustration of the guinea-pig house in Fig. 16 shows how this can be done by partitioning off a portion of the house · and making ventilating holes or small windows near the top.

A substantial double-decked house, similar to the one shown in the illustration, should be thirty-six inches long,

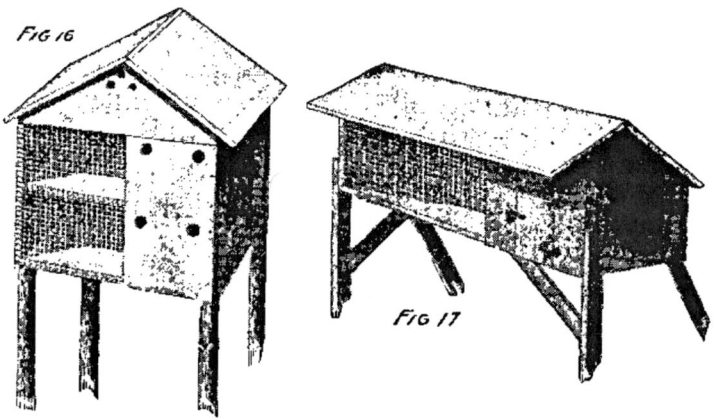

twenty-four inches wide, twenty-four inches high to the roof eaves and thirty-two inches to the peak. A small dry-goods case can be adapted to this use, and the floor nailed in mi way between the top and bottom.

The darkened compartment is fourteen inches wide and extends up on both floors. Holes three by four inches made in the sidings will permit the pigs to have access to the open and closed compartments. A door at one side is made high enough to open into both upper and lower compartments; this is swung on hinges, and for safety it may be provided with a hasp and padlock.

The open compartments are to be screened with square-mesh galvanized wire cloth substantially heavy to prevent the pigs escaping or dogs from entering and molesting them. This wire cloth can be purchased at a hardware store and attached to the wood with galvanized wire staples.

A guinea-pig house should not be placed on the ground, but attached to the tops of posts from twenty - four to thirty-six inches above the ground. Locust posts about four inches in diameter are the best for this purpose as they are tough and will not decay in the ground as quickly as other wood.

The guinea-pig hut shown in Fig. 17 has but one floor and it is much longer than the house, the floor plan being forty-two inches long and eighteen inches wide. The ends are fifteen inches high at the front, twelve at the back, and eighteen at the peak. The dark compartment is fifteen inches wide and the door at the front is six by eight inches, hung on hinges and fastened with a hasp and padlock.

At the front the roof extends over for six inches to shade the open compartment, and at both ends and the back it overhangs about two inches.

This hut is held up on sticks implanted in the ground, and braced so that the wind will not blow it over.

Chicken-coops

In the spring-time when little chickens are hatched, and it is not possible to let the hen wander about at random to scratch up the garden or the flower beds, some small coops and shelters should be constructed and placed in a corner of the back yard, or in some other vacant space, where the little chicks can run without being molested by the larger fowls, as they would be if put in the big chicken-coop or runway.

The easiest coop to make is shown in the illustration of the young chicken shelter (Fig. 18). It consists of a pitched roof mounted on three boards six inches high. This shelter may be three feet wide and two feet deep, and from the ground to the peak the distance is twenty-four inches.

Slats are nailed across the front to prevent the hen from getting out, although not so close as to prevent the chicks from squeezing through. A coat or two of paint will improve the appearance of this shelter, and each mother-hen should be provided with a separate coop for her family.

In the illustration of the young chicken coop (Fig. 19) a little more care is taken with the construction, and a canopy fly is arranged at the front to keep off rain and to shade the interior of the coop. This coop is three feet long, two feet wide, and thirty inches high at the front, but at the back it need not be more than twenty-four inches high.

It may be constructed from boards with matched edges, or perhaps from a dry-goods case, and if it is raised from the ground an inch or two, and a few holes bored in the bottom, it will insure a dry floor. The cross rail at the bottom to which the upright slats are nailed is three inches above the floor; and if made two inches wide and the slats one inch and a half in width, they will be heavy enough to resist dogs and cats, if they should try to disturb mother-hen and her brood.

Outriggers may be nailed at each end so that about fifteen inches of the wood projects beyond the sides. A strip of lath should be fastened between the ends, and light canvas or muslin may then be tacked fast to the roof and to the strip to serve as an awning.

Rabbit-hutches

Among animal pets rabbits seem to be general favorites all over the country, perhaps because they are such beautiful and harmless little creatures and so prettily marked. They are worthy of a comfortable home, and the boy who is fortunate enough to have some good rabbits should take pleasure in building a substantial hutch in which they can live and thrive.

In Fig. 20 a double-floored rabbit-hutch is shown, and if it is made large enough quite a family of rabbits can live in it, the larger ones down-stairs and the smaller ones up-stairs. An inclined plane will make it possible for the friends and relatives to visit each other.

This hutch should be from four to five feet long, twenty-four inches wide, and twenty-four inches high. The second floor is arranged so that it will be midway between the top and bottom, and at the rear an opening five inches wide and ten inches long will receive an inclined board, across which short sticks have been nailed to prevent the rabbits slipping when going up or coming down the stairs.

At one end a compartment is made eighteen inches wide, and provided with a door six inches wide hung on hinges and fastened with a hasp and lock. Openings five inches wide and six inches high are cut in the side of this compartment, so that the rabbits may enter it from either floor. A drop front, on hinges, will permit the hutch to be partially closed in very severe weather, but when it is pleasant the front should be raised and propped up with a stick, in the ends of which hooks are arranged that will fit into screw-eyes driven into the lid and along the side of the compartment, as shown in the illustration.

In the end of the hutch, opposite the bottom of the stairway, a feeding-doorway six inches square should be cut with a compass saw, and a door hung on hinges. This hutch should be supported on stout sticks or posts embedded in the ground for at least two feet, and it should be thirty to forty inches above the ground. Across the open runs, galvanized wire cloth, with half to three-quarter inch meshes, is to be nailed fast with staples. With a few coats of paint on the outside, this hutch will present a very good appearance.

The rabbit-house (Fig. 21) is a large, one-story structure, in which a family of rabbits can live very comfortably. It is thirty-six inches long, twenty-four inches wide, eighteen inches high at the back and twenty-two at the front. At one side a compartment is made twelve inches wide, and at the outer side a door seven by nine inches is hung and fastened with a lock. This house is supported on four posts, two or three feet above the ground, and when painted it should look very homelike to a rabbit's eyes.

A house of this same description, but larger, may be made for a monkey, a fox, an opossum, a raccoon, or even for bear cubs. For the latter, bars will have to be used instead of the wire cloth, for the bears would soon tear away the lighter material.

Squirrel Cages

For squirrels, chipmunks, and white rats very good cages can be made from wire cloth, tin boxes, and wood, and in the illustration of a squirrel cage (Fig. 22) a simple house is shown.

To make it, a base-board is cut twenty-eight inches long, fifteen inches wide, and one inch and a quarter thick. Ten inches from one end the edges of the board are sawed off so

that the end will be six inches wide. Eleven inches from
the small end a square piece of wood is mounted on the base-
board to form the back to the square compartment. This
is covered with tin on the inside, so that the rodents cannot
gnaw the wood away at the edges or about the hole that
leads into the cylinder.

A wedge-shaped piece of wood, six inches broad at the
bottom and two inches at the top, is attached to the small
end of the base-board, and from the top of this piece to the
top of the back-board a connection strip is nailed fast.

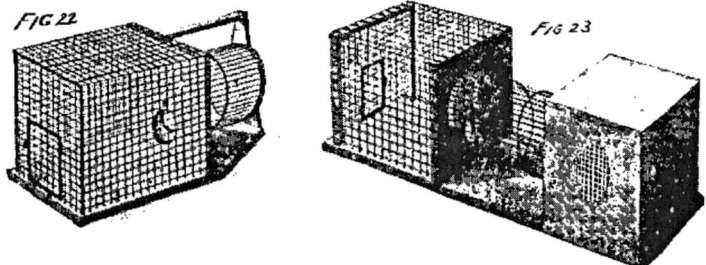

FIG 22

FIG 23

From thick wire or quarter-inch iron rod a wicket is made
and driven into holes at the wide end of the board. It
should be the same size as the back-board, and is placed
there to support the wire cloth of which the cage is made.

Small holes are made in the base-board with an awl, so
that the ends of the wire cloth will slip into them. When
the edges of the cloth are tacked to the back-board and
wired to the wicket, the ends in the holes will remain in
place.

A wire door made from the cloth can be hung on hinges,
which should be soldered to the galvanized cloth. With

straight wires or wire cloth an exercising cylinder can be made with wooden or tin ends. It is supported between the back of the cage and the wedge-shaped upright. Tacks driven around the hole that leads into the cylinder will prevent the occupants from gnawing away the edges of the wood-work.

The squirrel house (Fig. 23) is constructed in the same manner as the cage, but it has the advantage of a covered shelter at one end of the base-board. This is made from a tin cracker-box with the lid removed, and inverted so the bottom acts as the roof. In one side an oval opening is cut and a wire screen is fastened to it at the inside.

The wire cylinder is seven inches in diameter and twelve inches long, quite large enough for two squirrels to run a great race at the same time. A piece of hair felt, an old woollen cloth, or some curled hair will be comfortable for the squirrels to lie on in the enclosed cage.

Reptile Pens

In some parts of the country pets are made of reptiles, and very interesting and tame ones are found among the lizard family.

When making a reptile pen, care should be taken to get the joints tight and not have any small openings or cracks between boards, for snakes can get through a very small space, often much smaller than you would think it possible, judging from the size of their bodies.

In Fig. 24, the design for a very substantial reptile pen is shown, and instead of fine wire screening, two heavy plates of glass may be used at the front of each compartment. This is a double pen, and one side can be used for snakes, while the other may harbor some lizards or small land-turtles.

This pen is forty-eight inches long, twenty-four deep, and twenty-six high. The bottom rail at the front is four inches wide, and the top and upright ones are two inches wide.

The wood from which the pen is made should be tongue-and-grooved, and planed on both sides. It may be from

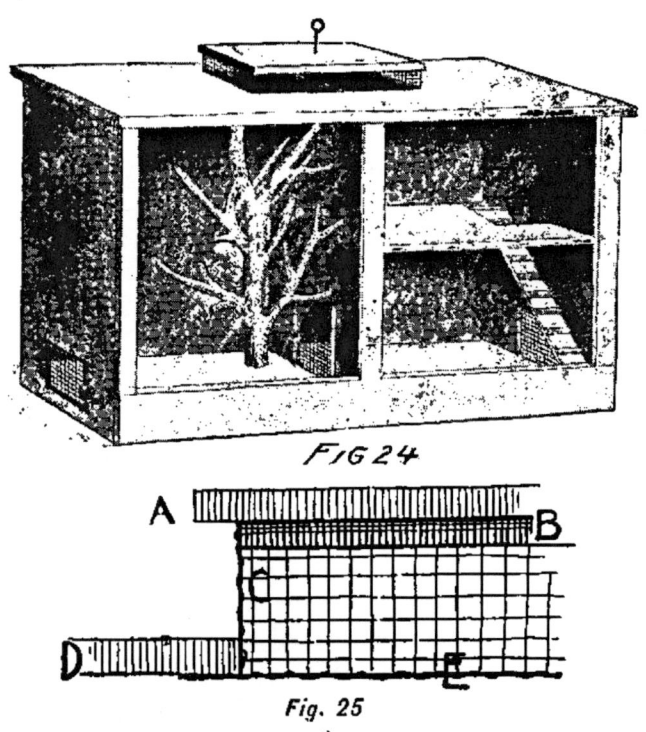

F/G 24

Fig. 25

48

three-quarters to one inch and a quarter thick, and narrow boards are preferable to wide ones.

In the lizard compartment an upper floor is fastened in, having an opening at one side where an inclined board, with cross sticks attached, is arranged so that the animals may climb up and down.

The snake pen should have a portion of a small tree fastened at top and bottom, on which the reptiles may climb and coil. The more short branches it has, the better, for it will then give the snakes a more satisfactory perch to move about on. At the bottom of each end a small trap doorway four inches high and six inches long is cut, and protected by a stout wire-cloth door, hinged and locked. These trapdoors are for the purpose of removing refuse or for feeding the reptiles; or a smaller opening at the back, near the top, and about two inches in diameter, can be used as a food door.

A ventilator is cut in the roof twelve inches long and six inches wide, so that each compartment gets the advantage of an opening about six inches square. Over this a roof is made three inches above the main roof, and with stout wire cloth the opening is covered first at the under side. Then the strip of wire cloth, four inches wide, is tacked around the inside of the opening and to a board the same size as the hole, or six by twelve inches, attached to the under side of the cap.

This arrangement is more clearly shown in Fig. 25, which is a sectional view, A being the cap, B the board to which the upper edge of the wire cloth is attached, C the wire cloth, and D the main roof to the pen. The line E represents the wire cloth tacked to the under side of the opening, to prevent the reptiles crawling up and over the partition.

At the lower end of the partition an opening four inches square may be made and fitted with a wire-netting door that can be raised and lowered by a rod that extends through the cap of the ventilator. One or two staples driven over the rod at the inside of the reptile pen will prevent the rod from bending, and the wire door should slide on runners provided with a rabbet at the inside, so that it cannot be dislodged.

With this construction, the reptiles may be allowed to mingle if they are peaceable, but if the snakes molest the small lizards they must be driven into their own side and the

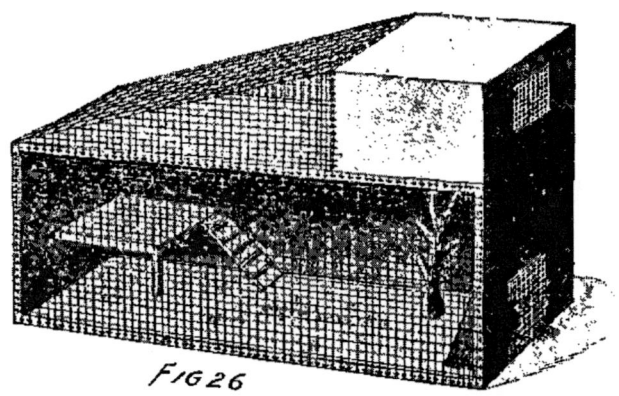

FIG 26

trap-door closed. With the outer doors at the bottom and the ventilator at the top, a free circulation of air can be had; and if the floor is kept well sanded and clean, this reptile pen will make a comfortable home for a collection of such pets.

The lizard run shown in Fig. 26 is made from a wooden

shoe-case open at the front, and on top of which a smaller box is mounted and connected with the lower one by means of an inclined board and an opening, through which the lizards can crawl. A ventilator is cut in the upper box and covered with wire netting; and in the lower box, at one end, a doorway is made, four by six inches, and protected by a heavy wire screen door on hinges.

A raised platform and ladder is made at one end of the large box, and in the open space one or two branches should be made fast on which the lizards can climb.

The top of the box should be enclosed with wire netting, as shown in the illustration. A doorway three inches square cut in the side of the upper box will allow access to this roof-garden.

A few coats of dark-green paint will finish these reptile pens on the outside, and they should be enamelled cream color, buff, or light green on the inside, so that the reptiles may be seen against the light background.

5

Chapter III

A Simple Summer-house

FOR the back yard, or in the fields and woods near the house, a summer-house or pergola will be found a comfortable nook in which to spend many pleasant hours.

A simple summer-house is shown in the illustration, Fig. 1. This is made of four posts, has a shingled roof, and is provided with seats on three sides. Obtain four spruce posts four inches square, or four tree-trunks from four to six inches in diameter. Plant them in the ground, forming a square of six feet. The posts should be embedded for at least two feet, and, to insure them from decaying too quickly, tar or pitch the bottoms, or give them two or three good coats of asphaltum varnish. The posts should stand seven feet above ground. Across the tops of the posts nail two-by-four-inch joist, with lap joints as shown at A in Fig. 2. With four more pieces of joist form the roof rafters, cutting a notch in each joist where it fits over the corners at the head of the posts. At the peak, the joist are bevelled where they meet.

Join two of the pieces at first; then lap the remaining two on both sides of them, nailing all the ends securely with steel wire nails. Put one middle rafter in on each side between

eaves to the roof.   It would not look well to have the roof
the corner ones; then nail shingle lath or scantling on the
four sides to receive the shingles.   The rafters should overhang the top frame about twelve inches, so as to form the

stop on a line with the posts.   Begin at the bottom and a
the middle of each side to shingle the roof, working out to
the corners and up through the middle to the peak.   To
prevent the roof leaking at the corners, bevel the shingles at
one side, then lap those on the other side over them and bevel
the edges.   Some builders lay a strip of tin flashing over the
edges as well as in the valleys of a roof to insure a perfectly
water-tight joint.   Use galvanized nails.   To hide the rough
rafters and shingle lath, the inside of the roof may be lined
with narrow, matched boards; then the wood-work may be
given a coat or two of paint in some desirable color.

A Back-yard Pergola

A back-yard pergola is constructed from two upright posts
four inches square, a cross beam two by six inches, and eight

joists laid across from the post bar to the top of the back fence. This style of pergola is particularly adapted to city yards and those surrounded by a board fence. In the event of there being no fence, the ends of the joist or roofing beams may bear on a two-by-six-inch cross bar that rests on two more posts corresponding with the front ones.

The posts are four inches square, of spruce or any other available wood, and are planed on all four sides. They are embedded in the ground for about two feet, and, to prevent them from sinking or shifting, place a large, flat stone in the hole on which the post will rest, and around it pack earth and stones instead of earth only. A lap cut in the front top end of the post will admit the two-by-six-inch cross beam. The posts are seven feet apart, and the cross beam ten feet long, with the ends cut as shown in Fig. 3 on page 56. The front end of each joist is rounded under as shown, and to make a more secure anchorage a notch two inches long and an inch deep may be cut at the under side of each joist, so that they will fit down over the upper edge of the cross beam. Make all the joints and laps fast with steel wire nails; then give the wood-work a few coats of paint.

Seats may be built in on two sides and supported with under braces or brackets to prop up the front edge, and a back-board may be nailed fast to the posts and fence.

A Toadstool Tree Canopy

Where there is a large tree on the place or near the house, a toadstool canopy (Fig. 4) may be constructed above a comfortable seat. The framing of the canopy is shown in Fig. 5, where the arrangement of corner rafters and braces can be clearly seen. The tree end of each rafter is bevelled (or cut on a slant) and nailed fast with steel wire nails. The under braces are keyed to the tree by cutting out a wedge of the bark, so that the lower end or point of the bracket will fit into it. These ends are to be well nailed to the tree-trunk, as they are the main props to hold up the roof. Between the corner rafters let one rafter in on each side; then nail shingle lath on the top of the rafters, and to these the shingles are fastened.

A seat eighteen inches wide may be built about the foot of the trunk and supported by two-by-three-inch joist let into the ground a foot or eighteen inches. Instead of shingling this roof, it may be thatched with salt hay arranged in flat tufts and nailed onto the lath. Begin at the lower edge to do this and thatch one line first; then begin on the end of the line above it and arrange the tufts closely side by side, and nail them fast. The last line at the top should have tar paper under it, closely fitted, and nailed to the tree trunk with copper tacks and painted. This will deflect the water and prevent it from running down the trunk and wetting the seat.

A Rustic Pergola

A simple but effective and useful rustic pergola is shown in Fig. 6. All the posts, cross-pieces, braces, and stringers at the top are of undressed wood, having the bark on. The corner posts are from four to six inches in diameter, and are embedded two feet in the ground. They are seven feet above the ground, and on top of two sets cross-stringers are made fast and braced with angle brackets. A sharp hatchet, a saw, and a hammer will be the only tools required for this work; and where an angle piece is attached to a post, the bark and wood should be cut away on the post, so that the bevelled edge of the bracket will lie snugly against it.

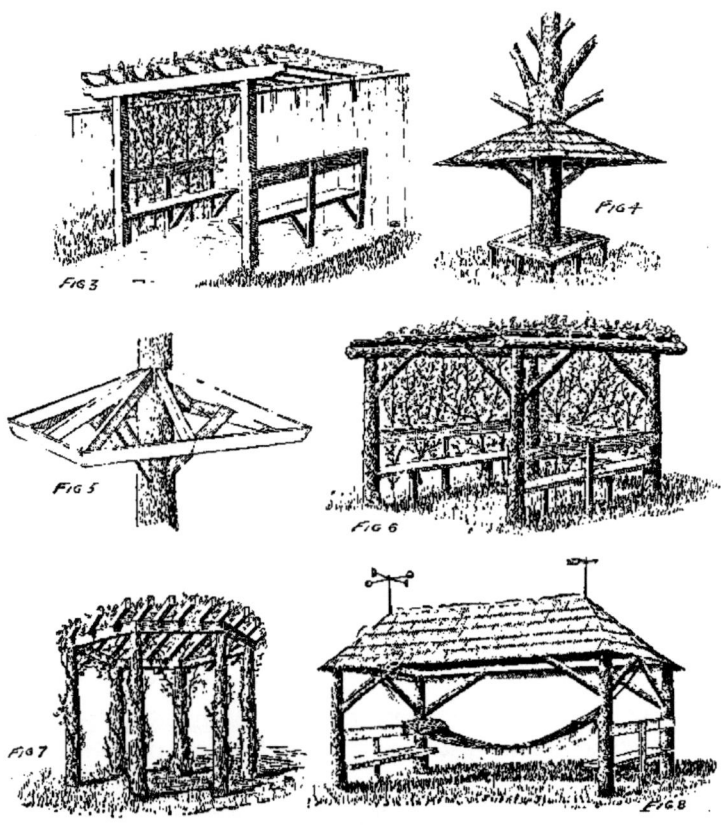

FIG 3

FIG 4

FIG 5

FIG 6

FIG 7

FIG 8

It should then be nailed fast with long steel wire nails. This pergola can be made of almost any size, but for one of moderate proportions it should measure eight feet square and seven feet high. Seats of smooth boards may be arranged on three sides between posts, and wires may be run up and down and crosswise, on which climbing vines may be supported.

A Circular Pergola

A circular pergola will present a pleasing appearance in any yard. It is made from six rustic posts, six supporting beams, and eleven top rafters, as shown in Fig. 7.

Tree-trunks of the proper size and length may be cut in the woods, or some locust posts can be purchased at a lumber-yard. The bark is to be left on, and the posts are to be planted two feet in the ground in a circle eight feet in diameter. The tops of the posts should be sawed off so that they are all an equal distance from the ground. On top of them nail six pieces of joist, two by four inches, with the narrower side resting on the posts.

The joist must be bevelled or mitred so that they will fit snugly at the posts. Spike them fast to each other and to the posts with large steel wire nails. The top rafters should be of two-by-three or two-by-four inch spruce, planed or left rough, and arranged equal distances apart, so that they will form a large circle on the supporting beams. These are to be nailed fast and painted if desired. Vines may be planted close to the posts, so that as they grow the thick mass of foliage will make a shady top to the pergola.

If desired, a few seats may be arranged between the posts

57

or columns, but portable seats would be more in keeping with this style of pergola.

A Summer Shelter

A design for a comfortable summer-house is shown in Fig. 8. The posts are set on an oblong, seven feet wide and twelve feet long. Seven or eight inch posts are planted in the ground, and the top rails are arranged as shown in Fig. 2. The rails can be of two-by-four-inch joist, and should be cut and neatly lapped at the ends, as shown at A in Fig. 2. A ridge-pole forms the centre support to this roof, and from it the rafters are run down to the top rails. Over these the shingle lath are nailed, and then the thatching of salt hay or shingles may be laid on. A wind-speeder and a weather-vane may be arranged at either end of the roof, as shown in the drawing, and seats may be built in between the end posts, with a supporting rib at the middle and braces under the seats. There is room enough under this roof to swing a hammock.

Chapter IV

WEATHER-VANES AND WINDMILLS

FROM the time of the earliest habitation of the earth, nature's great forces, wind and water, have been employed to furnish power for man's uses. Wind engines and mills for motive power have become almost obsolete in and about the great cities, as they are so cumbersome and uncertain, but in the country they are still used to a great extent for pumping water, milling, and operating light machinery.

Windmills have been made in a number of shapes by the people of different nations, and some of them are very picturesque, especially the Dutch wheels and those made in the eastern part of the United States a century or more ago, many of which are still working.

Windmills will never go out of use entirely, no matter what cheap motive power will eventually run the world; for when they are once set up properly they cost nothing to operate, and it a wheel is well made it will last for years with but trifling cost for repairs.

Windmills, weather-vanes, pinion-wheels, and wind toys of all descriptions have been made by boys in every age, and each generation goes on to invent or think of something new for the same old wind to play with that has toyed with the world's wheels for centuries. The illustrations and descriptions on this and the following pages will be found helpful in the construction of wind machinery that shall be both novel and practicable.

A Pinion-wheel Weather-vane

The easiest sort of a pinion-wheel and weather-vane to construct is shown in Fig. 1. It consists of a piece of stout

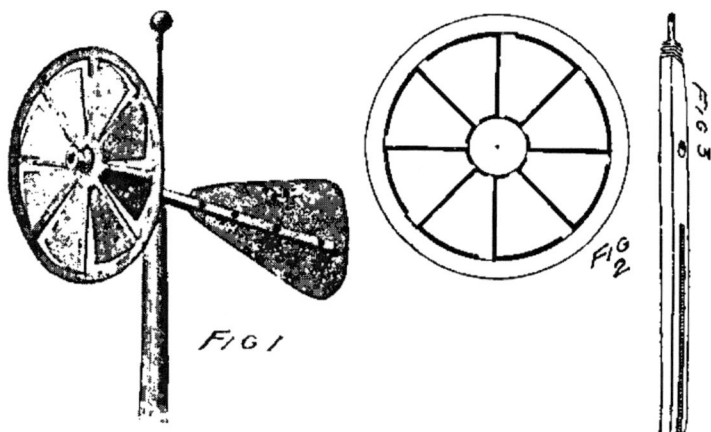

tin or sheet-iron, a wooden shaft twenty inches long, and a fan-tail twelve inches long and seven inches wide at the rear end.

Punch a small hole in the centre of a sheet of tin or iron not less than ten inches square, and with a lead-pencil compass draw a circle ten inches in diameter. Half an inch inside of this draw another one nine inches in diameter, as

indicated by the light lines in Fig. 2. One inch from the
centre draw a third circle making it two inches in diameter;
then divide the disk into eight equal parts.

With a cold chisel cut on the lines, as indicated in Fig. 2,
and bend the metal ears as shown in drawing No. 1, so that
the corners will set back an inch from the rim. With a
stout pair of shears cut around the outside line and free
the wheel from the sheet of metal.

At the front of the wheel fasten a spool with steel wire
nails driven through the tin to act as a hub. Then give them
both a coat or two of paint.

Make a shaft from hard wood an inch square, and cut
it in from one end about ten inches, as shown in Fig. 3.
At the other end bind the wood for an inch or two with
linen line or fine wire to prevent its splitting, and bore a
hole in the end with an awl. Through the spool and disk,
and into the hole in the shaft, drive a flat-headed steel wire
nail or a screw, three-sixteenths of an inch in diameter, to
act as the pinion on which the wheel may revolve.

From light wood, three-eighths of an inch in thickness,
cut a fan-tail seven inches wide at one end and two at the
other, and, having passed it through the cut in the shaft,
make it fast with small nails or screws.

Balance the shaft and wheel on your finger to determine
where to pierce the hole through which the upright shaft on
the pole should pass; then bore it out with bit and brace so
that the shaft will fit snug but not tight.

To the top of the shaft, over the hole, attach another
spool, so as to form a longer bearing; or a strap of metal may
be tacked so that it will bridge up over the hole about two

inches. In this bridge a corresponding hole may be cut, through which the vertical shaft or pin will pass. This is to hold the vane steady on the long pin of quarter-inch round iron driven into the top of the pole, and prevent it from dipping forward or backward.

Place this vane on a shed, the end of a barn roof, or on a high pole where the wind has free access to it.

A Wind-speeder

Wind-speeders may be constructed of metal or partly of wood, but one that can easily be made by a boy consists of two sticks, four ordinary tin funnels having their ends stopped up with a plug of wood, and a pole, into the end of which a long iron pin is driven and on which the hub revolves. Fig. 4.

Two hard - wood sticks thirty inches long and three-quarters of an inch square are cut at the middle so that they will lap, and with steel nails they are attached to a hub three-quarters of an inch thick and three inches in diameter, in the centre of which a quarter-inch hole is bored. The end of each stick or arm is cut in to receive the funnels, and they are held in place by straps of tin passed around each neck and tacked fast to the top and bottom of the cross sticks.

With a sharp-pointed awl or punch a small hole is made through the strap and neck, and a long, slim steel nail is driven through both into the end of the sticks to give the funnels an additional purchase.

To reduce the friction and to prevent the wood from

62

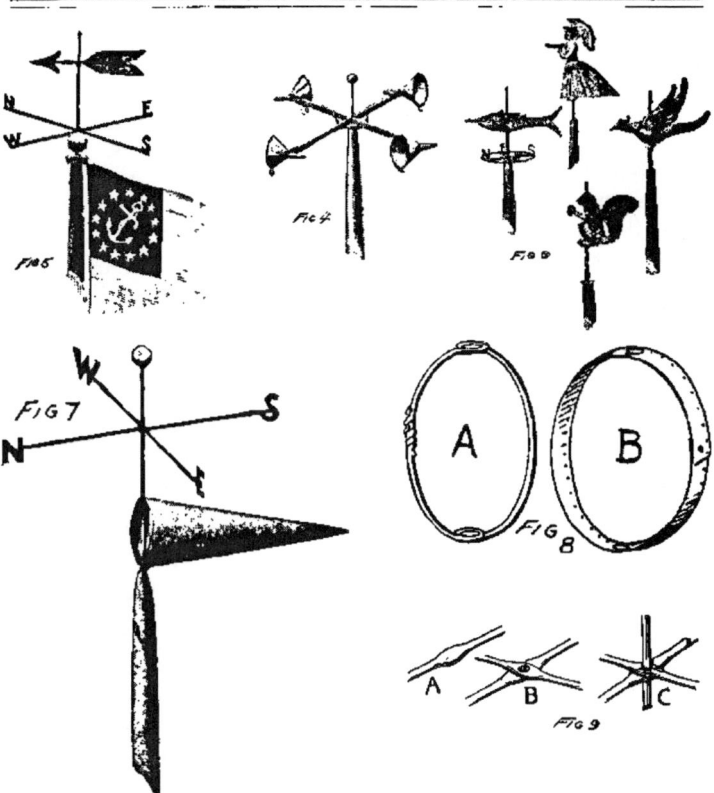

wearing away at the under side of the hub, a large flat washer should be attached to the wood with copper tacks driven closely all around the outer edge. Before the speeder is slipped over the upright pin, a short piece of small gas-pipe or tubing should be placed over it so it will rest be-tween the hub and the top of the pole. Two coats of white

63

or light-colored paint will improve the appearance of this speeder.

The Arrow Weather-vane

Of all the weather-vanes that have ever been made, the balanced arrow is undoubtedly the oldest and most popular; it is the universal type of its class, and, from the simple arrow that a boy can whittle from a shingle to the beautifully gilded vane that crowns the pinnacle of some great building, it is everywhere in evidence. Fig. 5.

The arrow-vane can be made any length to suit the height at which it may be placed, but for the house, barn, flag-pole, or tower not more than fifty or sixty feet high, it should be from twenty-four to thirty-six inches long, with the blade from five to six inches in width.

The most substantial vane is made in three pieces, the point, shaft, and blade. The shaft is made from hard wood, three-quarters of an inch square, in the ends of which cuts are made to receive a tin or sheet-metal point and blade. These are held in place with steel nails driven through the wood and clinched on the opposite side. The arrow is balanced and a hole is then made in the shaft through which the upright pin or rod will pass.

A ferule or ring is driven on the upright rod to hold the arrow in the proper place, and below it two rods should be arranged at right angles, at the ends of which the letters N, E, S, W are soldered. These rods may be of brass or wood, and if the wood is used it should be of hickory or locust, half an inch square or round, and slit at the ends to receive the letters of tin or sheet metal. These latter are held in place with slim steel wire nails driven through the wood and metal.

At the top of a flag-pole these arms should be mounted above a gilded ball, and they should be, if of brass or copper, held securely in place with wire or solder. If they are of iron, it would be well to have a blacksmith weld them, so that they will be rigid and stay in place.

Wooden Vanes

In Fig. 6 some suggestions for wooden vanes are shown that can be followed with the scroll saw and jackknife or a compass saw and carving chisels. These vanes can be made in almost any size that will not be out of proportion to the building or pole they are to be mounted on.

The fish is cut from wood five-eighths of an inch thick, and all around the edges the wood is bevelled so as to give the fish a rounded effect. The fish is balanced on the edge of a piece of wood to determine where the rod will pass through it; then with a quarter-inch bit the hole is carefully bored through from top to bottom. The compass-point letters can be made from sheet tin and supported on two cross sticks and a stout wire hoop from twelve to fifteen inches in diameter.

The lady with the parasol is cut from wood half an inch in thickness. She is fifteen inches high and twelve inches wide across the bottom of the skirt. From the shoes to the hat, a quarter-inch hole is bored entirely through the body, but if this be found too difficult, a staple at the top and bottom will answer instead. Through these staples the rod will pass.

65

The squirrel is made in the same manner as the lady, and either balanced on the rod which passes through the body or by means of staples driven at one side. A ring and washer should be provided on the rod for the bottom of the vane to rest on, as there would be too much friction if the vane rested on the top end of the pole into which the rod is driven.

The bird vane is cut out and balanced the same as the fish, and the modelling may be carved in the wood or painted, to give shape and character to the vane. Otherwise it would be but a blank piece of thin board cut in the shape of the outline.

In all of these vanes it is necessary, of course, to have the greatest overhang on the side opposite to that facing the wind, otherwise they would not indicate properly.

A Wind-pennant

An excellent and reliable wind indicator is shown in Fig. 7, the illustration of the wind-pennant. It consists of a metal hoop on which a funnel-shaped silk or cotton fabric pennant is sewed fast, and when this latter is filled by a breeze it stands out, as the illustration shows.

A pennant fifteen inches long should have a hoop five inches in diameter, and it can be made either from wire rings bent as shown in Fig. 8 A, or from sheet metal, as shown at Fig. 8 B.

The sheet metal should be perforated with small holes all around one edge to pass the thread through, when sewing the fabric fast, and the edges should be smoothed so as not to cut the threads. If the hoop is made of wire, a ring should be formed at top and bottom for the upright rod to pass through; but if it is of sheet metal a hole at the top and bottom will admit the rod.

This pennant is very useful at the mast-head of a boat, and is much more satisfactory to watch than the perpetually bobbing flat pennant, as it does not break or fall down unless it is calm, and only shifts from side to side as the wind blows it.

On a flag-pole or staff above the pennant the compass points are arranged; and if these are made from copper or brass, the letters may be soldered fast to the ends of the arms. Where the arms cross, they are to be flattened as shown in Fig. 9 A, and lapped together, as shown in Fig. 9 B. After the hole is bored they should be bound to the upright rod with copper wire and soldered so they will remain in a fixed position that the wind cannot alter. Fig. 9 C.

Sticks of hard wood may be substituted for the metal arms, and the sheet-metal letters let into saw cuts made at the outer ends.

A Basket-ball Vane

An odd wind indicator is shown in Fig. 10, illustrating a ball vane in a basket. It consists of a flat basket, with a rim six inches high, made of wire cloth with square meshes; inside of this a silk or cotton covered ball of wire is placed and blown by the wind from one side to the other of the basket. Of course, the direction the wind is coming from is opposite to that taken by the ball.

The basket should be twenty-four inches in diameter, six

inches high, and supported at the top of a pole by wires attached from the upper and lower edge of the outer rim, and leading up and down to the pole, the ends being made fast to staples or screw-eyes.

The ball, which is made of wire hoops and fastened together with fine wires, should be from four to six inches in

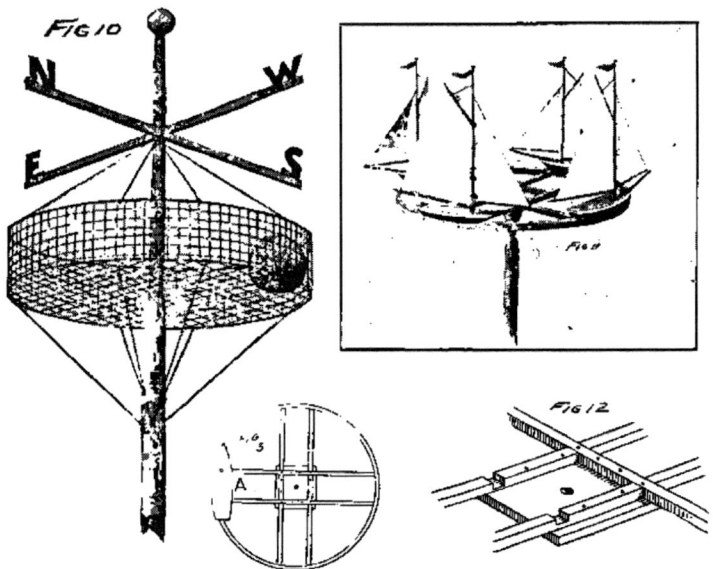

diameter. It is covered with silk or thin muslin sewed on in the same manner in which a baseball is covered with leather. The frame-work must be of light spring brass or copper wire, and where the hoops cross it would be well to touch the unions with solder to insure a firm joint and make the ball rigid.

If the ball should blow out of the basket at any time, it may be necessary to lace wires across the outer rim at the top, so as to form a confining net-work.

Above the basket the compass points can be arranged on wood or metal arms, and when complete and mounted this weather-vane will present a most unique appearance.

A Merry-go-round

A merry-go-round like the one shown in Fig. 11 is an interesting wind toy and pleasing to watch, as the boats keep sailing round and round. It is made from a child's hoople properly braced with cross sticks and mounted on a hub. Four flat-boats are made and attached to the outer edge of the frame. When rigged with sails and placed at the top of a post, on a rod, the boats will keep up a continual sailing so long as there is any breeze. A hoople three feet in diameter is best for this purpose, as it gives more space between the boats.

Double sets of braces or cross strips are arranged inside the hoople, and, where they meet at the middle, laps are cut in the sticks so that they will fit flush, as shown in Fig. 12.

The sticks are placed seven inches apart, and are five-eighths of an inch square; under the lap joints a plate of wood nine inches square is attached by means of screws or steel wire nails, to strengthen the unions of the cross sticks as well as to make a platform, at the under side of which the hub is arranged. A plan of the hoople, the cross sticks, and the location of one boat is shown in Fig. 13.

The boats are placed so that the outer edges of the bottoms rest on the top of the hoople. The inner edges rest on two of the cross sticks, where they are securely attached with long, slim screws passed up through the sticks and hoople and into the bottoms of the boats.

A block of wood four or five inches square and six inches long is to be shaved down at one end so that it is round and about one inch and a half in diameter. This is attached to the under side of the plate, at the middle of the hoople frame, so that the small end projects down; and through it a half-inch hole is bored.

An iron pin half an inch in thickness and eighteen inches long is to be driven into the upper end of a post over which the hub and hoople frame will fit. The upper end of the iron pin is threaded and provided with two nuts. One of these should be screwed down tight on the other with a washer between to act as a lock-nut, so that the revolution of the merry-go-round will not tighten or loosen them when once adjusted.

The boats are ten inches long and three inches wide at the middle, but they taper fore and aft, as shown in Fig. 13 A. They are cut from pine or whitewood two inches thick, and painted in gay colors. The masts are fifteen inches high, and the sails are provided with booms, gaffs, and jib-booms, also with rings which hold the sails close to the masts. The rigging is of copper wire, as the constant motion would soon wear out string or line and the sails would fly loose.

Each boat must be in good trim to keep the motion uniform, and if the sails wear out too soon, tin ones should be made or the muslin ones may be given a coat or two of white paint. Pennants at the tops of the masts will add to the effect.

A Wind Turbine

The wind turbine shown in Fig. 14, on the following page, is made of two hooples about thirty inches in diameter, four cross sticks, two wire hoops, and eight V-shaped tin blades.

The cross sticks, thirty inches long, are cut and lapped at the middle and attached to the edge of each hoop with screws or nails. The wire hoops are twenty-two inches in diameter, and are fastened to the cross sticks with staples. The plan of one hoople and the cross sticks, the wire hoop and the location of the blades, is shown in Fig. 15.

The outer corners of each blade are tacked fast to both the upper and lower hoople, while the inner corners are wired fast to the stout wire hoop. The blades are made from tin or sheet iron twelve inches long and six inches wide, and, when bent in the shape of a V, the width across the open end should be four inches.

The blades are depended upon to hold the upper and lower frames in place, and when the turbine is on the top of a post with a rod running through the middle of the cross sticks, around which it revolves, the wind will keep it spinning at a high speed.

Power can be developed with this turbine, but only a very small percentage as compared with a windmill the entire surface of which is continually exposed to the breeze. In the turbine only two or three of the blades are effective at any one time.

A Barrel-hoop Pinion-wheel

From a flat hoop, a few pieces of tin or sheet iron, and some thin wood, a barrel-hoop pinion-wheel may be made similar to the one shown in Fig. 16.

The barrel-hoop will measure about twenty-one inches in diameter, and the hub should be made five inches in diameter,

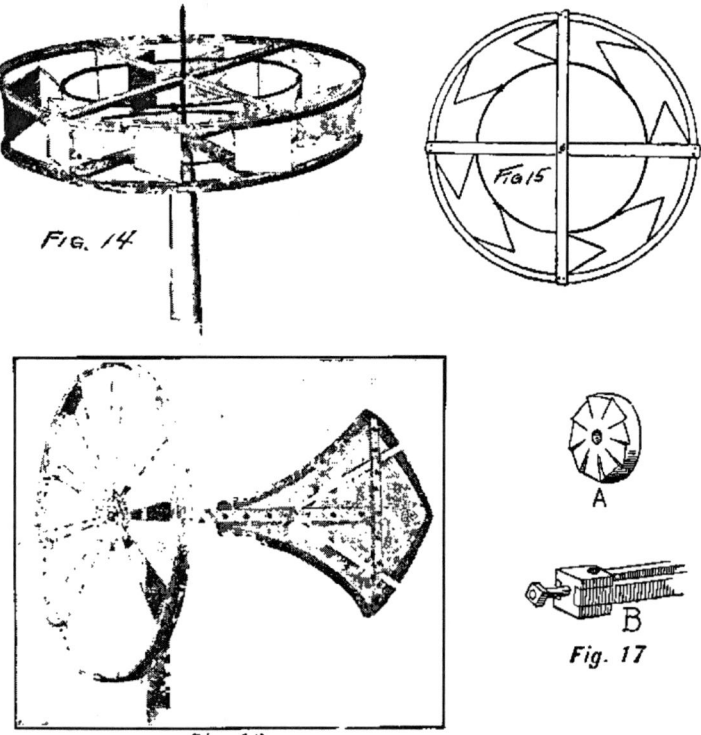

Fig. 14

Fig. 15

Fig. 16

A

B

Fig. 17

two inches thick, and cut in, as shown in Fig. 17 A, with nine places to receive the small ends of the metal blades. The hub revolves on a pin which is driven into a block of wood three inches square, as shown at Fig. 17 B. A hole is made in the block from top to bottom, through which a half-inch rod will pass. The rails that support the tail are let into each side of the block and are securely fastened with screws, as shown also at Fig. 17 B.

The fan-tails are twenty-four inches long, one inch and a half wide, and half an inch thick, made of ash or hickory that will bend easily, so as to be drawn in against the blades forming the tail.

The tin blades are cut five inches wide at one end and one inch and a half at the other, and fastened to both the hoop and hub with tacks, as shown in the illustration.

The blades forming the fan are of half-inch wood, one V-shaped piece and two end slats cut as shown in the illustration. They are all held in position by the two rails that extend back from the pinion block and two that are set at right angles to them, and which hold the upper and lower edge blades.

This wheel may be placed at the top of a post two or three inches square or round, in which a half-inch iron rod or long pin has been driven, leaving about six or eight inches of it projecting above the top of the post. On this the block turns as the wind acts on the fan-tail.

A Pumping Windmill

A simple wheel, with spokes and sails, that is commonly employed on canal-boats and barges, and in a small way for raising water in a suction-pump, is shown in the illustration of a pumping windmill. Fig. 18.

It consists of a hub, six spokes, a fan-tail, and a trunk or upright to which the wheel is attached. The hub is a hex-

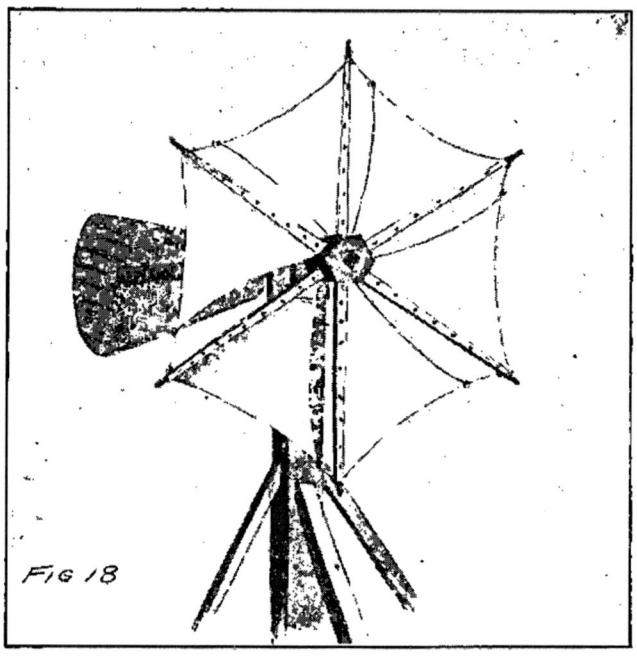

FIG 18

agon of six inches and six inches long, so that one spoke can be driven into a hole made in each side, as shown in Fig. 19. The spokes are three feet long, three by one inch and a half at the hub end, and one by one inch and a half at the outer end. They are driven snugly into holes in the hub three inches long and one inch and a half wide, and pinned to hold them in place.

The hub should be made of hard wood, and it would be well to have a blacksmith put a thin iron band around each end to prevent it from splitting. The holes may be cut with a mortise chisel and mallet, and care must be taken to shape them evenly, so that the spokes will line properly.

Triangular pieces of twilled muslin sheeting are tacked to the face of each spoke, and the loose corner of each is caught to the next spoke end with a rope and snap. This makes an outlet between the leech and spoke of each space between spokes for the wind to pass through, thereby causing the wheel to revolve.

The wheel is held in place to the head of the supporting post by a shaft which passes through the hub and is bolted fast at the front of it with a nut. A blacksmith will make this shaft, as it is somewhat beyond a boy's ability unless he has had some experience in blacksmithing. It should be shaped as shown in Fig. 20.

The shaft is an inch square where it passes through the hub, and at the front end it is threaded and provided with a nut and washer. At the end of the square part, A, where the rear of the hub will stop, a shoulder, B, should be welded on to hold the hub in the proper place.

An inch beyond this square shoulder, another one, C, is welded on the shaft, which for the balance of its length is three-quarters of an inch in diameter.

Just beyond the shoulder or collar, C, the crank is formed, two inches wide and three inches out from the shaft. Beyond the crank another collar, C C, is welded on, and beyond this the shaft should measure six inches in length.

The total length of the shaft is fifteen inches, and all the collars and smooth surfaces should be dressed down with a file and then painted. The head to which the fan-tail is attached is made of two blocks, cut as shown in Fig. 21, and fastened five inches apart on the lower rails that support the long rails to which, in turn, the tail is attached.

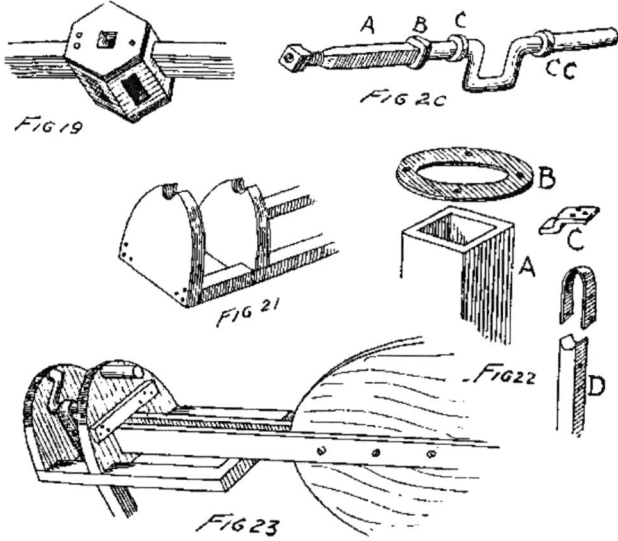

FIG 19

FIG 20

FIG 21

FIG 22

FIG 23

The upper ends of the blocks are cut out so as to admit the shaft. The collars, C, and C C, are at the inside of the blocks. To hold the shaft in place, straps of iron are screwed fast over the top of each block.

This head rests on the top of a trunk or hollow square

post, through which the rod passes that connects the crank with the piston-rod of a pump. This trunk is of three-quarter-inch wood and seven inches square, as shown in Fig. 22 A; and at the top of it a flat iron collar, B, is screwed fast.

To hold the head on and keep it in the proper place, four iron cleats (Fig. 22 C) are screwed fast to the under corners of the head to grip the projecting edge of the collar. This arrangement will hold the head stiff, but will allow it to move about as impelled by the wind acting on the tail.

A little grease or vaseline should be placed on top of the collar, so that the head will move on it easily. The top of the connection rod should be attached to the crank, as shown in Fig. 22 D, where a strap of iron passes over the crank and is bolted to the top of the hard-wood rod.

The tail is attached to the head as shown in Fig. 23, which is a rear view of the head block and a portion of the forward part of the tail.

The tail is thirty-three inches long and twenty-four inches wide at the rear end, and is made of boards three-quarters of an inch in thickness. If the mill is to be placed over a pump, a platform should be erected to which the trunk may be braced with props, as shown in the illustration, and on which the lower end of the trunk may rest.

Guy rods or wires can also be carried from the upper part of the trunk down to pegs driven in the ground, which will lend additional support and steadiness to the upright shaft. To start the wheel, snap the ends of the sheets to the spoke ends; to stop it, unsnap the ends and furl the sails around the spokes, and tie them securely with a cotton cord.

A Windmill and Tower

Windmills, of course, can be put to many different uses and are generally of sufficient size to develop a considerable amount of power. Fig. 24 shows a windmill and tower that

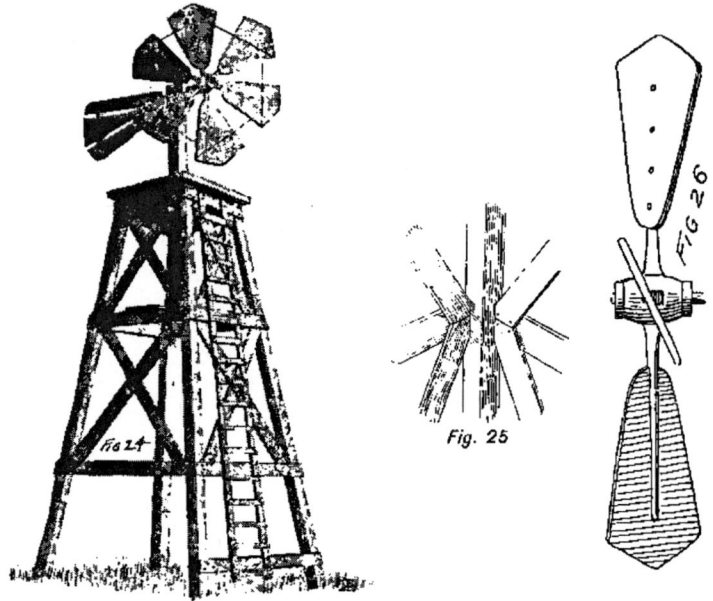

Fig. 25

any smart boy can make of wood, an old buggy wheel, and a few iron fittings that a blacksmith will make at a nominal cost.

The tower is the first thing to make, and it should be constructed of four spruce sticks sixteen feet long and four inches square, thirty inches square at the top and seventy-two inches square at the base.

The deck is thirty-six inches square, and projects two inches over the top rails all around. The rails and cross braces are of spruce or pine strips four inches wide and seven-eighths of an inch thick, and are attached to the corner posts with steel wire nails. The corner posts are embedded two feet in the ground, leaving fourteen feet of tower above the surface. The rail at the bottom, attached to the four posts, is three feet above the ground, and, midway between this and the top rail under the deck, the middle rail is run around the posts.

The cross braces are bevelled at the ends, so that they will fit snugly against the corner posts and in behind the rails where they are securely nailed to both posts and rails.

One of the posts with its binding of rails and cross brace is shown in Fig. 25, and this clearly illustrates how the union is made.

The posts, rails, and braces are all to be planed, so that they will present a good appearance when painted; and at one side of the tower a ladder can be made of scantling, and the lower end of it attached to a rail nailed to the corner posts a few inches above the ground.

Across two of the rails half-way up the tower a board is nailed, to which the lower end of a trunk is made fast, if a wheel similar to the pumping-mill is to be used. But if a wooden mill is desired, it can be constructed from a buggy-wheel and six blades of wood, to appear as shown in the illustration.

At a wagon-shop an old wheel can be had for little or nothing, and with a little work it may be converted into the frame of a windmill.

Each spoke is to be cut at an angle on one side so that the blades, when attached to them, will have the necessary pitch to make the wind act on them. This can be seen in Fig. 26, which is an edge view of the wheel showing a top, bottom, and middle blade.

The blades are eighteen inches long, twelve inches wide at the outer end, and six inches in width next the hub. They are three-quarters of an inch thick, and are attached to the spokes with screws. If it is found necessary, a wire can be run from the outer end of each blade to the end of the next spoke, to steady the blades, as shown in the illustration.

The crank and shaft can be arranged as described for the pumping-mill, and a fan-tail to keep the wheel up into the wind is made in proportion to the size of the mill.

All the wood-work should be painted to give it a good appearance. A mill of this size will develop at least quarter of a horse-power in a fifteen-mile breeze.

Chapter V

AËRIAL TOYS

The Elastic Flying-machine

TO have a flying - machine is the dream of every boy. To build a large one is exceedingly difficult, but a small one run by a rubber band can be easily constructed. You will not be able to fly up to the roofs of houses and spires of churches, but it will furnish you much amusement, without the danger of a broken neck.

I will tell you exactly how I constructed one of these machines, and then you can make one for yourself. The backbone was a knitting-needle. The wings, or more properly aëroplanes, were light bamboo strips (taken from a Japanese fan) and covered with the Japanese paper which is used for napkins. (Fig. 1.)

Fig. 2 shows the backbone and its parts. Cut from thin brass or copper a piece shaped like No. 1, and bend the top over, as shown at No. 2. Brass suitable for this may be bought at any hardware-store, or an old article made of proper metal may be cut up. The shell of a metallic cartridge is excellent. The brass should be as thin as possible, to be light, and so that it may be cut with an old pair of shears and bent easily. First cut the piece out roughly with the shears, and then trim it into shape with a small file. Scrape that part of the metal bright and clean which will form the inside of the roll, and then bend it around the ' needle so that it will fit nicely and snugly.

This must be fastened to the forward end of the backbone. The best and lightest way is to braze it, as the tin-

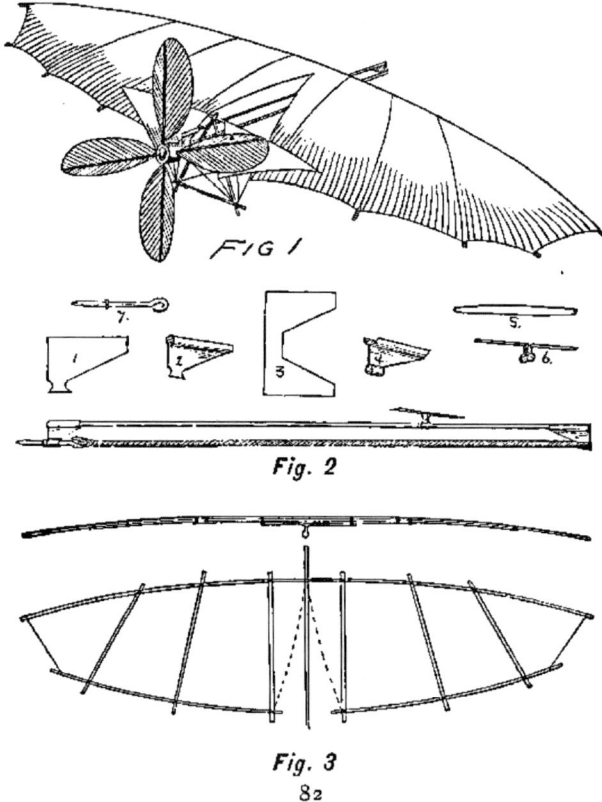

FIG 1

Fig. 2

Fig. 3

82

smiths call it   File the polish from the end of the needle,
and wet it with soldering fluid, which may be bought at a
tinner's, or made by adding zinc to muriatic acid until no
more is dissolved.   Slip on the brass support just where
you want it, and lay on a piece of solder about half the size
of a grain of wheat.   Now hold this in the flame of a candle,
in the gas, or near a hot stove, until the solder melts.   Take
it away and let it cool, and you will find that the solder has
run into all the cracks and joined the pieces beautifully.
File off any excess of solder or rough ends, and you will have
a neat and workman-like joint, as well as a very light one.

Cut out the piece No. 3, and bend it into the shape shown
at No. 4.   In this case you will need to file the upper surface
of the groove bright and clean.   Take off the polish from
the other end of the needle, and then put the stern-post, as
it may be called, in place, and hold it there by twisting a
fine wire around it and the needle.   Be careful to get both
supports turned the same way.   Then braze and finish it as
before.

Make the piece No. 5, and form it into the shape No. 6.
This is fastened by brazing to the backbone, as shown in
the lower diagram.   Take a piece of another knitting-needle,
and make a shaft like No. 7 by heating red-hot and pound-
ing the end into a hook with a small hammer.

Put the straight end of this shaft through the hole in the
stern-post which was formed by bending the metal, and
then make a shoulder on it, as follows: bend a piece of fine
wire into a ring the size of the needle, and braze this to the
shaft about a quarter-inch from the stern-post.   This ring
of wire keeps the shaft from slipping through the hole when

the rubber is stretched. File a flat point on the straight end of the shaft.

Next make the wings. For the ribs I used the thin bamboo strips taken from a Japanese fan. The paper is pulled or soaked off, and the thin strips cut close to the handle. The front of the wings is made as in the upper diagram of Fig. 3. Take one of the largest and stiffest strips of the bamboo, find the exact middle, and lay it evenly across the wing-support (No. 6 in Fig. 2), which is already in place on the backbone. Lash it to the support with waxed sewing-silk. Over this piece lay two others of equal length, making them come together (but not lap over) just above the backbone. When well secured, add three pieces of the same length above the two, placing them in such a way that the joinings shall not come over the joinings of either of the other pieces, and thus weaken the wings.

The ribs are made from the bamboo strips, cut the proper length and lashed to the front edge. The other ends are fastened to a cross-rib to make them take the same curvature. The lower diagram of Fig. 3 shows how the ribs are spaced.

Cover the wings with thin, strong paper. The best is Japanese paper, such as is used in making napkins. This is exceedingly light and very strong. It should be sewed, not gummed, as the gum makes the paper tear easily, and your sticky fingers spoil the whole cover very quickly. The paper is tough enough to be sewed, using a fine needle and white cotton, and you will get a neater and much more satisfactory job.

Make a triangle by lashing together three pieces of bamboo, two being about two inches long, and the third one inch. This triangle is lashed to the backbone just behind the wings, with the short side down; its position may be seen by a glance at the picture of the finished machine. It is kept rigid by running stays, made of waxed sewing-silk, from the lower corners to the stern-post, from the right-hand corner to the middle of the left wing, and from the left-hand corner to the middle of the right wing.

Just in front of this triangle fasten a piece of the bamboo, and make two small guiding vanes or rudders. These are made in a similar manner to the wings. Tie threads to the lower corners of the wings, and then to the triangle, drawing them down until they have the proper angle. The guiding-vanes should have a greater angle than the wings—that is, they should be drawn farther down.

It only remains now to make the screw and attach the rubber band. For the hub of the wheel you will need a small cork. This cork must be kept from turning on the end of the shaft. If the sharpened end of the shaft carrying the hook for the rudder was simply stuck into the cork, it would soon wear loose and turn easily. To make a firm hold for the shaft, bore a hole through the cork about a quarter-inch from the large end, and drive a plug of soft wood into this hole. The flat-pointed end of the shaft can now pass into the cork and be forced into the wood, being careful to have the end of the point parallel to the grain of the wood. This will give a firm hold and prevent the screw slipping.

The blades of the screw are made of thin paper gummed on to short pieces of bamboo. Lay one of the bamboo spokes on a piece of thin, stiff paper, and then gum over it a small strip of the thin Japanese paper before referred to. When this is dry, cut it down to the proper shape and sharpen the end of the spoke. Force these spokes into the cork so that all the blades will turn the same way, as shown in the picture—*i. e.*, so that when the screw is turned the blades will all strike the air in the same manner and tend to force the machine forward, not so that some try to push it forward and some backward.

Select a rubber band of the proper size—such a one as will stretch the length of the backbone easily and not be so strong that, when stretched, the backbone is bent into a bow. Tie this band to the forward support with a string, and then draw it back and slip it over the hook on the shaft.

To wind up the machine, hold it by the backbone and turn the screw the wrong way until the rubber is twisted tight. Then hold the machine up, let go the screw, and when it is revolving rapidly, give it a gentle push forward. If it pitches head-first, draw down the wings; if tail-first, let up the wings or turn the screw the other way. If the wheel does not revolve rapidly cut off part of the blades or use a stronger rubber. Some little adjustment of the kind is usually required before the thing moves properly.

A contrivance of this sort should be very light. The one before me has wings two feet from tip to tip, and it weighs when complete—backbone, wings, rubber, screw, etc.—only one-third of an ounce.

Self-acting Aërial Car

Here is an idea for a mechanical toy to be used either on a kite-string or a cord stretched from a flag-pole in the yard or a handy tree. The only condition is that the lower end of the cord is directly against the wind. The elevation at which the car can run will depend on the strength of the wind and sail area of the machine. The only wood used is the lightest and driest pine that can be procured. The carriage is made entirely of one-half by one-quarter inch wood, and is composed of two strips, fourteen inches long, placed one inch apart. The two guiders are two inches from each end, and have a small screw-eye on the lower extremity, through which the cord is passed. On the upper side of the carriage, exactly in the centre, are screwed two eyes, which should measure a little over a half-inch in diameter of the inside of their circle. Through these is passed the spar of the sail, allowing enough space to insure easy turning, as the spar acts as an axis on which the sail turns when on its downward trip. This spar is at right angles with the carriage. Two upright sticks measuring twenty inches, and the same dimensions as the material used for the construction of the carriage, are next added. These should be slightly pointed at both ends, and a cross-bar at the top of these uprights securely fastened gives additional strength. The balancing-bar is made of three-eighths by three-eighths inch pine, tapering at the lower end, and is ten inches in length, and fastened to the carriage by two strips of wood'—five by one-quarter by one-eighth inch. The wheels are formed as follows: Take a piece of one-eighth inch pine, which should be at least three inches wide. On this place a strip of wood, we will say, for instance, ten by one-quarter by one-half inch. By driving a small wire nail through both pieces of wood, and inserting a sharp

knife-blade through the upper piece of wood, and turning (the upper piece) slowly from left to right, you will
find you can cut a perfect circle in the lower piece of wood.
The wheels are formed by this process. It takes four pieces
of stiff card-board and two of wood to make the wheels for
the carriage. The diameter of the wooden wheel is one and

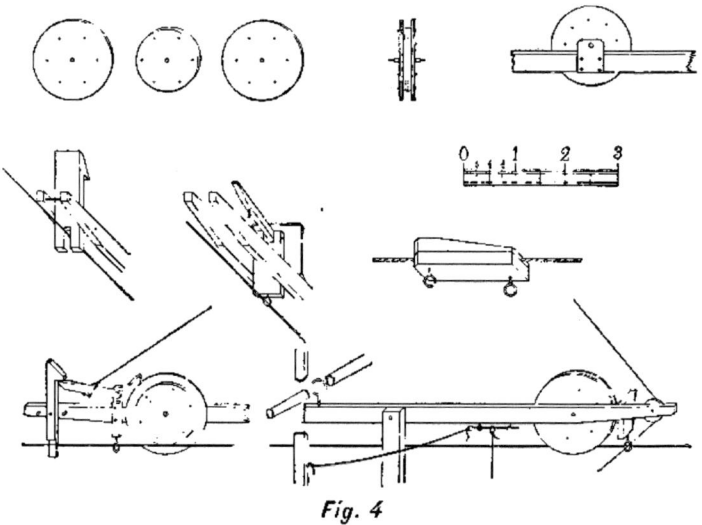

Fig. 4

one-half inches, while the card-board disks are two and one-
quarter inches. The wheels in the draught are a trifle smaller,
but by experiments it is found that the above-sized wheel
makes faster time. You will see that after cutting out your
disks the hole made by the wire nail is exactly in the centre.
Run a small wire nail through the three disks, placing the
wooden disk in the centre and the card-board ones on each

88

side (this makes three disks for each wheel). Put some glue on touching surface, and clinch the three together with pins or wire brads. The place where these nails go is shown by the spots on side draught of the wheel. The axle-tree is made of oak, and at the extremities a piece of stout wire is inserted, which extends one-eighth of an inch beyond the wood of the axle-tree. The hardest axle-tree is one made from the shafts of an old clock. Take particular care that the wheels run very true, as the success of the machine depends to a great extent upon this.

From the lower extremity of the balancing-rod hangs a weight. The easiest way to make this weight is to take a small bag, and fill it with sand until the machine balances (the sail in horizontal position). Having progressed thus far in the construction of the machine, turn the sail in a horizontal position, and attach a cord from one side of the cross-bar to a small grooved wheel at the aft end of the carriage. From the screw-eye at lower extremity of the balancing-bar is attached a small rubber band; when stretched it will reach within three-quarters of an inch of the small wheel at the aft end of the carriage. It will be found, after the cord and rubber band have been joined, that upon letting go the perpendicular bars the sail will turn in a horizontal position. At the forward end of the carriage is a catch, to which is fastened a ring. The catch comes in contact with a block (previously placed three-quarters up the string). The detail drawings show the formation and working of the catch. Fig. 4.

The sail is made of light muslin, and extends in the form of a pair of wings, the cloth only reaching from the outside

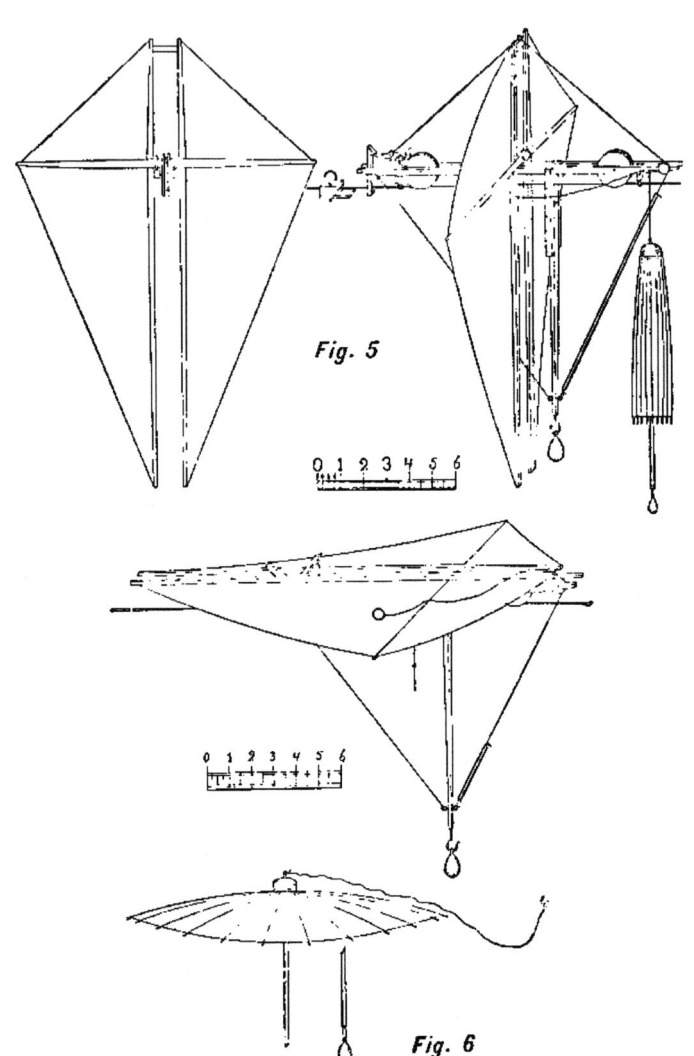

Fig. 5

0 1 2 3 4 5 6

0 1 2 3 4 5 6

Fig. 6

of the uprights to the ends of the spar, leaving a free space in the centre for the sail to pass through the carriage. The parachute is a small Chinese umbrella (pick out one that opens easily), and can be bought for a few cents. A small weight is attached to the handle with a few feet of cord. We will say that now you have completed the machine— you have a kite flying; run the string through the two guiders, place the two wheels of the carriage upon the kite-string, set the sail perpendicular, and fasten the catch with the cord. A stop-block has been previously placed on the cord twenty feet from the kite; now attach the parachute (Chinese umbrella). The force of the wind acting on the sail forces the machine up the incline of the kite-string at a rapid rate, skyward, until it reaches the block, which throws off the catch. The sail swings back to a horizontal position, letting the parachute drop. The sail being folded and presenting no resistance to the wind, the force of gravitation acting on the weight of the machine causes it to descend the kite-cord quickly, and return to the original starting-point of its flight. See Fig. 5, a side and end view, and Fig. 6, the parachute and the car on its return.

Aërial Boat-sailing

Study with care the accompanying plans. The materials are one-half by one-quarter-inch pine, free from knots, ten common brass rings three-quarters of an inch in diameter, two round-headed brass screws one inch in length, two flat-headed ones of the same dimensions, two small screw-hooks, and eight assorted brass screw-eyes, there be-

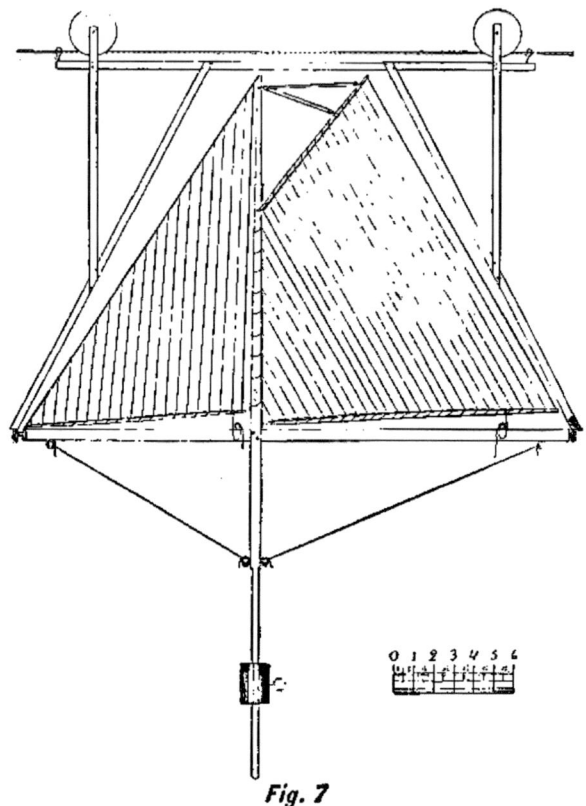

Fig. 7

ing two of each size. Now that we have the material for the frames, we will begin with Fig. 7, which shows the sail and sheer plan. The frame is made of six pieces of wood. The top piece is exactly two feet in length. The two uprights which hold the wheels are each one foot and one inch long. The two angle pieces are one foot nine inches each. The lower horizontal strip measures two feet three and one-half inches, and is joined to the two angle strips by means of a screw-eye and screw at each extremity. Now cut a strip of pine, making it exactly three feet in length. Set it on the frame in an upright position, allowing a half-inch clearance from the upper horizontal piece. It should be eleven inches from one of the angle pieces at the lower end. Round the upper part above the horizontal strip; it should be brought to a taper at the upper end. This forms the mast. The lower part is uniform, and allows the weight to be moved up and down to insure a correct balance, which is regulated according to the force of the wind. The weight is made of one-and-a-half-inch lead pipe, and is two inches in length. A round plug of pine is driven in the centre of the lead pipe, and a hole is bored in the centre of the plug to fit the balancing-bar.

One of the screw-eyes is inserted through the piece of lead pipe, and by this means the weight can be elevated or brought down the shaft and held firmly in the required place, which will depend on the force of the wind. In regard to the wheels, Fig. 8 shows the simplest constructed. They are made in three parts. Take two of the largest-sized wooden button moulds and a piece of thin board (cut in a circle) smaller than the button moulds. We will say, for instance, the button moulds are one and one-half inches in diameter, and the centre piece of pine is one inch in diameter and one-eighth of an inch thick. The way to get a true circle on this soft pine is to take the one-eighth-inch wood and measure on a separate piece of pine one-half inch, drive in a small wire nail in one extreme of the previously measured strip, and on the other extremity insert the point of a sharp knife. Place on the board used for centre of wheel, and turn in a circle from right to left several times. If the distance between the knife-blade and nail is one-half inch, the wheel cut out will be exactly one inch in diameter.

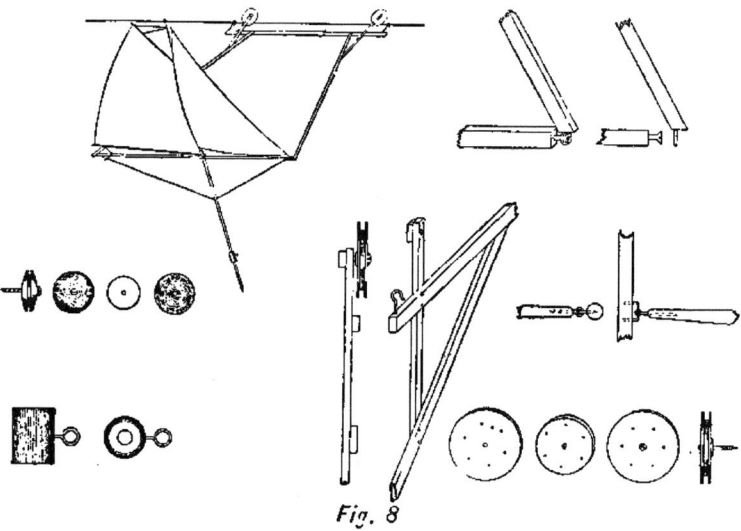

Fig. 8

Insert a wire nail through the two button moulds, and place the inch wheel in the centre, gluing it at each contact surface. This will give you the grooved wheel.

The drawing (Fig. 7) indicates how this wheel is fastened to the frame. The wheel can be made of two card-board disks two and one-half inches in diameter, and one wooden wheel two inches in diameter placed between them. They

94

are joined by clinched pins, shown by the circle of dots in Fig. 8.

The dimensions of the sail are as follows: Main-sail—hoist, ten and one-half inches; gaff, eight and one-half inches; leech, nineteen and one-quarter inches; boom, fourteen and one-half inches. Jib—foot, eleven inches; hoist, sixteen inches—on the stay, twenty and one-quarter inches. The jib carries a boom, and the main-sail a gaff and boom. The material used for the sails is light muslin with hemmed edges.

Take a long chalk-line or heavy cord, and stretch at right angles to the direction of the wind. If the wind is from the north, the cord must reach east and west. Each extremity of the cord must be the same height from the ground, and can be attached from tree to tree, or from an upper-story window to a house near by.

When the boat reaches the extremity of the cord the operator at that end of the cord turns it, and starts it on the return journey.

If the cord is strung between two houses you will find the boat will sail back and forth, except when the wind is dead ahead or a few points either way.

A "High-flyer"

To make the "flyer" you will need a piece of thin sheet tin, zinc, or iron, that may be purchased from a tinsmith for a few cents; and for the engine a linen-thread spool, a piece of hard-wood stick, and a few steel wire nails will be required.

To begin with, obtain an empty linen-thread spool having a smooth hole through it, and in one end drive four one-inch steel-wire nails at regular distances apart, so as to form the corners of a perfect square; drive the nails in half-way, then file the heads off, and the spool will appear like Fig. 9. Next get a round hard-wood stick seven inches long, and around it, two inches from one end, make a deep cut with your knife. From this cut to the end of the stick shave the wood away so it will look like Fig. 11.

These two parts will complete the engine, and the next thing to make will be the flyer. Thin sheet-zinc will be found the best to make it of; and having obtained a piece, mark on it with a compass a circle five inches in diameter; mark two lines across this circle from edge to edge, at right angles, as shown by the dotted lines in Fig. 14.

From a piece of stiff paper cut a pattern in the form of one of the ears shown in Fig. 14. Lay this pattern on the zinc so that one of the lines will be in the centre of it, and mark the shape on the zinc; mark the other three ears in a similar manner, and then with a stout pair of shears cut out the flyer.

In the centre of it make a hole large enough for the small end of the stick to pass through it, and around it make four small holes at the centre of each ear, to correspond with the pins on the spool.

The flyer will then fit over the stick and pins and lay flat on top of the spool; bend its ears with your fingers so they appear like the propeller-blades of a steamboat, or like a windmill, and it will then be ready to fly. Fig. 10.

When bending the ears they must be arranged so that the

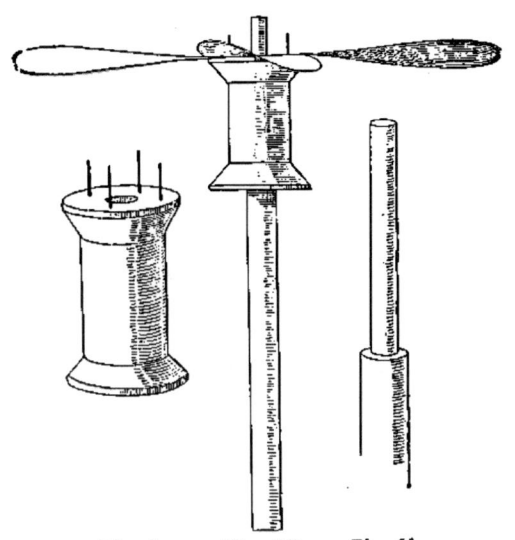

Fig. 9   *Fig. 10*   *Fig. 11*

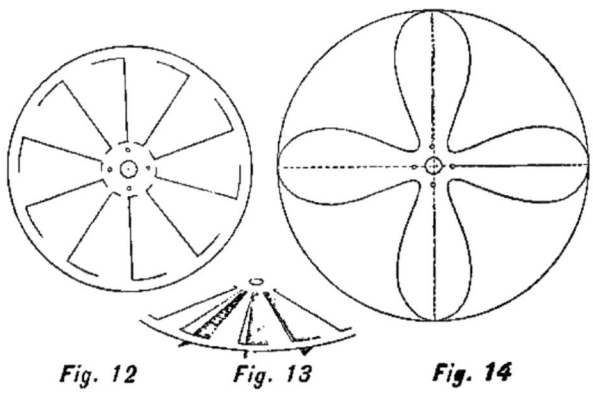

Fig. 12   *Fig. 13*   *Fig. 14*

A "HIGH-FLYER"

edge that catches the wind first will be inclined upward, as otherwise the flyer, instead of flying, will hug the spool tightly.

Another style of flyer is shown in Fig. 12, and is made of a circular disk of zinc four inches in diameter.

Make the five holes in the centre fit over the stick and pins. When all the places have been cut, bend the ears down as shown in Fig. 13, and when flying it turn it upsidedown, letting the ears project upward.

To put the flyer in action, take the stick in your left hand, and over the small end of it place the spool, against which put your thumb to keep it from slipping. Wind strong cord around the spool, to the end of which a button is fastened to keep the cord from slipping through your fingers; on top of the spool place the flyer, and give the string a vigorous pull, at the same time releasing the spool with your thumb, and the centrifugal force will cause the flyer to revolve rapidly, shoot upward, and sail to a height of fifty or a hundred feet in the air, slowly descending as the revolutions diminish.

Larger flyers can be made in a similar manner; and to make a very large one, plant a post in the ground, having its upper end reduced to form a shoulder, as explained for the small stick. Get a round piece of wood several inches in diameter, and arrange four very stout steel-wire nails in the top of it. Make a tin or iron flyer twelve or fifteen inches in diameter, and use a piece of small clothes-line or cotton line to spin it with.

To operate it, wind the spool with the rope, and have some one under it to keep it from slipping. When you are ready to pull the rope, place the flyer on the pins, and as the spool is released give the rope a quick, strong pull, and the flyer will rise.

Part **II**

A F I E L D

Chapter VI

COASTERS, SKEES, AND SNOW-SHOES

ALL real boys welcome the approach of the winter season with its glorious opportunities for sport on the snow and ice. Toboggans, double-runners, skees, and snow-shoes—the very words make the blood tingle in one's veins, and happy is the boy whose home is in the Northern climes where there is real winter for at least four months out of the year.

Nowadays it is possible to purchase almost everything for winter sports, but the boy who is handy with tools and of an inventive turn of mind will take more pleasure in constructing his own things than in buying them out of a shop.

Very few boys would care to make their own skates, as the modern steel-clamp skates are superior in lightness and durability to anything he could construct; but the various varieties of sleds, coasters, and snow-shoes are quite within the measure of his abilities, and their making will fill most pleasurably the leisure hours after school and on Saturdays.

All the cold-weather countries have their distinctive and peculiar forms of winter amusements. Tobogganing and snow-shoeing are particularly popular in Canada; skeeing is the national sport of Norway. But it is the American boy who has reduced coasting to an exact science, and the

Yankee bob-sleds and "jumper-coasters" are now pre-eminent wherever the snow flies. To take the best wherever we find it is the sportsman's motto.

Toboggans

There is no more enjoyable winter sport than tobogganing, and in many parts of America, notably Montreal, large and expensively constructed artificial slides are in constant use throughout the winter season.

For ordinary hill - coasting most American boys prefer bob-sleds and coasters, but in the extreme Northern States and throughout Canada the plain toboggan is the favorite coaster.

A boy who is at all clever with tools can make a good toboggan from three or four thin hickory boards, a few cross-battens, and some rails. For the bottom quarter-inch hickory should be employed, as that is strong and will bend easily when steamed.

To make an eight-foot toboggan with a width of twenty inches, obtain the hickory boards and batten them with three pieces of hard - wood two inches wide and three-quarters of an inch thick. Make the fastenings with brass screws or copper rivets having the heads countersunk in the bottom. At the front ends rivet on a wood batten long enough to project two inches beyond the boards at each end.

From a curtain-pole cut six pieces two inches long and bore a quarter-inch hole through each one from end to end. Cut two hickory rails three-quarters of an inch square and plane off the sharp corners; then with copper or iron rods, to act as long rivets, attach the rails to the toboggan so that they are separated from the battens by means of the wooden blocks, as shown in the illustration of the plain toboggan. Fig. 1.

At both ends of the rod-rivets place washers or burrs to rivet on, as otherwise the rivet would pull through the wood, tearing the hole larger and at the same time making the

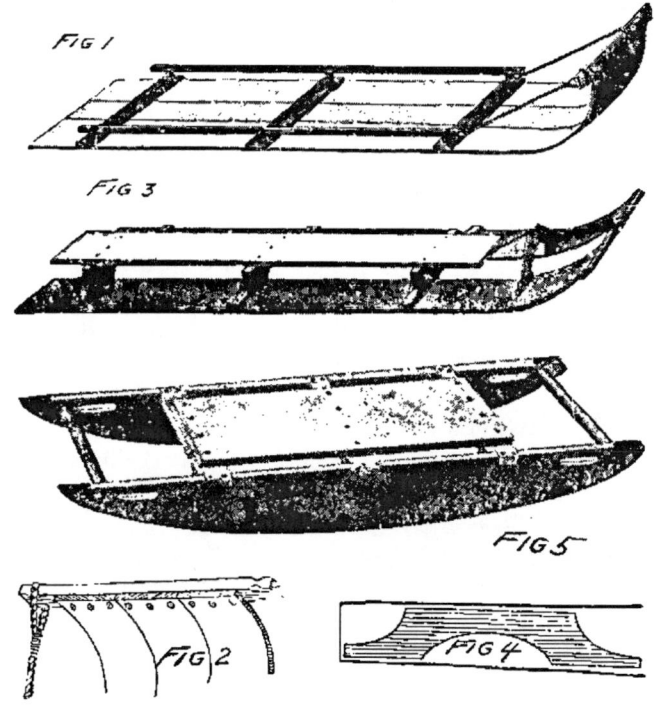

FIG 1

FIG 3

FIG 5

FIG 2

FIG 4

anchorage insecure. Cut notches in the projecting ends of the front stick as shown at the right side of Fig. 2, so that ropes can be lashed fast to the stick as shown at the left side of Fig. 2.

Steam the boards between the front end and the first batten, or pour boiling hot water over both sides of the boards; then bend the wood up and with the ropes as a help to hold the boards in place continue the wetting and bending until the proper curve has been gained, as shown in the illustration. Lash the ropes fast, and when the wood is dry sand-paper it smooth and give it several good coats of varnish.

A sled-toboggan (Fig. 3) is made from two hickory boards eight feet long and a quarter of an inch in thickness. If the toboggan is to be twenty-two inches wide each runner should be several inches wide.

Three hard-wood bridges twenty-two inches long and four inches high are cut, as shown in Fig. 4, and attached to the runners with screws (Fig. 3). They support a seat eight inches wide which is screwed down to the top of the bridges.

In front of the first bridge and behind the last one short bracket-braces are attached to prevent the bridges from rocking, and these as well as the bridges can be cut from wood about an inch and a half in thickness.

The front ends of the boards are attached to a batten, and by steaming the boards may be curved up as shown and held in place with a stanchion-rope lashed fast to the batten and to the front bridge. A supporting bridge should be used to give it additional power. Fig. 3.

When the varnish wears off the bottom give it another coat, as the smooth, hard finish helps the toboggan to slide easily over the snow.

A Rocker-coaster

A very good coasting-sled is shown in the illustration of a rocker-coaster (Fig. 5), and for short hills a sled of this sort will prove very fast and easy to steer.

It is from four to five feet long, twenty inches broad, and seven inches high at the middle. The lower edge of each runner is curved from end to end with a long, sweeping line, and it is grooved to receive a round runner of steel, which a blacksmith will make and attach.

The frame of the coaster should be made of hard-wood five-eighths of an inch in thickness, and the three cross-ribs are one inch and a half in width and one inch in thickness. Laps are cut in the top edges of the sides, and the cross-ribs are let into them and made fast with screws. Wooden brackets or cleats are attached to the sides and to the under side of each cross-rib to strengthen the construction, and at both ends a piece of round curtain-pole is made fast as shown in Fig. 5.

The ends of the poles are trimmed off so as to form dowel ends, and these fit into holes made in the ends of the sides.

Hand-holes are cut with a bit and compass-saw at the ends of the sides; a deck of half-inch wood is laid over the ribs and held down with screws. Have the blacksmith flatten the ends of each runner and bend them over so they will lie on top at the end of each side.

A few good coats of paint will finish the wood-work nicely, and the rocker-coaster will then be ready for use.

A Single-runner Coaster

A few years ago the boys of New England invented a new kind of sled and called it a single-runner coaster or jumper-coaster. They sit upon it, keeping their balance with the feet, and it is remarkable how rapidly and easily they go downhill on this queer-looking affair, and without the slightest danger of toppling over. Fig. 6.

The coaster is very simple in construction and any boy can make it from pine or hard-wood, the latter being preferable as it has more body and is heavier. The runner is forty-two inches long, one inch and a half thick, and four inches high, curved at one end and cut at an angle at the other. The upright is of wood the same thickness and width, and eleven or twelve inches high, so that with the top board or seat and the height of the runner the coaster is sixteen or seventeen inches high; and for taller boys it can be made still higher. The seat is ten inches long and seven inches wide, and attached to the upright with screws, as shown at Fig. 7. The upright is cut from wood about ten inches wide, so that, with a compass-saw, a broad foot may be shaped at the bottom which will give a better bearing on the runner than would a narrower one.

From wood two inches wide, make two side-plates or braces to run from under the seat down half-way over the runner as shown in Fig. 7. To steady the seat at the top of the uprights cut two angle-brackets and attach them as shown in the figure drawing. A blacksmith will fashion a runner from quarter-round or thin tire iron and attach it as shown in the illustration. The runners can be held on with flat-headed screws countersunk in the iron, and after a few trips the surface of the metal will be worn bright and smooth, insuring easy and rapid running.

A Bob-sled

Every boy wants a double-runner of his own, for there seems to be nothing quite like bobbing on a sled carrying from six to ten boys—enough to give it weight and a good impetus on its downward course. A bob-sled is not at all difficult to construct, and a very satisfactory and substantial one may be made from inexpensive materials and with the tools that nearly every boy possesses. Fig. 8.

For the seat obtain a clear spruce plank ten feet long, ten inches wide, and one inch and a half thick, planed on both sides and edges. The front sled is thirty inches long and fourteen inches wide, with the sides five inches high. The rear sled is forty inches long from prow to end of runners, and is the same width and height as the front one. The sides are of hard-wood seven-eighths of an inch in thickness, and braced with cross-pieces of hard-wood two inches wide and one inch and a half thick.

Laps are cut in the top of the sides, and with screws the ends of the braces are securely held in place. Under each cross-piece and at the sides brackets must be securely fastened with screws as shown at Fig. 9, to strengthen the sides and take some of the strain from the cross-piece fastenings. Eight inches from the rear end a stout block is set in the runners through which the king-bolt passes that fastens the seat to the sled. This is of hard-wood fourteen inches long, two inches and a half wide, and four inches

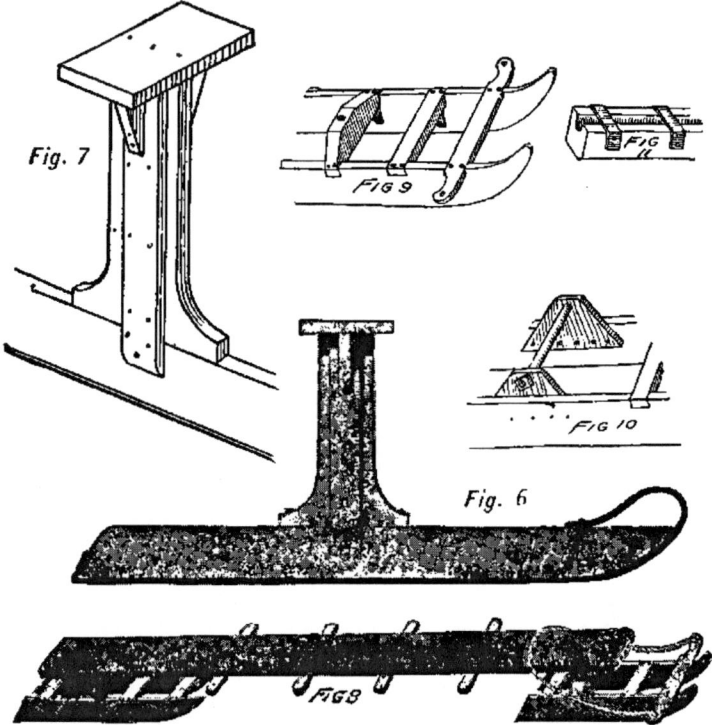

Fig. 7

Fig. 6

high at the middle, as shown in Fig. 9. A similar block two inches high is attached to the under side of the plank and bears on the lower block. Between the two blocks and on the bolt, two large, flat iron washers are placed, so that it will be an easy matter to turn the sled when there is a heavy weight on the plank.

The head of the five-eighths-inch king-bolt should be embedded in the top of the block that is fast to the plank before it is attached, and the bolt should be provided with two nuts for safety. In the summer-time, when the bob is stored away, the forward sled can be removed by unscrewing the nuts from the lower end of the bolt under the sled.

To steer the bob a hard-wood cross-bar piece is let into the runners as shown in Fig. 9. It projects six inches at each side, and foot-notches are cut at the rear edge as shown in the illustration. The rear sled is attached to the plank by means of a block and bolts.

Two triangular hard-wood blocks one inch in thickness, with the grain running vertically, are screwed fast to the inside sides of the runners as shown in Fig. 10, and through holes in the upper end a long half-inch bolt is passed from side to side. This bolt fits in a groove made at the under side of the block that is attached to the plank; and across the groove in several places straps of iron are fastened as shown in the inverted block at Fig. 11. A hinge-joint is the result, and to prevent the rear sled from dropping too far when jumping over a bump a rope should be passed under the forward cross-piece and attached to a staple driven at the under side of the plank.

The plank can be padded with hair from an old mattress and covered with a strip of carpet nailed all around the edges of the board. Cross-pieces screwed fast to the under side of the plank will serve as foot-rests, and with a coat or two of paint this bob-sled will be ready for use.

Skees

Skee running and jumping is one of the favorite winter sports in Norway and Sweden and is steadily growing in favor both in the Northern United States and in Canada. On very steep hills it is a dangerous sport, but it is perfectly

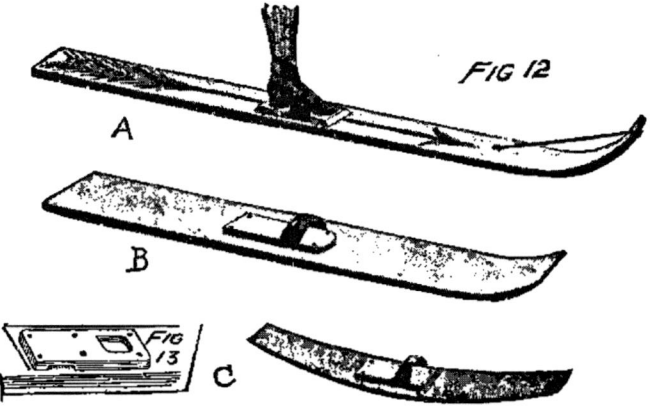

safe to use the skees on either short hills or on long ones that are not too steep. Once you start you must go to the bottom, and a good skee-jumper should be as agile as a cat, for he must always land feet down when jumping.

A skee of the right proportions should be seven feet long and four inches wide. Hickory, oak, or other hard-wood three-quarters of an inch in thickness will be the best material from which to make the skees. Two or three grooves cut in a straight line along the entire bottom length will hold the skee slider on his course, as the keel does a boat.

The skees are tapered and bent up at the front ends as shown in Fig. 12. This can be done by steaming and bending until the proper pitch is obtained; but if a high curve is desired it would be well to attach a thong to the end and draw it back to the body of the skee as shown in Fig. 12 A.

At the middle of the skee a foot-block is attached and provided with a toe-strap as shown in Fig. 13. This strap fits under the block and can be removed if necessary as a lap is cut at the under side of the block.

A shorter and broader skee is shown in Fig. 12 B. This is safer for smaller boys to use as it is five feet long and six inches wide.

Many of the Norwegian skees are beautifully carved and ornamented, and the boy who has some decorative ability can embellish the tops of his skees and varnish them all over to improve their appearance and make them smooth, so that they will slide easily.

A skee made from a hogshead or crockery-cask stave i. shown in Fig. 12 C; and a great deal of fun can be had with this makeshift on short hills.

Snow-shoes

For travelling over the snow the most widely known and useful appliance is the snow-shoe in one form or another. The Esquimau and the American Indian do all their winter travelling on snow-shoes, and through the Alps and in the snow-bound parts of Europe and Asia they are commonly employed as a means of locomotion from place to place.

The long snow-shoe shown in Fig. 14 A is the one commonly used by the Iroquois Indians, and it measures from three to four feet in length and from twelve to fifteen inches in width. It is usually made from one long strip of hickory bent while green and dried in the desired shape, then braced and interlaced with thongs of rawhide or deer-gut.

The rim is usually from three-quarters to seven-eighths of an inch square and is rounded on the outer edges. The braces or spreaders are let into the inner edges of the rim as shown in Fig. 15 A, and are held securely in place with a thong passed through a hole in the end of the piece and wrapped around the rim as shown in Fig. 15 B. The spreaders are of seasoned hickory two inches wide and five-eighths of an inch thick. The edges are bevelled slightly, and near the centre line two rows of holes are made through which to lace the thongs. Two smaller sticks are arranged at each side of the broad spreaders, and the lattice weaving is caught around them as shown in the illustration. Some of the thongs are caught over the rim while others are passed through holes made in the edge similar to the manner in which a tennis racket is laced. Foot-laces are fastened at the front spreader to which the shoe-toes are lashed, for when travelling the heels should be free to lift while the ball of the foot and the entire snow-shoe remains flat on the snow.

The shoe in the form of a tennis racket (Fig. 14 B) is the shape commonly used by the Esquimaux and is about thirty-four inches long and fifteen inches wide. It is made some-

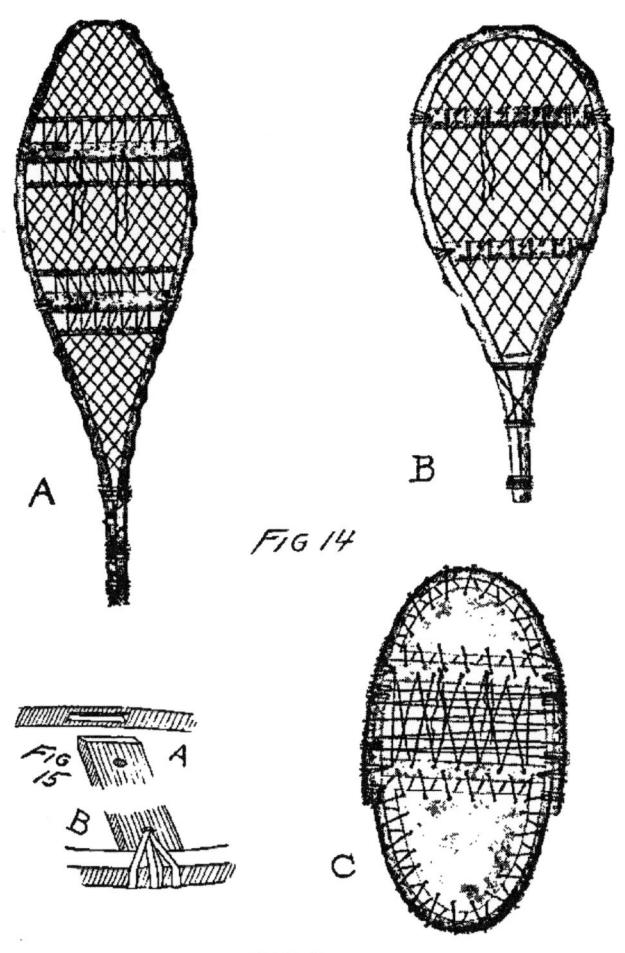

A

B

FIG 14

FIG 15

A

B

C

SNOW-SHOES

what similar to the Iroquois shoe but the mesh is more open.

The oval shoe (Fig. 14 C) is made from two U-shaped rims lashed together at the middle and provided with two spreaders. Two stout pieces of rawhide are laced in the ends, and through the middle a lacing of thongs is woven across between the spreaders and sides of the rim.

These and many other forms of snow-shoes can be made by the boy who is interested in snow-shoe travelling. The wood can be procured anywhere and the rawhide thongs may be purchased at a hardware store. They are sold as belt-lacings for machinery, but they can be easily split and so made available for snow-shoe use.

Chapter VII

SAIL-SKATING AND SNOWBALL ARTILLERY

A Skating-sail

SAIL-SKATING is a very enjoyable means of getting over the ice, and with properly constructed frames and sails a very respectable rate of speed can be maintained. In using a sail the boy is the boat, and by his manipulation of the sheets he can go where he pleases, either before the wind or tacking, as in a boat.

The skating-sail shown in Fig. 1 is an improvement over the old style of attaching two diamond-shaped cloths to the ends of yard-arms. To make the frame obtain two clear pine or white-wood sticks twelve feet long, one inch and a quarter square, and taper them slightly towards the ends with a plane. At the same time round the corners at the top of one stick and bottom of the other as shown in Fig. 2 C, which represents a sawed-off section of both sticks. With linen line wind the sticks for an inch or two for every nine or ten inches of their entire length to strengthen them. Paint these windings a dark color and then varnish the sticks or color them with a stain.

Now procure two other sticks, each five feet six inches long and seven-eighths of an inch square, and plane them smooth, at the same time tapering the ends slightly. These are for the cross-arms, and at the middle of each one lash fast a block five inches long and seven-eighths of an inch square having a pin driven in each end as shown in Fig. 2 A. These pins fit in small holes made at the inside of the yard-arms four feet and six inches from either end.

The yard-arms are lashed together at the ends, then sprung apart at the middle so that the cross-arm blocks will fit between them. To properly hold the arms in place a strap should be drawn around the sticks at the middle, and to insure a good prop a block six inches long, two inches wide, and seven-eighths of an inch thick is to be cut and provided with two pins at each end as shown in Fig. 2 C. The pins will fit into small holes made in the long sticks, and when the strap is buckled tight the block will be held securely in place.

A large flat hook should be lashed fast to this block, and when sailing along before the wind this can be caught over a stout leather belt to help support the weight of the sail.

Two twilled-cotton sails are made in the shape shown in the illustration and provided with snaps at the three outer ends so that they may catch into eyes lashed fast to the ends of the arms and to the long sticks as shown in Fig. 2 B. The sails should be drawn taut at the inner ends with rings and a strap or light rope. If there should be too much sail-area for the wind that may be blowing the sail can be feathered—that is, bent down or up so that it allows some of the wind to pass under it instead of pressing against the sails with its full force.

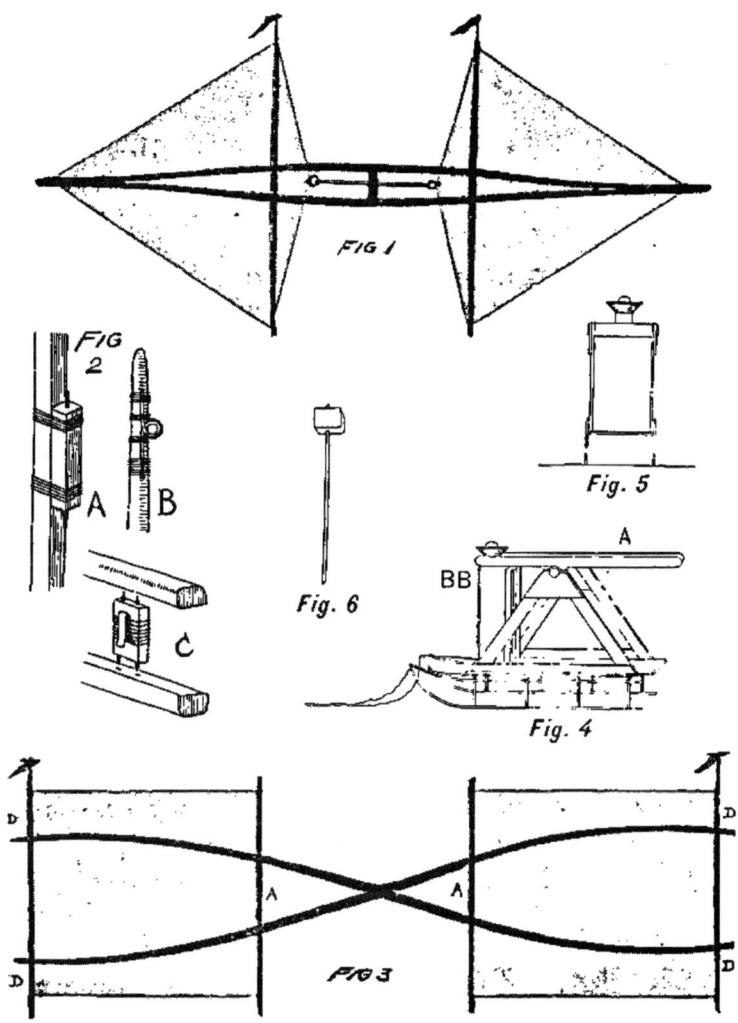

FIG 1

FIG 2

A   B

C

Fig. 6

Fig. 5

A

BB

Fig. 4

D   D

A   A

FIG 3

D   D

A SKATING-SAIL, A SQUARE-RIGGED ICE-SAIL, AND A SNOWBALL MORTAR

A Square-rigged Ice-sail

In Fig. 3 two square sails are supported at the ends of crossed yard-arms fourteen feet long. Four cross-sticks of equal length are made, the same as those for the skating-sail first described, and at the middle a long block is attached to two of them as shown in Fig. 2 A. Pins in the ends of the blocks fit into holes in the long arms, and when the ends of the long arms are bent in they grip the pins and blocks.

Short blocks provided with a single pin are lashed to the outer cross-sticks eight inches in from the ends. Holes made in the outer ends of the long sticks will receive these pins, the spring of the stick holding both inner and outer cross-sticks in place at the same time.

Heavy sheeting or unbleached muslin sails may be stretched and bound to the cross-sticks and when detached they can be rolled up on the sticks. This sail is handled the same as the skating-sail but is more powerful as the sheets are larger.

A Snowball Mortar

For snowball fights a mortar is an effective weapon for it throws a shot upward into the air. It may be mounted on a hand-sled.

Make two triangles of boards as shown in Fig. 4. The bottom strip should project far enough below the two legs to permit of screwing it firmly to the edge of the bottom board, which is the width of the top of the sled and is attached to it by straps.

The pivot-bar or axle-tree rests in grooves cut in the

points of the triangles. The propulsion-bar (A) is a stout piece of oak fastened securely to the pivot-bar and at right angles to it. Two uprights (BB) fastened to the bottom board by screws or nails driven from underneath and braced to the legs of the triangles support a cross-piece which keeps the propulsion-bar horizontal when the spring is attached. A small tin basin is secured to the extreme forward end of the propulsion-bar.

To use the mortar place a snowball or other missile in the basin and strike the other end of the bar a hard blow with a long-handled wooden-mallet.

The range may be regulated by the force of the blow and by moving the sled to and fro and right and left. Dimensions of mortar shown in diagram: Length of bottom board, three feet ten inches; length of legs, two feet six inches; uprights, two feet three inches; propulsion-bar, four feet two inches by two and one-half by four inches; width of frame, thirteen inches.

Should the snow be too dry to make compact snowballs a small piece of sheep-skin or cotton-batting should be inserted in the breech of the gun or the basin of the mortar and tacked in place. This will tend to prevent the snowballs from breaking.

Fig. 5 is an end-view of the mortar and Fig. 6 is the wooden mallet used in firing.

Chapter VIII

KITES AND AEROPLANES

The Ship Kite

THE ship kite (Fig. 1) is an odd shape for a wind-toy but a good sailer in any breeze. It is quite easy to make and requires but one mast, four yard-arms, a keel, some thin, strong twine, and the necessary covering materials. The mast is thirty-six inches long, the lowest spar twenty-four inches long, the top one twelve, and the two middle ones proportioned in length to the two side-strings tied at the ends of the top and bottom sticks—that is, at A and B on both sides of Fig. 2.

The keel of the frame is made from a thin piece of hardwood that will spring and keep its shape, such as hickory, oak, or birch; and after soaking it in boiling hot water for a few minutes lash it fast to the bottom of the mast and draw up the ends with the strings C, C (Fig. 2), and carry the ends up over two yard-arms so the pressure of the keel will not draw the lower yard-arm out of shape. The sticks should be of good clear and tough white or North Carolina pine, spruce, or white-wood, three-eighths of an inch square for the mast and the same size but tapered at the ends for the yard-arms. Use strong cotton or linen twine for the connections between spars and mast and draw them taut but not so tight that they would spring the sticks out of shape.

From the ends of each yard-arm strings D D D are stretched and tied to the mast so as to make an opening at the bottom of each sail. In kite-making it is found a much better plan to have a number of planes against which

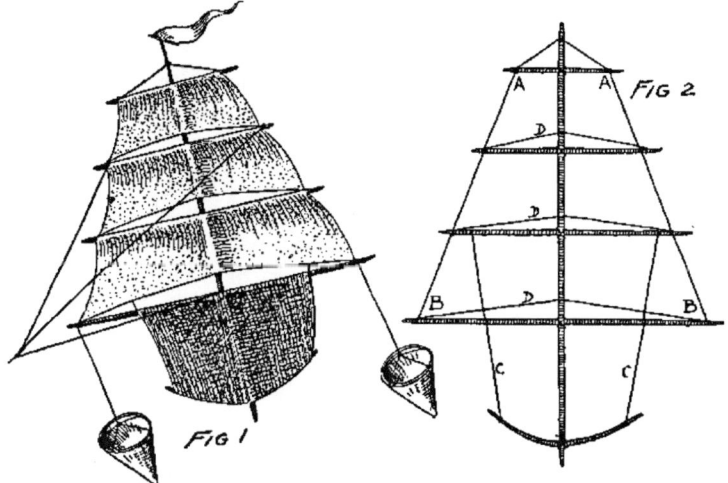

the wind can act instead of one large one that is often unwieldy and difficult to handle.

This frame should be covered with thin paper muslin, sewed all around the edges over the string-ribs and to the frame-sticks with strong cotton thread. Do not have too much muslin overlap the edges, and after going around the edges twice with the needle and fine cotton thread it would be well to cut away all the unnecessary material as it only adds weight with no benefit to the kite. Do not use paste or glue to fasten the fabric covering on a frame; it only adds weight and does not stick well.

Arrange the yoke as shown in the illustration of the ship kite (Fig. 1), and to balance it make two funnel-drags or wind-anchors from thin wire or wood hoops, nine inches in diameter, the funnel proper being of paper muslin twelve inches deep. Use hickory or green birch for the hoops and lap the ends for three inches; then bind them together with strong linen thread.

Make the funnel-shaped bag of paper muslin and drop the hoop into it, taking care to get an equal space all around from point of cone to edge of hoop. Then sew the bag fast to the hoop and cut away all surplus material. The yoke is made of two strong, thin cross-wires or strings and the drop-string is fastened where they cross, as may be seen in Fig. 1.

The Chinese-junk Kite

The Chinese-junk kite (Fig. 3), is made in a similar manner to the ship kite, but there are two masts, as the kite is broader and larger; consequently the frame should be braced so that it will not rack in a strong breeze.

The masts are forty-two inches high, the lowest yard-arm thirty-six inches long, and the top one thirty inches in length. The bottom of the hull is made from a piece of green hickory or birch sprung into place and lashed fast with linen line. There are three inches of space between the hull and lower sail and from two to three inches of space between the other sails.

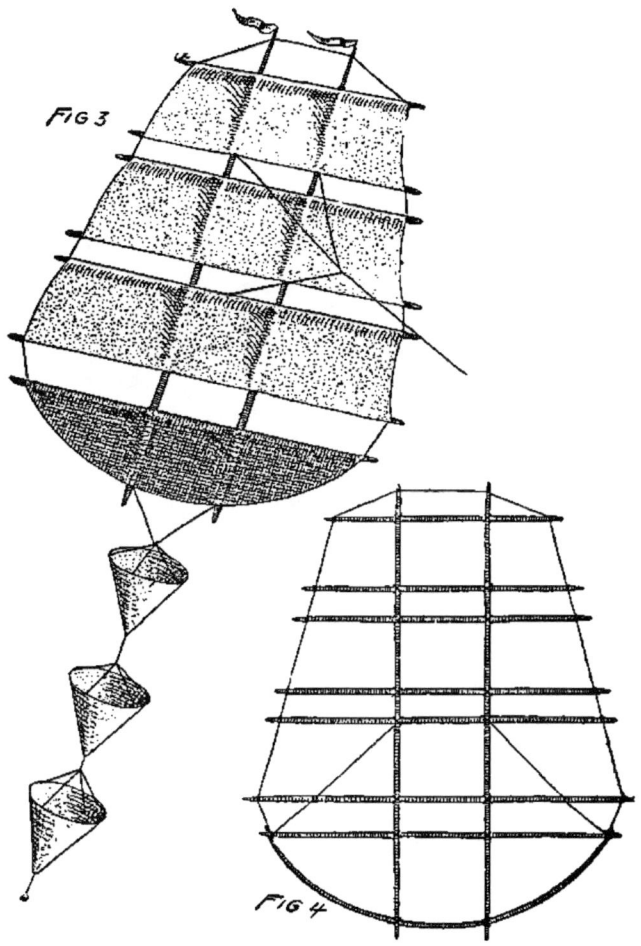

FIG 3

FIG 4

THE CHINESE-JUNK KITE

The masts and spars may be of any light, strong wood, the masts half an inch square and the yard-arms three-eighths of an inch tapered towards the ends. The spars and masts are bound securely with fine linen line as shown in the junk kite-frame (Fig. 4). It would look well to cover the sail-frames of all these boat kites with white or very light-colored muslin and the hulls with dark-brown, green, or black goods so as to lend contrast and make the kites when in the air appear more like real boats.

Arrange the yoke to this kite as shown in the drawing (Fig. 3), and add as many funnel-drags as may be found necessary to steady this kite. Instead of placing these wind-anchors close to the foot of the kite it is often better to drop a cord five or ten feet with the funnel on the end of it. While the funnel weighs but very little it is acted on by the wind and is better than a heavy tail. As the wind blows stronger the funnel is forced back and holds the wind, thereby dragging on the foot of the kite and automatically shifting it to different angles so that the wind will pass down along the planes and out through the spaces underneath.

The Schooner Kite

The schooner kite (Fig. 5) is an attractive one when sailing up in the wind, and for a kite the shape is very close to a real schooner in proportions. The frame is built on a deck-stick thirty-seven inches long, and six inches below it is the keel-stick twenty inches long. The main-mast or aft-stick is thirty-three inches long and the foremast is thirty inches from tip to tip. The foremast is set in twelve inches from the bow end of the deck-stick and the main-mast is ten inches from this. The gaffs are each nine inches long and are caught to both mast and a top-stick, which is in turn lashed fast to the upper part of each mast. Strings are run from place to place on these sticks as shown at Fig. 6, then the sails and hull are cut from muslin and sewed to the strings and spars.

The yoke is composed of three strings as shown in the drawing (Fig. 5), and from the muslin cut two pennants and float them from the top of the masts.

When up in the air this schooner kite will have a very real appearance as the breeze will bulge the sails and give it the effect of tacking on the wind. If the schooner is inclined to pitch or roll too much attach two wind-anchors, one at the foot of each mast, and pay them out about five or six feet.

A Balloon Kite

From four sticks and a long hickory rib the balloon kite-frame (Fig. 7) is made. The cross-sticks are three feet and three inches long and the uprights are each four feet long. The uprights are set apart six inches at the foot and eleven inches at the top, while the cross-sticks are twelve inches apart at both sides of the frame. Where the sticks cross they are to be lashed and bound with linen twine; then the hickory rib is sprung into position and lashed fast at the ends of the cross-sticks and upper ends of the vertical sticks. A thong is to be bound to each end of the rib and drawn down to the foot of the frame so that the curve over the top formed by the hickory rib is even and symmetrical.

Cover this frame with dark-gray or green paper muslin, then make the car from a hoop fifteen inches in diameter and a muslin funnel twenty inches deep. Suspend the car on four strings attached to the foot of the kite, and having arranged the yoke from the places where the sticks cross, as shown in Fig. 8, this interesting sky-scraper will be ready for an ascension.

An Air-ship Kite

The air-ship kite (Fig. 9), if large and well made, will present a very realistic appearance when well up in the air.

The frame is made from dry spruce or pine sticks half an inch square for the long ones and a trifle smaller for the shorter ones. The frame as shown in Fig. 10 is seven feet long from A to A, and at the middle the balloon is twenty-eight inches—that is, from B to B. The middle upright stick is four feet long and the end sticks C C that support the car are forty-five inches long. The middle upright B B is first lashed to the middle of the long stick A A. The ends of the curved sticks are then brought together and lashed to ends A A, and at the same time the unions are made with sticks C C. After that the sticks between B and C are set in place and securely lashed fast. The long sticks D D, forming the top and bottom of the car, are four feet and four inches long. One is lashed to the lower ends of the three long drop-sticks and ten inches above that the top one is made fast.

With thin spring or hard brass wire bind the forms of the two occupants of the car and make them fast to sticks D D with string. Then cover the entire balloon and car as well

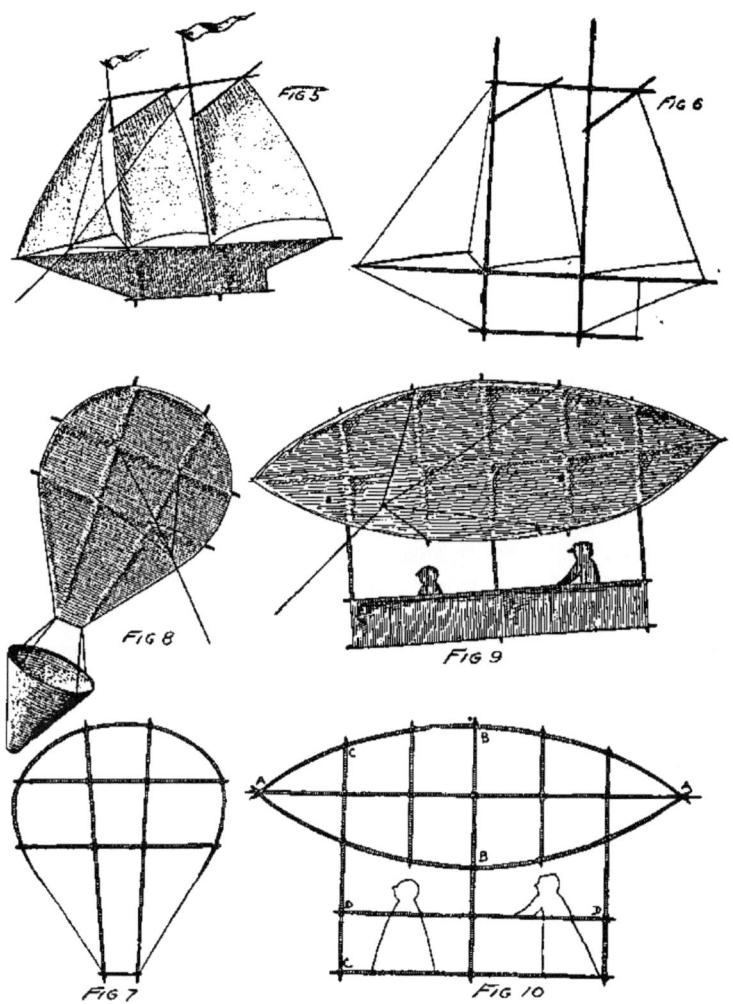

THE SCHOONER, BALLOON, AND AN AIR-SHIP KITE

as the men with dark-colored paper muslin. Make the yoke of linen thread so that the kite will balance well.

Bat-wing and Crown-top Kites

Of the many odd shapes in which kites can be made perhaps the bat-wing and crown-top are the most unique. The bat-wing (Fig. 11) is made up on a frame composed of half-inch square sticks for the longest ones and three-eighths-inch square ones for the cross-ribs. The two long sticks (Fig. 12, AA) are six feet and six inches, slightly tapered at the ends and separated about eight inches. The long uprights B B are four feet and three inches and are separated fifteen inches. These two sets of sticks are lashed fast where they cross and the horizontal ones are bound at the outer ends with short sticks twelve inches in length. Fifteen inches up from the bottom a cross-stick, C, four feet long is lashed fast; then the shape is described with stout cotton or linen cord. This frame is to be covered with muslin and sewed at the edges, and when ready to fly it arrange the yoke as shown in the illustration (Fig. 11).

The crown-top kite (Fig. 13) is three feet and six inches wide, three feet high, and one foot across the bottom. These sizes are for a kite of medium size; if a larger one is desired it can be made five feet and three inches wide, four feet and three inches high, and eighteen inches across the foot. The sticks are from a quarter to half an inch square and bound together with strong, thin cord (Fig. 14). Muslin is the proper covering for this frame, but if thin, strong paper is preferred it can be used to good advantage.

KITES AND AEROPLANES

Sandwich Islands Bird Kite

One afternoon in the village of Paihiihi, on Maui, one of the Sandwich Islands, I saw, at a considerable distance from me, a curious object floating in the air and at first mistook it for a large bird. It would glide about in graceful curves or dart suddenly towards the ground only to soar upward just as suddenly, or poise motionless save for a slight flapping of its wings.

But my blissful ignorance was soon dispelled by the laughter of a friend who assured me that I was gazing at one of the kites of the cannibals—a name sportively applied to a number of natives of the Gilbert Islands who immigrated to Maui some time since. They are a more barbarous people than the Hawaiians but seem to be amiable, and I have never known them to eat anything *worse* than a shark.

Wishing to see this new variety of kite, I started immediately for the scene of action, and was soon in the midst of a dozen or more men and women about half of whom had kites, which were larger than I had supposed, being from thirteen to fifteen feet wide and two to three feet high. When I arrived several were floating high in the air almost directly over the men who held the strings — sometimes, indeed, sailing directly over them.

I watched for some time their graceful, birdlike motion and then tried to buy one. They seemed loath to part with them, however, and it was only after I had exhausted nearly all my persuasive powers and all the small change in my pockets that I succeeded in obtaining one. My awkward

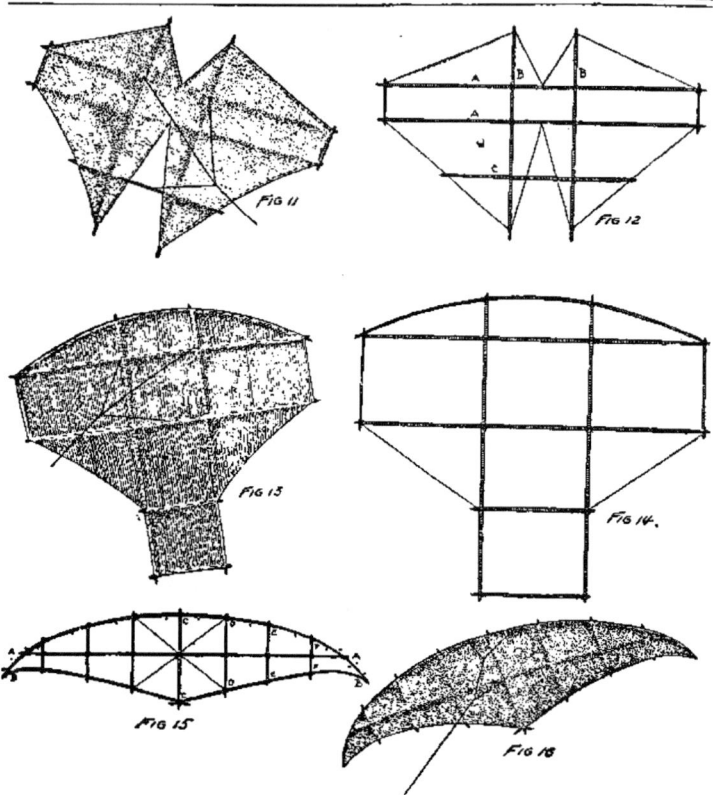

Fig 11

Fig 12

Fig 13

Fig 14.

Fig 15

Fig 16

endeavors to carry it away with me were greeted with much laughter until one of the cannibals showed me the proper way to handle it.

The drawings which I have made of one of these kites will enable any enterprising boy to make one. As no tail is used great care must be taken to make it perfectly symmetrical. It is also desirable to have the kite very light and yet as stiff as possible.

The proper construction of the frame is shown in Fig. 15. The total width of this kite is thirteen feet and the height at the middle is thirty-two inches. First cut the middle stick C C thirty-two inches long and lay it on the floor of a barn where a few nails can be driven in temporarily to hold the sticks while bending them into the proper shapes. Cut sticks D D, E E, and F F, and place them on the floor either side of the middle one. The long, straight stick A A is twelve feet in length, of half-inch basswood or pine, and slightly tapered with a plane at both ends. Lash this to each of the cross-sticks, then with a long stick bend the bow around nails driven in the floor as indicated by the dots under the bow-piece in Fig. 15.

This bow-piece is half an inch square and tapered with a plane at both ends. It would be well to pour boiling water on this stick for a distance of three feet at both ends, so as to make it easier to bend. Leave it in this position for a few hours until the water dries out and the wood is shaped, then lash the top ends of the cross-sticks to the bow-piece.

While bending the bow the two lower sticks may be shaped at the same time. They should be of hickory or birch and tapered at the outer ends. These must be shaped over nails the same as the bow-piece, then when they are dry they are to be lashed to all the cross-ribs and the ends of the bow with fine linen line. The cross-sticks need not be more than three-eighths of an inch square, but the middle and top sticks should be half an inch thick for strength.

Draw cross-strings from the top and lower ends of sticks D D, as shown in Fig. 15, to act as braces; then cover the frame with thin, strong paper or muslin, sewing it fast to the ribs with linen thread. The construction of the yoke is clearly shown in Fig. 16.

Box Kites

High up in the air, much too high for the boys on the ground to see the mechanical details, several queer-looking but powerful kites, or "gigs," were tugging at their strings in a stiff breeze. When these flying-gigs were hauled down a big crowd of boys gathered to see them at close range, and here are the pictures of them as well as the plan-drawings showing how they are made. Any bright boy can easily follow these plans and produce equally good and powerful kites.

The construction of the box kite is shown in Fig. 17, where the oblong measures thirty-six inches high and twenty-four inches wide. These oblongs are held apart at the top and bottom by sticks A A which measure twelve inches in length. At the middle of the framework the corner sticks B B are braced with two cross-sticks C, which are notched at the ends, so that the inside corners of the sticks B B will fit snugly and can be securely held with a slim steel-wire nail. This frame is made of light pine sticks about three-eighths or half an inch square.

Eight inches below the top of the frame tie a cord, and nine inches below this tie another one to the front upright sticks as shown at D D. Cover the front, sides, and back of the frame with strong, thin Manila paper or light, closely woven muslin, having the top and bottom open, also the space at the front between the strings D D. A yoke caught at the top corner of the box, as shown in Fig. 18, will be sufficient in a light breeze, but for a strong wind add another

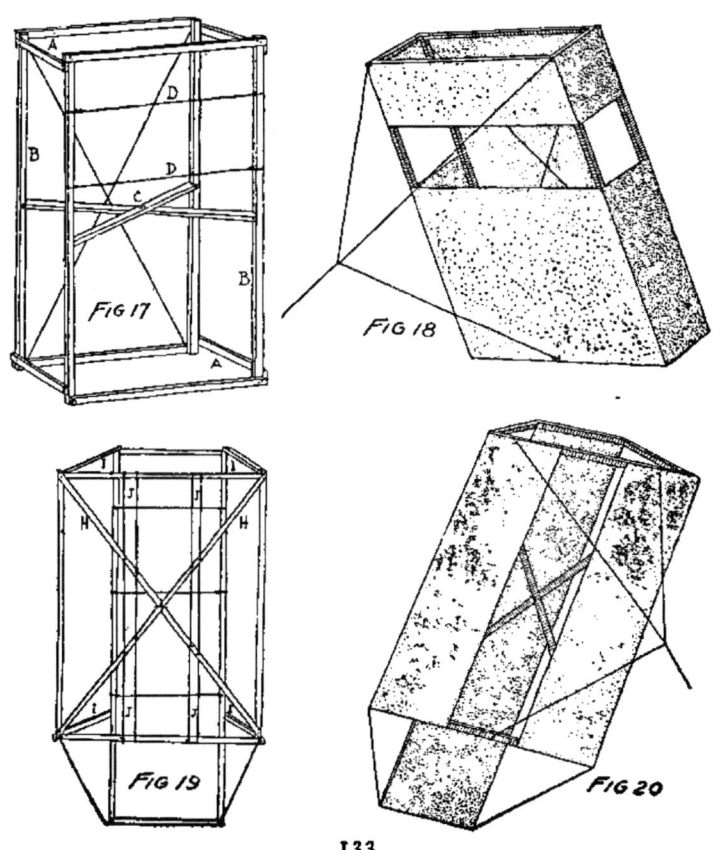

FIG 17

FIG 18

FIG 19

FIG 20

from the side-sticks where the top or bottom cord D is tied; this will steady the flying-box and prevent its pitching.

The "paralleloplane" is another powerful kite which is easily constructed according to the plan shown in Fig. 19. The front frame is thirty-six inches high and twenty-four inches wide and braced with cross-sticks H H. The rear frame is forty-four inches long and fifteen inches wide and is held in place ten inches behind the large frame with sticks I I. Strings are tied to the top and bottom cross-sticks of the large frame, and eight inches apart, as shown at J J, to which one end of the paper or muslin is made fast. Fig. 20 will show the three fields covered with cloth or paper, and when the paralleloplane is in the air the space between the front planes admits the wind to the rear plane with the extending tail, which tips the kite to the proper angle.

If these kites need balancing in very strong breezes, a yoke at the bottom of the kites from which a long string may be suspended will take some paper cross-bars, as shown in Fig. 21, or the wind-anchors can be used. One or two of them may be hung from the bottom on a long string or one at each lower end of the paralleloplane.

A messenger that will travel and travel fast is shown in Fig. 22, and as they are very easy to make a number of them should be prepared for use. Two thin sticks twelve inches long form the top and bottom yards for a strip of muslin or paper six inches wide. From the four ends some thin wire such as florists use is connected with a cork about twelve inches in the rear of the sail, where it is bound fast with a few wraps of the wire. A pin is passed through the middle of the top yard to the sail and is bent over forming a hook, and in the cork another one is arranged in a similar manner. The messenger can be hung on the string,

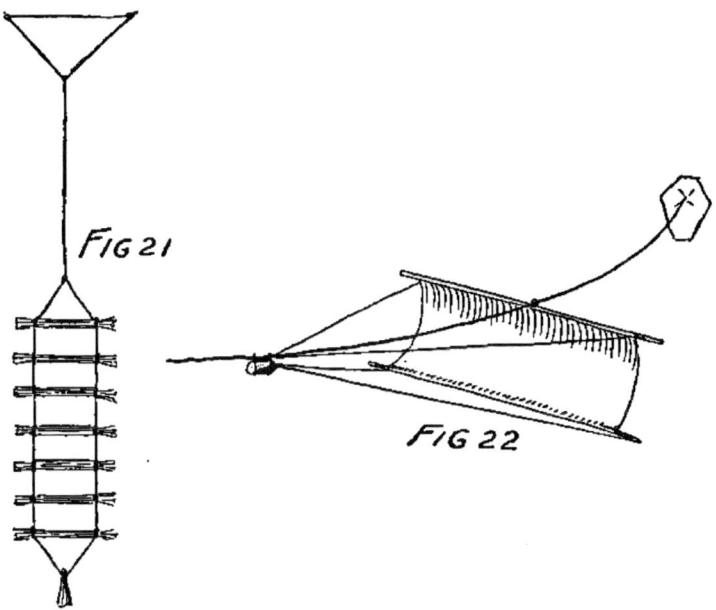

FIG 21

FIG 22

and if there are no knots to intercept its progress it will quickly speed away to the kite.

The Flying-wedge and Double-plane Kite

Flying-wedge or double-plane kites are made in several shapes and sizes with the planes arranged at different angles and in broken surfaces.

The flying - wedge is an interesting gig to make and

hold when up, for it is a strong puller. Its construction is shown in Fig. 23, and like the box kite the frame is made of half-inch pine sticks. The front frame is forty inches high and twenty-four inches wide, and the rear one two inches longer but the same width. The frames are attached at the top but held apart at the bottom by the sticks E E, which are eighteen inches long. Twelve inches below the top a cross-stick F is attached, and from the side-sticks down to the centre of the bottom cross-stick the sticks G G are made fast. Strings may be substituted for these sticks but they will not brace the framework so well. Diagonally across the back frame and at the bottom strings are made fast to brace the frame, while the back ones also help to relieve the strain of the wind on the paper or muslin drawn across the framework. Figure 24 will show the fields covered with paper or muslin, which are arranged so the wind passing through the triangular opening in front presses against the back plane and out at the sides and bottom, while some of it is forced up in the top behind the upper plane and helps in the lifting power. Small flags on sticks at the top add to the appearance of this flying-wedge which is an exceedingly unique sky-scraper.

The double-plane kite (Fig. 25) is another form of the wedge. The general plan and sizes for the frame of this wedge tally with those just given, but the slight changes in the arrangement of sticks can be seen in Fig. 26.

The plane at the front is just half the height of the kite, and at the back it would be well to use two cross-sticks from corner to corner as braces rather than string as suggested for the flying-wedge. Use paper muslin for the covering and stretch it taut; then sew it fast. Rig up two small flags on sticks for the top corners and arrange the yoke as shown in Fig. 25. If the wedge is inclined to wobble or dive hang two wind-anchors on the corners, preferably the front, as the action will be better than if hung at the back.

The wind strikes the front plane and upper part of rear

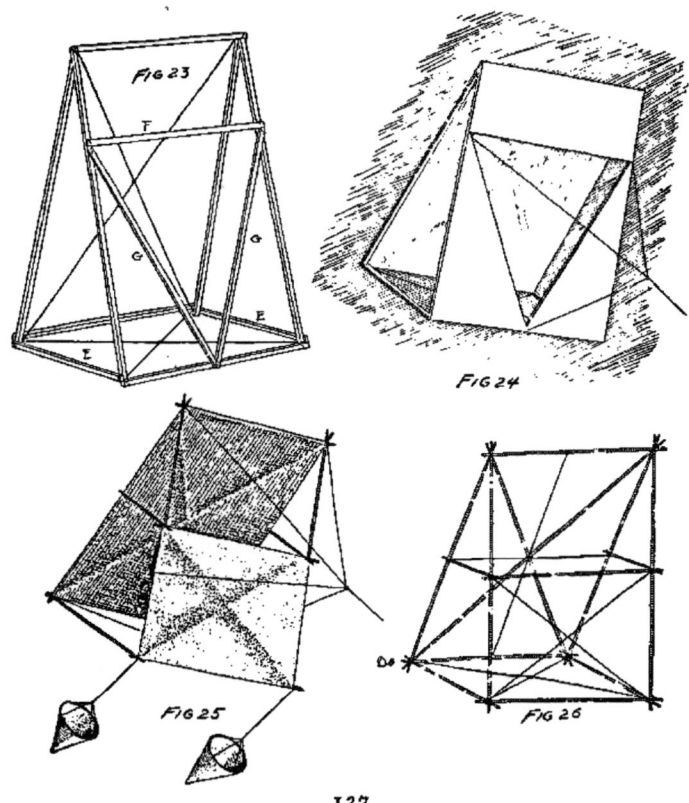

FIG 23

FIG 24

FIG 25

FIG 26

bevelled plane, also the outer edges of the rear plane, and in this manner a double kite is made that will be found a strong and steady puller.

Kite-reels

Kite-reels are always useful things to help haul in long lengths of string, and particularly if the kite is a strong puller and in a stiff breeze.

A reel for kites with a good pull is shown in Fig. 27, and a boy with a hammer, a saw, and a few nails can quickly put it together from some box-boards sawed in two-inch strips. The reel is made of two thin boards half an inch in thickness, cut circular with a compass-saw, and the hub is shaped from an old rolling-pin that perhaps has been discarded from the kitchen. It is impossible to give exact sizes owing to the possible difference in the lengths of rolling-pins, but the round sides should be at least six inches in diameter and placed twelve inches apart. One end of the pin, or the handle, should be sawed and cut square so a crank may be cut and nailed to it as shown at A in Fig. 28. From wood seven-eighths of an inch thick cut the crank B, and attach a handle to the outer end of it. Bore a hole with a bit in the end that fits over the axle, and with a compass-saw or small chisel cut the hole square so that the axle will fit snugly into it. The flanges are to be made fast to the ends of the rolling-pin hub with nails or screws, and this revolving barrel is hung in the inverted V-shaped frame of the reel. To hold this reel down when winding in a line make several hardwood stakes as shown at C. These are cut out with a saw; and to protect the head and prevent it from splitting off, bore two small holes through the head as indicated by the dotted lines and slip steel-wire nails through them. Place burrs over the pointed ends, cut the ends off, and with a light hammer rivet the nail-ends down on the burrs so as to bind the head securely. This is much better than winding wire about the head, since the nails act as pins and will prevent the head from splitting while the stake is being driven into the ground. The overhanging end of the head laps on the end cross-plates forming the platform of the reel, and two or three at the end opposite that at which the string is being hauled in will hold the reel securely to the ground.

Another form of reel is shown in the illustration of a chest-reel (Fig. 30). This is made from two flat, good barrel-hoops, some braces, and the reel and shaft as described in Fig. 28 A and B.

Two good, broad barrel-hoops are selected and cut so that they will measure eighteen inches on the segment or twelve inches across the line A A in Fig. 29. Two out-riggers B B are cut from pine or white-wood ten inches long, two inches wide, and three-quarters of an inch thick; these are bevelled at the end towards the hoop, where they are made fast with screws. The outer ends of these sticks are bound with the stick C, and near the inner ends and close to the hoop a binder-piece D is fastened with screws.

The reel should be made first and clamped in place when the frame is put together. The lower hoop is made fast to the short upright·pieces C C, shown in Fig. 30, and braced to the main out-riggers B B with bracket-strips. All the unions are made with screws or long copper rivets securely fastened at the blunt end with burrs over which the copper end is beaten and riveted.

Near the hoop-ends holes are to be made with a bit through which stout cotton line can be passed and made

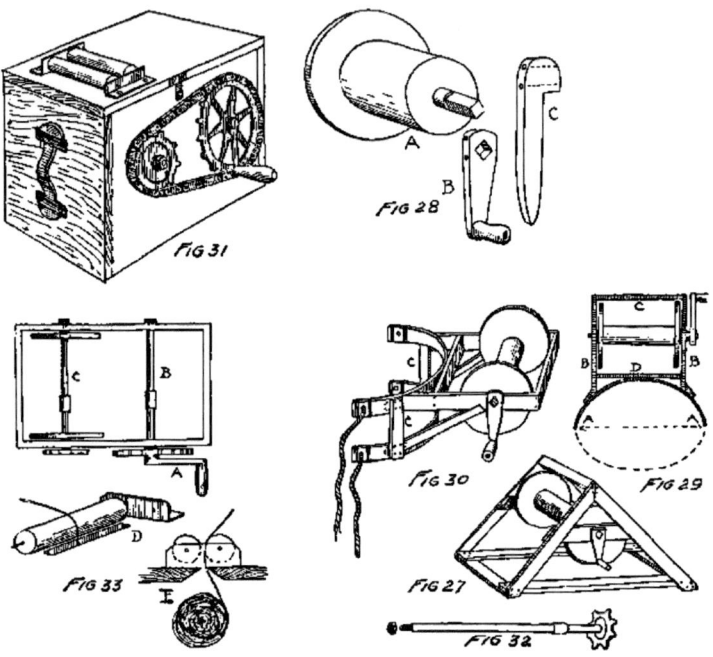

fast so as to tie the reel to a boy's body (Fig. 30). The hoop-end should be bound with linen line at either side of the hole so as to prevent the hoop splitting and the lashing-thongs tearing away. This is a very convenient form of portable reel and is easily carried about without having to touch it. A friction-brake can be made from a piece of sole-leather that will bear against the edge of one large end of the reel so that when paying out cord it may be regulated as the kite draws on it.

Leather or metal washers should be placed between the reel-ends and the frame that the axle is hung in so as to prevent friction and the consequent wearing of the wood.

Fig. 31 shows a simple, home-made box-reel that will wind up a thousand feet of line in short order. It consists of a box, to which the cover is hinged, and two sprocket-wheels from an old bicycle. One large one has a handle for turning it, the other, a smaller wheel, is fastened firmly to a spindle (Fig. 32) that runs through the box. The box is of pine or white-wood fourteen inches long inside measure, eight inches wide, and ten inches deep. The wood may be from one-half to seven-eighths of an inch thick, and the points should be made with glue and nails or screws to hold them securely and prevent the box from racking.

Find two old sprocket-wheels and a piece of bicycle chain and make the wheels fast to iron axles that will pass through holes made in the sides of the box. The ends of these axles should be threaded and provided with a nut so as to hold the axles in place when run through the box.

The arrangement of these wheels and the chain is clearly shown in the illustration of a box-reel (Fig. 31). The large wheel should be attached to an axle and one of the pedal-cranks made fast to it. Instead of the pedal a wooden handle will slip on the pedal axle where it can be secured by the nut that held the pedal in place. The relative positions of wheels, axles, and other parts of this reel can be seen at Fig. 33. A represents the crank, handle, and large wheel; B the axle that passes through the box; C the axle and flanges made fast to the small sprocket-wheel; and D shows how the wooden roller-wheels are arranged over the slot in the box so that the string can be drawn in without its touching the edge of the slot. The edges should be flared at the under side so that the cord will wind on a fat reel without touching the wood as shown at E.

Two wooden flanges should be cut from thin wood and made fast to the axle C to prevent the cord winding on the axle close to the box and thereby clogging its action. Leather washers separate the flanges and the boxes so as to reduce the possibility of friction.

The slot cut in the top of the box should be as long as the available winding-space on the axle, and protecting it at both sides are rollers cut from one-inch curtain-poles or broom-sticks. Steel-wire finishing-nails are driven in the end of each one, taking care to get the nail exactly in the middle.

Bend two L-pieces from stout sheet-iron, and having punched or drilled holes in the right place through the upright ear, make these bearings fast to the top of the box with screws as shown at D in Fig. 33. By turning the box slightly from side to side when winding in the string, the incoming line will travel from end to end of the slot so that the coil on the shaft will be equally thick from flange to flange.

A leather trunk-handle may be made fast to one end of the box for convenience in carrying.

This form of direct gearing with sprocket - wheels and chain makes it impossible for the cord-shaft to slip as it will do in the grooved wheel and string or leather-belt connections. It is simple and sure and quite as easy to pay out from as to wind in with.

Chapter IX

FISHING-TACKLE

Choice of Tackle

EVERY boy knows how to go a-fishing, but an intelligent boy is not long in learning that the mere getting of a lot of fish is a small part of the pleasure. That is why he prefers the rod to the seine, one big fish to many smaller ones, one cunning old trout or pickerel outwitted to a basket of stupid fish that contended for the bait. Presently he begins to desire more delicate tackle, and understands that he is fishing for sport, not fish. I take it that the whole art and mystery of angling is how to get the most sport and enjoyment out of it. But how?

To begin with, no one will destroy a fish which is not dangerous to man, nor will he fish just for amusement; in other words, he fishes only for desirable fish. The chief things that make a fish desirable, in the sense of a game or sport fish, are that it shall be good food, not too common and not too easily caught. If, besides, it be beautiful and found in beautiful places so much the better. It happens that by common consent certain fish—salmon and trout and their kindred—are in Europe and America esteemed above all others, and the opportunity to angle for them is not open

144

to every one, and most boys must get their sport with other less - esteemed kinds. "Boys' fish" they are sometimes slightingly called, but they have lots of sport to give to the boy who knows how to get it, and he will get more sport if he takes pains to make the fish better worth catching and better worth having after it is caught. It is better worth having, for instance, if you have caught it from the cleanest water you have access to. Clean water makes sweet fish. If a fish is to be kept kill it at once by a blow upon the back of the head where the backbone joins it. This is not only more merciful but makes firmer meat. If one is fishing from a boat or not moving about much the fish may be kept alive in a floating live-box or basket, and at the end of the fishing the best may be chosen for keeping and the rest let go. Fish are sweeter, too, if cleaned as soon as possible; besides, the cleaning is done more easily if done early. Learn to do it well yourself, and try to be at home in time to do it before supper. Cleaning fish by candle-light goes far to spoil the sport of a pleasant day. Do not clean fish with your pocket-knife. Have in your kit a stout one for the purpose which will also cut bait. Such knives made expressly are sold for a small sum, but a veteran kitchen-knife or a broken table-knife if kept in order will do excellent service.

Do not throw your fish in the dirt nor let them lie in the sun nor string them upon a twig or line if you wish them to be sweet. Have a basket with a cover, even if the cover be no more than a newspaper. Wash this basket and dry and air it in the sunshine if you can after every using. All these things you should do if you wish what you catch to be as good as it can be.

Now, how are you to increase the sport of the catching? Of course you want the largest fish and these are usually the oldest and the most wary. This wariness you do not expect to change, but you hope to defeat it. Study the habits of the fish, where and when and upon what it feeds or what it seeks. Let your fishing be governed by your discoveries. And while you are offering him what he wants and when and where he wants it, remember these old fellows are fussy about their table-service. They do not feel hungry if a boy throws his shadow across their table, or shakes it by rushing up to it. Stalk your fish, then, as quietly as you are able, and if you have alarmed it in any way stay out of sight and remain as quiet as possible for a long time until your clumsiness is forgotten, and then let your lure, whether bait or fly, drift into the fish's sight as if you had nothing to do with it. And remember that the finer your tackle the more likely this pretence will be to succeed.

You want also as good a fight as you can get. Remember that the fighting qualities of fish are as a rule best developed in those which live in rapid and turbulent water, and in those which pursue their prey and catch it by their own nimbleness. But any fish will fight better if you make the struggle more even by using delicate tackle. You win then only by dexterity of handling, which is one of the great charms of angling, and about the only one, as regards the mere catching of fish, on which the experienced angler sets much value. The secret of success with delicate tackle may be told in two words—care and coolness. Care in the preparation of the tackle, coolness in handling it.

When you put your tackle together you will make it far

safer if you consider it as one apparatus or machine from hook to reel and if you let the rod top, or "tip," be the weakest point of all, because by it you can best determine the strain upon the whole gear. For instance, a good line for fresh-water fishing will usually lift at least ten pounds, a good snell at least three pounds if new, the hook more than the snell, while the top of an ordinary light rod will rarely bear more than two pounds of dead weight, so that you may know by the strain upon the top joint just what the tackle is bearing; and if the joint is safe the whole is likewise safe.

By testing your tackle you raise your fishing from a rough-and-ready guesswork to something like certainty, the one point of doubt being always the security of the hook in the fish's mouth, and even of this you soon acquire the power of judging. But this testing is not done once for all. Good tackle which is put away wet to mildew, or gut which is frayed or put in the sun to rot, does not long remain sound. Therefore dry your line, carefully unwinding it from the reel if you have one and winding it upon a chair-back, for instance, when you come home. Look over and test your tackle every time you are going fishing—yes, and every time it gets caught on a stone or stump or in the bushes—if you wish to escape the loss of your best fish. All this means that tackle to be safe must be sound—that is, good all through. A line, for instance, which is strong in one place and weak in another will give you more trouble than one which is not so strong but uniform.

The strain upon the tackle is equalized by the elasticity of the rod, which to some extent makes up for want of dexterity. But never have a rod so flexible that it will not control the tackle, and, above all, avoid one which is weak in the middle.

Lastly, let the fish do the pulling if you wish to safely handle it. No angling-tackle is as strong as a boy. But if the rod be so held that its spring keeps the line taut and a gentle, steady pull upon the fish the latter soon exhausts himself fighting this elasticity. Any excess of line not easily controlled by the rod alone should be at once taken up by the reel. Draw the tired fish out gently, without "yanking," or if heavy lead it into the landing-net.

Rods vary according to the kind of fishing, and the "all-round" fisherman will probably have, without being finicky, as many rods as a golf-player has clubs. But the boy for whom this is written must make his pocket-money go as far as possible, and he will probably have but one. Rod-making is an interesting amusement, but it would better be deferred until one knows fairly well the use of a rod and just what kind he wants. The making of rods is not very economical, since nowadays factories turn out really good ones at prices little above what one must pay for reliable rod-wood. Roughly speaking, there are two kinds of rods, bait-rods and fly-rods. Bait-rods are nearly always stiffer than fly-rods; the latter must have sufficient flexibility and elasticity to throw a line quite a distance, often several times the length of the rod. But in choosing a bait-rod a different selection will be made according to the particular sort of fishing within reach. Thus if one fishes ponds or wide streams from the bank, a rod a dozen feet long would not be too long; but if from a boat, a shorter rod not above ten feet will be more convenient. Still, shorter rods are better if bait is to be cast long distances, as is done in minnow-casting or some kinds of sea-fishing. A jointed-rod is convenient for carrying, but if one lives within walking or driving distance of his fishing a rod in one piece, such as is easily made from a slender bamboo with an elastic tip of good wood spliced on, is as good for bait-fishing as any. If besides bait-fishing one desires to use the fly, then the best rod is a rather stout fly-rod about ten feet in length, because it can be used for bait-fishing, while a bait-rod cannot be used to cast a fly.

Beautiful and excellent rods are made of split bamboo, and some of moderate cost, but avoid very cheap ones. But for beginners' use the writer prefers a solid-wood rod of good quality, because it is less liable to injury and because of the greater ease with which it is repaired; the boy himself may do it if he be handy. Whatever rod you have, let the line-guides be of the sort known as "standing-guides" rather than rings, if you have the choice.

Lines should be sound and strong but not too heavy for the rod; twisted lines are more easily found of good quality but braided lines kink less. Twenty yards are quite enough for any fishing of the kind we are considering and half as much would usually suffice. In fly-fishing for large trout or bass the reel usually carries forty to fifty yards.

Hooks should be of the best quality to be had. Good hooks are still practically all made in England. Shapes which have received names are many, and most of them have advantages for particular kinds of fishing. Among the best are O'Shaughnessy, Limerick, Sneckbend, Aberdeen, and Sproat. The last-named we think will meet more kinds of need than any other one. As to size it should be remembered that the hook is to fit the bait, not the fish's mouth; a very small fish can take any ordinary hook.

A reel is not so absolutely necessary as the rod, line, and hook, but it is a prime convenience. A well-made single-click reel is better than any multiplier except for the one matter of making long casts from the reel, which a beginner is not likely to do.

For fly-casting a leader or casting-line of gut between the fly and the main line is necessary for making a light cast, but for ordinary bait-fishing the gut-snells which are nowadays so generally sold attached to hook are bottom line enough. If, however, you can get some white, gray, or cream-colored hairs from the tail of a young stallion you can make bottom lines or leaders for light fishing without expense.

A gaudy float is pretty sure to form part of the first angling outfit, and it is useful to keep the bait out of the weeds and to notify the inexperienced angler that a fish is biting. Choose one that is slender in shape and not large. A dry stick makes a good enough extemporaneous float, and if fish are shy may be better than a more showy one.

For sinkers split shot B B size and buckshot or strips of thin lead, such as comes from tea-chests, wound around the line are as good as any and very easily gotten.

Do not buy a bait-box: It is not so good as a bag with a draw-string, which will allow your hand to be inserted and will also close the aperture snugly. The same string will serve to fasten the bag to your button-hole or creel-strap. The bag is best made of flannel. Wash it after using.

Worms are much better if dug a day or two before using and "scoured" by putting them into soft moss wrung out of water. They become brighter and firmer by scouring and are more attractive to fish. If live minnows or small fish are used for bait, of course they must be kept in water, which must be changed from time to time. A pail is the most convenient vessel to carry them in.

A landing-net is convenient if you fish for game which is heavy in proportion to your tackle—say for fish upward of a pound in weight with a light rod. Very low-priced ones are now sold in the shops and sufficiently good ones can be made at home.

We give no details about flies as their name is legion. A beginner would better have but few kinds and of moderate size; a few hackles will probably be all he needs.

There are a multitude of things sold in the tackle-shops which are tempting but not at all necessary, not to mention many which could have been devised only by a person who was no angler. Those already spoken of are all that seem essential.

Bait-rods and Fly-rods

Probably most boys are too sensible to fall into the error which seems to beset many adults—namely, that the possession of tackle makes an angler. It is necessary to know how to use it.

Begin by putting your rod together properly; put the tip into the middle first, and then the middle into the butt. See that the ferrules are well "home" and that the guides are all on the same side so that the line will run freely.

Place the reel, if you have one, in the reel-seat and see that the reel-bands are snug and will not slip. Then lead off the lines through the rings and the tip-ring. These details are the same whatever kind of fishing is in hand; the others depend upon what is to be done.

Let us suppose that you are to fish with bait and that bait a worm. If you have a short gut line—two or three feet long—it will be well to fasten it to the end of the line and to the other end of the gut attach the snell of the hook. But when seeking many fish which are not very shy, the snell may be fastened directly to the line. In fishing in a gently moving stream no lead may be needed; if the current be quick a little will probably be required to keep the bait near the bottom. In pond - fishing or reaches of a stream which are very quiet a float as well as lead may be convenient. Some veteran anglers still enjoy the bobbing of the float. The hook may be put into the side of the worm as shown at A, or into the head as at B (Fig. 1). A is rather more attractive to the fish; B more likely to be taken in such a way as to insure that the hook is in the fish's mouth. When the worm is dead or has slipped down into a bunch at the bend of the hook no fish that you want will be likely to take it.

Now, do not make a splash when you put it into the water. If you have to cast it out into still water do not use your rod and line as if it were a thresher's flail. Holding your rod nearly straight up, give the line a gentle swing forward, and when the bait has swung well out reach after it with the rod so that the bait (and float, too, if there be one) shall fall as lightly as possible. Do not be in too great a hurry to change its place. If you are fishing in running water, drop the bait quietly into the water and so manage the rod that it shall neither hasten nor hinder the movement of the bait, which should travel as nearly as possible as it would if it were not upon a hook. All the time you are to keep as much as possible out of sight. When you feel the pluck of the fish drop the point of your rod and wait a second or two before you attempt to strike the hook into the flesh.

It sometimes happens that the place you wish to fish is so encumbered with bushes that it cannot be approached. In such a case, if you can find an opening in the bushes you may get at the water by shortening the line and winding what is left around and around the top of the rod. Then pass it through the opening, and, reaching out over the water, roll the rod over and over in the hands until the line is unwound and the bait goes dropping down to the water, as a spider lets himself down from his web. If you have a bite, give the fish time to make sure of the bait. Strike, and, when you can, shorten your line still farther if necessary and draw your fish out.

On the other hand, if in a fairly open place you wish to reach a point at some distance, you may throw your bait out by pulling sufficient line from the reel, and, gathering it in coils upon the left hand, swing the bait out with sufficient force to carry the coils of line after it and so reach the desired point.

To tell in a few words how to cast a fly is hardly practicable. It is not done by force but by knack. A cast consists of a back cast which carries the line upward and backward, and a forward cast which propels it towards the desired spot.

The knack consists in giving with the wrist such a quick motion to the rod as shall set its elasticity to work, and this carries the line. One must not thrash with the rod.

As useful a way as any to help the reader will be to describe how the writer has tried to help lads who are learning to cast. It is in this way: The boy takes the rod, fitted with its reel and line only, to a water's-edge free of bushes or trees or to a lawn recently mowed. If the grass is slightly damp all the better as it holds the line more nearly as does the water. He pulls off from the reel enough line so that the free part shall be once and a half or twice the length of the rod. This he throws out in front of him as well as he can. He then is told to keep his elbow close against his side to prevent moving the arm above the elbow. He then tries with a quick movement of the wrist, and with as little movement of the forearm as possible, to lift the line upward and backward until it straightens out behind him, and then with another similar motion to make it go straight out before him.

The accompanying drawing (Figs. 2 and 3) show how the wrist and thumb really do all the work, and how little the forearm really moves in good casting. They show, too, what should be the limits of the motion in the butt of the rod. If it goes farther back the back cast is apt to be low and the line if not the rod may get into trouble in bushes or grass. If it goes farther forward the line is apt to go down with a splash.

After this restraint of motion has become habitual the rule of holding the elbow against the side may be relaxed a little, especially in making long casts.

154

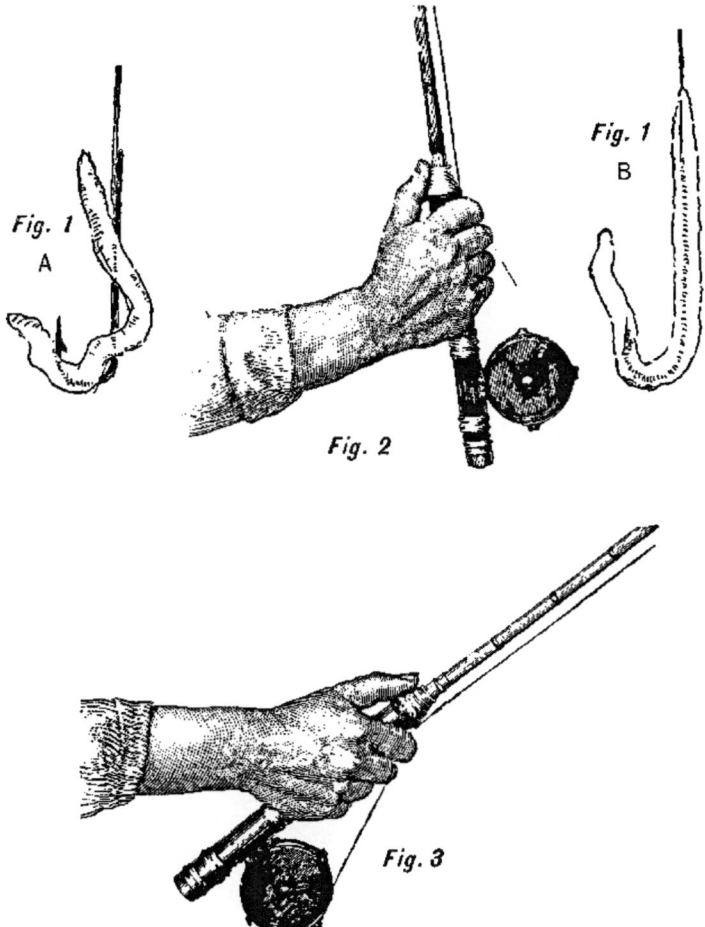

Fig. 1
A

Fig. 1
B

Fig. 2

Fig. 3

HOOK-BAITING AND FLY-CASTING

Do not try to lift a sunken line suddenly from the water. Coax it to the surface, as else the resistance of the line will probably snap your rod.

Do not try to make the forward cast on just the same plane as the back cast for fear that the end of the line should snap like a whip-lash, which if you were actually fishing would crack off your flies pretty certainly. Therefore make the lift of the back cast with a slight sweep (generally inward towards the body is the more natural), and deliver the forward cast straight out towards its destination. But always aim about your own height above the spot on the water you mean to reach to insure the line falling lightly.

In all your practising remember that the key-note of good casting is in getting a good, clean, high back cast, and in never sending the line forward until it is quite straight out behind and above you in the back cast. If you have with you some one to guide you as to when it is straightened out it will be a great gain, particularly as the time required for the straightening varies with the length of line that is used.

Do not try to cast a long line until you have learned to cast a short one well; and well means not only with a high back cast and straight forward, but also accurately as to aim and delicately.

Repairs, Knots, and Splices

As has been said already it hardly pays nowadays to make one's own tackle, at least for a beginner. But a few things it is useful to know so that repairs and supplies of a sort can be made in an emergency. But emergencies are to

a great degree prevented by care—by cleaning and looking
over the rod and the reel whenever you come home, and
keeping it safe. The reel may need a drop of oil now and
then, and it should be always kept out of the dust, in a box
or drawer, and above all from falls or blows.

The repairs most commonly called for are the splicing of

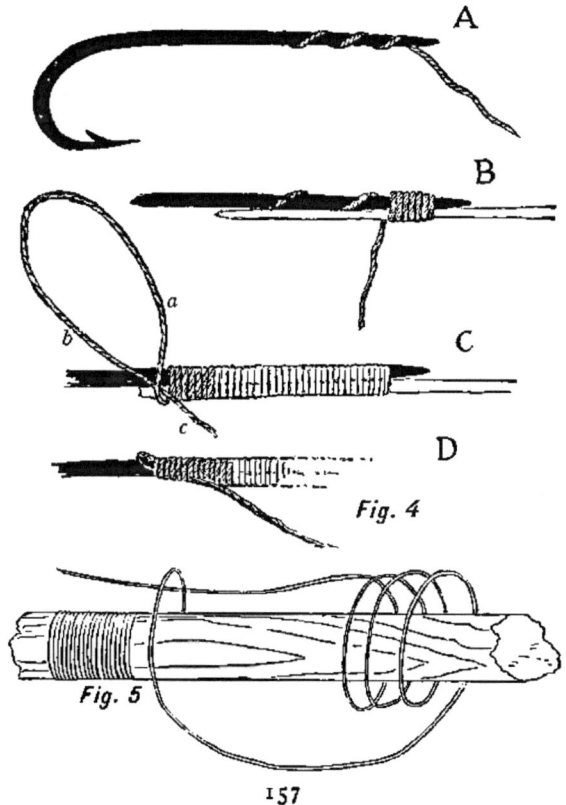

Fig. 4

Fig. 5

157

a broken rod, the replacing a lost tip-ring or guide-ring, the knotting of gut, and the putting a hook to gut. The repair-kit, to use a cyclist's phrase, consists of a piece of shoemaker's wax, some moderately stout sewing-silk—number A being the best suited for quick work of all sorts—some bits of flexible brass wire, and a pocket-knife. As the method of wrapping used in all repairs is essentially the same let us begin with the simplest, the putting the hook to gut.

First wax well a piece of silk half a yard or more in length. Choose your hook and the piece of gut (or line if you do not use gut) to which it is to be fastened. Take the bend of the hook firmly between the left thumb and forefinger and with the right take two or three turns of the silk about the other end of the shank (Fig. 4 A). Then lay the gut on the under side of the hook, reaching two-thirds down the shank, and wind the silk snugly, coil against coil, over both hook and gut towards the bend of the hook B. When the gut is nearly covered make a loop as at C, but relatively larger than in the figure and keep on winding so that the part a covers in not only hook and gut but the part b, clearing the silk from the bend of the hook at each turn. When four or five turns have been taken draw on c and pull it snug. (D shows the loop not quite drawn down.) When snug cut off the end and you have the "invisible knot" or "whip-finish" universally used by fishermen. The same whipping and finish are used for the other repairs mentioned above.

Suppose that a joint of the rod has broken with a slanting break. It may be that the surfaces can be fitted together neatly. In this case they may be joined at once, but if any part has been lost or broken away, then the broken surfaces must be trimmed and smoothed with the knife until they do fit. They are spliced thus: Rub the surfaces with your shoemaker's wax, press them together, and if you cannot easily hold them, tie them temporarily with a piece of string, or perhaps still better, make open coils over the joined parts as at A in Fig. 4. Then wind back over these coils and the joined parts, making close, snug coils just as you did on the hook. The whip-finish must be managed a little differently. Fig. 5 shows how this is done. When ready to finish drop a loop and make four or five loose turns. Carry the end under the beginning of the loop, wind down the loose coils firmly, and pull the end through as before.

A lost tip-ring or guide-ring can be made good by a piece of wire bent into proper shape and whipped on with well waxed silk thread.

We need say but a few words about knots. In order to knot your gut it must be first softened, which is done by laying it in water; it softens much more rapidly in luke-warm water than in cold. Two lengths of gut are joined together by lapping the end of one by the end of the other and making a knot in both together. Fig. 6 A shows this knot, only the end is put through twice for greater security. If the fishing is such as does not need strong tackle a single knot will suffice.

A loop at the end of a piece of gut is made by making the knot as at B, which is the commonly used knot.

A better knot is that shown at C, which looks complicated as drawn, but really is not so, as in tying it the two loops a and b are made, the end c laid between them, and then b is drawn through a.

D shows the ordinary simple method of fastening a line to the loop of a leader or of a snell. It is the "becket hitch" of the seaman. It explains itself. Its great advantage is

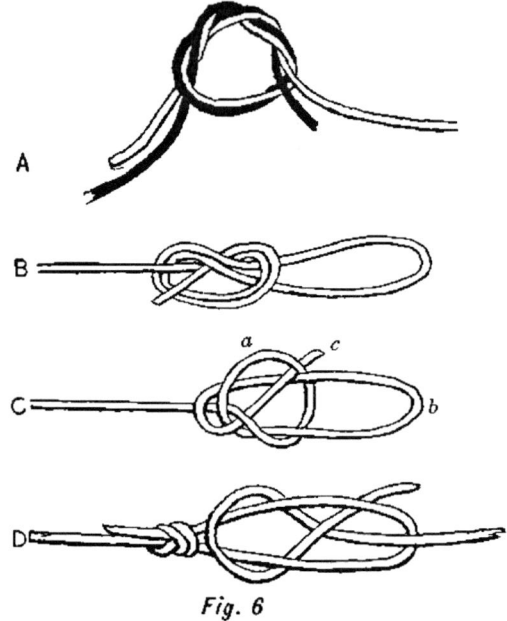

Fig. 6

that it cannot slip if drawn down snugly and can be instantly loosened by pushing the main line back a little way.

Aids for Young Anglers

How often has it happened that on reaching a camping-ground, hotel, or boarding-house near river or lake where pickerel, bass, and large perch abounded no provision is found for the angler's sport but a boat—no lines, sinkers, or floats; no nets for catching live bait, and no bait but worms. For sunfish, catfish, and small perch, worms are very fair bait; but for pickerel, bass, and large perch live bait is best. Here are some makeshifts and aids that may be gotten up at short notice and at small expense.

Fig. 7 is an end-section of a mosquito-net seine for taking live bait. The length of the seine is thirty-eight feet, depth five feet. The "cork-line" A A consists of a small-sized clothes-line. Corks not always being obtainable, I have used pieces of thoroughly seasoned white pine three inches in length and one inch in diameter (C C C). Through these rounded pieces of wood holes are bored through which the clothes-line passes. These floats are placed eight inches apart and are kept in position by the clothes-line fitting tightly in the holes. At the bottom of the seine another clothes-line is sewed to the netting (B B). This is called the "lead line" and is for the purpose of keeping the lower part of the seine close to the bottom of the water. In the lead line pieces of sheet-lead one inch in length are fastened (H H H) twenty-eight inches apart. The "staff" D is a well-seasoned piece of hickory six feet long, to the lower end of which sheet-lead is also fastened at E to keep it down. To the staff is attached the staff line F F F, thirty feet long, which is for the purpose of drawing in the seine after it has been cast.

A seine of this size is generally worked by two persons and two boats. Each person takes one of the staff lines in his boat, and rowing towards the shore with the extended seine describes a semicircle between the boats. As the shore is approached each boat closes in, thereby causing the two staffs to meet and imprison all the fish that have come within the bounds of the seine. When one person works the seine one of the staff lines is tied to a rock or stake on

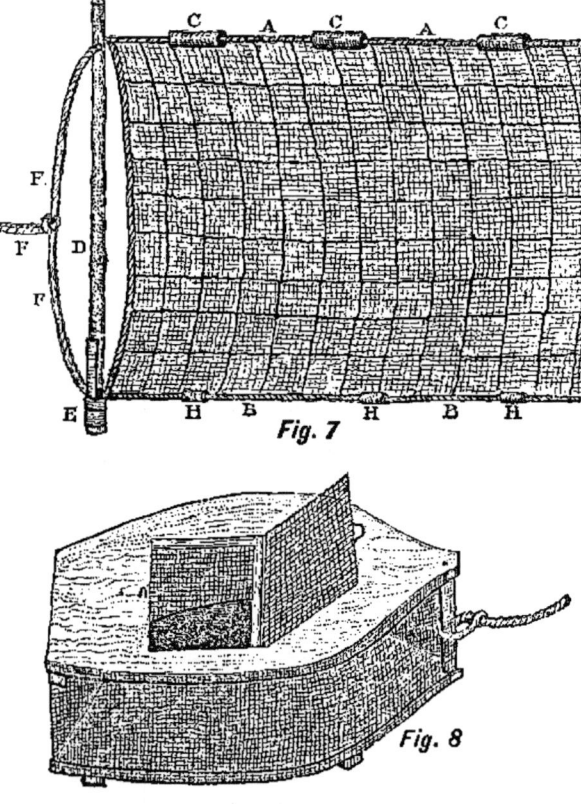

Fig. 7

Fig. 8

the shore and the other line is taken into a boat, or the operator wades out and causes his end of the seine to describe a circle until the two shafts meet. Great care must be taken to keep the lead line close to the bottom otherwise the fish will escape. In the selection of the seining-ground always avoid stony bottoms, snags, and brush, which will cause the seine to "roll up" and tear.

The cost of the above-described seine ranges from three to four dollars, and is capable of lasting two seasons if carefully handled and spread out on the grass to dry after using it. A much superior article to mosquito-net is bobinet, which will last several seasons.

Fig. 8 is a bait-boat for keeping the bait alive. It is towed behind or kept by the side when fishing. The top and bottom pieces consist of half-inch pine; in the centre of each piece square openings are cut; that on the top is protected by a door made of wire-cloth or quarter-inch mesh fastened to two small staples which answer the purpose of hinges; over the opening in the bottom piece wire-cloth is nailed to admit of a free circulation of water. Under the back end of the top piece a cleat is nailed, also two cleats on the bottom piece as shown in the drawing. At the bow of the boat an upright piece of wood is fastened to the top and bottom of the bait-boat by means of screws. The sides of the boat consist of one piece of wire-cloth, the ends of which meet at the upright piece of wood at the bow and are nailed with broad-headed galvanized nails. The top and bottom of the wire-cloth are also fastened with nails to the edges of the top and bottom of the boat as shown in the drawing. A tow-line is fastened to the bow and the boat is complete.

When handling the bait a small hand-net (Fig. 9) is used, consisting of a stout piece of wire as shown in the drawing. The straight parts of the wire are bound together with fishing-line and constitute the handle; to this frame netting is sewed to form the net-bag.

For a makeshift float nothing is better than a good-sized bottle-cork into which a cut has been made with a sharp knife or razor extending from the side to the centre of the cork. Into this cut the line is drawn as shown in Fig. 10 A.

Sheet-lead is always a useful aid in makeshift fishing-tackle, and for light lines makes excellent sinkers when bent and compressed around the line as shown at Fig. 10 B.

For cleaning out a boat a stiff whisk-broom made of fine birch twigs bound together with wire or fishing-line, as shown at Fig. 11, will be found very useful.

Fig. 12 A and B are hand-made sinkers beaten and carved out of old lead pipe. The carved one, B, is first roughed out with a jack-knife and finished up with fine emery or sand paper. A is beaten into shape with a railroad spike on an anvil or smooth stone. This beating and carving of lead is very pleasant work, the lead being of such an easy and good-natured temper.

For a cheap and easy-obtainable bailer make use of an empty tomato or corned-beef can as shown in Fig. 13. A hole sufficiently large to admit of the handle is punched in the side of the can; the inside of the handle is chamfered off so as to fit close to the inner side of the can. Through the can and into the end of the handle a stout nail is driven as at A.

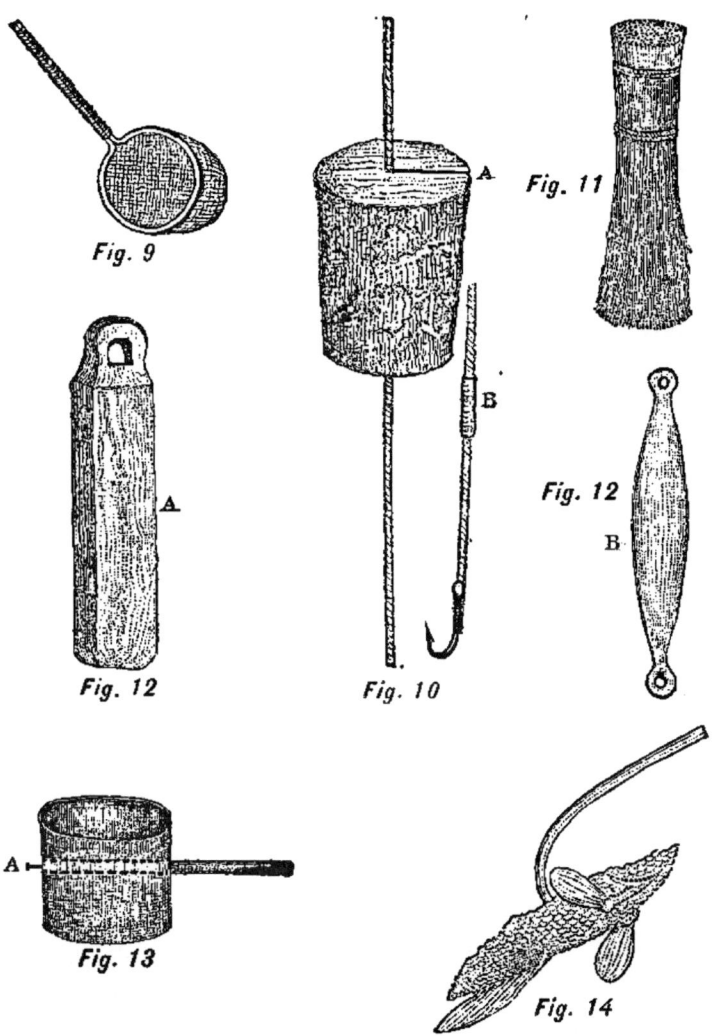

Fig. 9

Fig. 11

Fig. 12

A

Fig. 12

Fig. 10

Fig. 13

Fig. 14

SOME USEFUL HINTS

A good bait for large fish is a strip cut from the under side of a small pickerel, perch, or sunfish, which is placed on the hook as shown in Fig. 14.

Baits, and Where to Find Them

As a rule, the young fisherman naturally considers the angle-worm to be the only bait he need have when he goes fishing, and, taking a spade, he seeks a moist, loamy spot in the garden and proceeds to fill his box. But there is a choice even in worms, and those of a clear, dark, amber color are the best.

Just at night, and after a soft, warm rain, worms of the size of a lead-pencil will be found crawling over the ground. These are excellent bait for bass, chub, perch, and large trout early in the season. If you step very lightly, so as not to jar the ground, you can easily pick up a box of these large fellows.

It is well enough to have worms with you on all occasions, but there are many other baits. Frogs, crabs, grubs, dobsons, minnows, June-bugs, grasshoppers, and crickets, as well as artificial baits, are more successful lures with certain fish. A few words telling where to find these baits and the proper manner of keeping them fresh and lively may prove of value.

Frogs are most plentiful on the shores of ponds or streams filled with plant growth, and in low, moist places in meadows. In searching for them in grass, wait till you see one jump, then catch it in your hands. They are not so easily gotten from the shores, as they are apt to take to the water at the first alarm.

Crabs are usually found under stones along the shores of a stream or pond, and in some localities in low, moist places in grass-lands. Seize the crab back of the pincers and it cannot nip you.

Dobsons are only found under mossy stones in swift-running waters. They are of a dark-gray color, have many legs, and when fully grown are about three inches long. The head is shield-shaped and armed with good, stout pincers, so handle the dobson as you would a crab. The best way to get a supply of dobsons is to have some one hold one edge of a fine-meshed net on the bottom of the stream while you turn over the stones above the net with a hoe. The dobsons, loosing their hold on the bottom, will be carried by the current into the net. Put frogs, crabs, and dobsons into a pail with plenty of grass and some water. If you are to keep them for some time change the water occasionally.

Grubs are excellent bait for trout early in the season. They are found in partially decayed tree-trunks, stumps, and old timbers left in moist places. Cut into the wood with an axe, and if you find it full of holes of the size of a lead-pencil, knock it to pieces and pick out the grubs. Put them in a tin bait-box with some of the rotten wood you found them in.

Minnows of a size suitable for perch and bass fishing can usually be procured from a spring hole or the pools of a small stream. Take a rather baggy net with a small mesh, and after setting it at one end of the pool drive the minnows into it by striking on the water with a pole and punching about on the bottom. If you stir up the water the little fish will drive more easily. If your supply must be procured from a lake or pond, look among the shallows close inshore until you have found a school, then draw a small seine around them. Large minnows for pickerel or pike fishing can be caught with a hook and line. Those you are to use for skittering had better be packed in salt. The minnows you would keep alive should be put into the bait-pail as soon as caught. Bait-pails, as usually made, consist of one pail freely perforated with holes to be set into a tight outer pail. By this arrangement the water can be changed frequently without inconveniencing the little fellows. If the bait is to be carried some distance, and there is no chance to change the water, pack the space between the two pails loosely with grass. The water trickling down through the grass will take up the air needed by the fish.

Crickets are to be found under stones, loose sods, and old planks. Select the largest you can find. June-bugs, sometimes called May-bugs, hide through the heat of the day among the leaves of the trees, and sometimes by shaking a tree quite a number will fall to the ground. Grasshoppers are plentiful in meadow and pasture lands, and may easily be caught in the hands. Put June-bugs, crickets, and grasshoppers in a wide-mouthed bottle loosely stuffed with grass. Do not cork the bottle tight.

I never esteemed artificial baits, such as the rubber frog and crab, very highly. It is impossible to give the semblance of life to them in the water, and most game fish prefer live food to dead. The spoon-hook and the artificial fly, however, have proved their worth. The spoon should be of a size in keeping with the size of the game fished for, and it is well enough to have two—one bright, for use early in the morning and late in the afternoon and on dark days, the other dull-colored for use in the brightest part of the day. It is an excellent plan to bait a spoon-hook with a large worm, a minnow, or a piece of meat; then if the fish strikes and misses the hook it may get a portion of the bait and will strike again with truer aim.

There are many other things that can be used for bait, which are to be found only in your locality. What they are you can learn by observation and experiment. One can always learn something. Only recently I discovered that bass were fond of darning-needles.

Sometimes the fish have very fickle appetites, and it is well to have as many kinds of bait as you can conveniently carry. It is also a good plan to open the stomach of the first fish you catch, and offer to its companions the same kind of food found inside of it.

A Trap for Small Fish

Many of the boys and girls who live near the sea-side are interested in making and stocking aquariums, and many, no doubt, have experienced the same difficulty which I did when I used to stock aquariums myself.

I always found that the scoop-net which we use to catch the fish with is good enough for certain kinds of minnows, but there are others which are too lively or too shy to be caught in that way; so I set to work to devise some plan for their capture. I claim no originality for this trap—it is hundreds of years old; but as it answered my purpose better than anything else, I used it. The way I made it was as follows:

I took a piece of wire-netting about three feet square and bent it so as to form a tube three feet long and about one foot in diameter (Fig. 15). I then took two other strips of

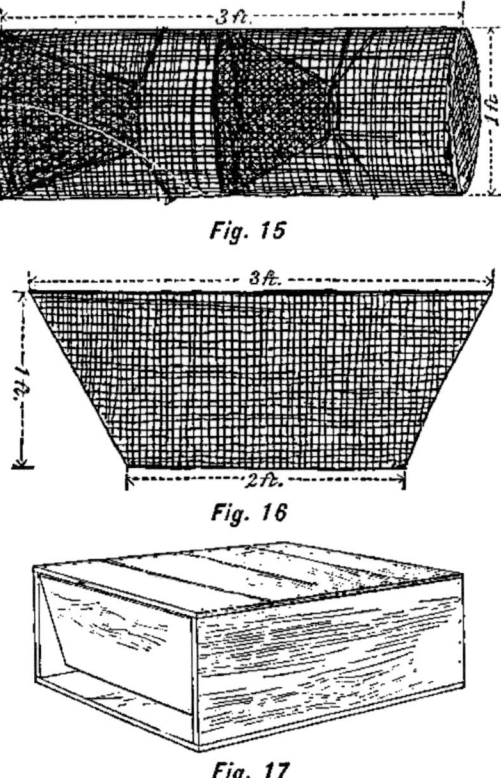

Fig. 15

Fig. 16

Fig. 17

wire-netting, three feet long at the top, one foot wide, and two feet at the bottom (Fig. 16); these I bent into funnel shape. I sewed one funnel in about the middle of my cylinder and another in one end, as shown in Fig. 15, strengthening them in their position with strings from the small ends to the sides of the cylinder. The other end of the cylinder I closed with a piece of strong bagging so sewed on that there was a space left at one side which could be untied when I wished to empty the trap.

The manner of setting the trap is as simple as its manufacture. A handful of clams or mussels, crushed so that the minnows can get at the flesh, is thrown in between the first and second funnels. The fish, little crabs, small eels, and the like, go in, and when they try to get out they find it much easier to swim through the second funnel than to find the small hole in the first. I have had several of these traps, or "pots," as the fishermen call them, in operation at one time, and have caught as many as half a bushel of small fish in one night.

The trap can be made by making a frame of hoops and lath and covering it with mosquito-netting, but it is not so desirable as the fine wire, being more easily torn.

A Water-turtle Trap

Some time ago, while spending the summer in the country, I began the pleasing amusement of making an aquarium. I used various methods to procure the inmates of the great glass box which I had made for the purpose, and was successful, except that I could not get a water-turtle. There they would lie on logs in the pond sunning themselves, but the moment I came within reaching distance, plump they would go into the water. At last I took an old soap-box, and after carefully removing one end I nailed on the cover. I then fastened the end to the cover by hinges, so that it would swing inward, and after throwing in a few bones and scraps of meat, I sunk the box in the pond close beside a big log where the turtles were accustomed to sun themselves. I put a heavy stone on the box, so as to keep it steady, and awaited the next morning for developments. Fig. 17.

Here I may say that this trap takes advantage of a peculiarity in the nature of the water-turtle—namely, if there is a log or stone that he cannot get under, that is just the place that he wants to get; and I calculated that the slight resistance offered by my swinging door would be just enough to make the turtles determined to get into my box. The next morning when I went to my trap I found several turtles of all sizes, from one tiny, yellow-spotted fellow, or mud-turtle, not larger than a half-dollar, to an ugly, great snapper as big as your hat, and so ill-tempered that I let him go again, glad enough at having got rid of so troublesome a visitor. After that I set my trap several times and caught a number of turtles. The smaller ones furnish a charming addition to an aquarium, and the larger ones, if properly dressed, make a capital stew.

An Eel-pot

All along the Atlantic coast eel-pots are made on the same general plan, a bottle-shaped basket having a funnel fitted at the bottom and provided with a hat that is held on by two straps of green oak.

Three forms are used on which to build up the basket-work. The large form is usually ten inches in diameter and shaped down to eight inches at the top or neck. This form is two feet long and has a round stick driven in the small end. This in turn rests in a hole bored in a solid piece of plank, so that it is held in an inverted position and revolves in the hole. Green oak is used for the ribs and bands. This is cut as straight and free from knots as possible, and is soaked in water for weeks before it is split and slivered. Green oak will sliver in an even and uniform manner if it is started right, and from the trunk of an oak-tree six inches in diameter enough material can be had to make several dozen eel-pots. The ribs are three-quarters of an inch wide and about one-eighth of an inch thick, while the bands are a trifle thinner and wider. A number of the ribs are tied around the form as shown in Fig. 18, and beginning at the bottom the bands are woven in and out around the form, turning it as the work progresses so that the immediate parts are always in sight. Where the ends join they are shaved down thin so that one laps over the other; then the weaving continues until the top is reached. The ends of the ribs are then shaved thin and bent back and slipped under some of the straps. A thin ribbon of the oak is sewed over and over around the edge to finish it. The top or small end of the basket is finished in a similar manner.

The cone or funnel form is fifteen inches long, nine inches in diameter at the large end, and tapers down to two inches at the bottom as shown in Fig. 19. Ribs are tied to this form the same as in the case of the large one, and the weaving begins at the bottom and is carried to the top, where the ends of the ribs are shaved and turned in as before described.

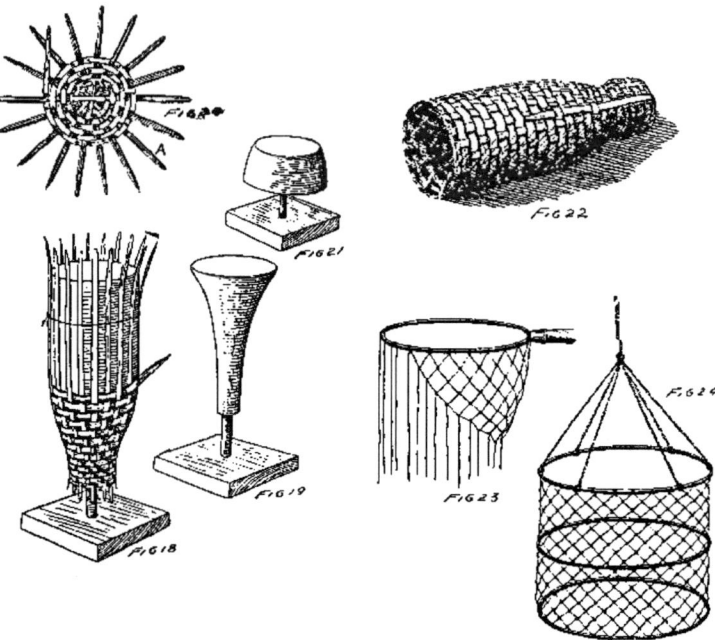

The bottom or small end of the funnel is the trap, and here the long, thin ends of the ribs are left, so that the eel, when he goes through the funnel and into the pot, cannot get back again.

The hat is woven the same as a basket by crossing the ribs and adding a half-rib from the centre anywhere on the circle, so as to make an uneven number of ribs; thus the weaving will not duplicate after the first turn around the circle. This extra rib is shown at A in Fig. 20. A hat form, shown in Fig. 21, is made of wood and mounted on a block so that it will revolve the same as the other forms. When a part of the hat is woven it is placed on the form and two small nails driven through the ribs into the form to hold the weaving in place. It is then shaped down over the rounded edges of the form and carried one or two inches below the form so the lower edges of the ribs can be shaved and bent easily. A long strap of the green oak is passed under one of the ribs in the hat and caught under bands of the body as shown in the drawing of a complete eel-pot. Fig. 22.

The funnel is sewed to the bottom edge of the body with thin bands. As soon as the pots are finished they should be sunk in shallow water to keep them wet and get them thoroughly water-soaked.

Stakes or poles are to be driven or worked down into the bottom of the bay and the eel-pots made fast to them with ropes. To bait an eel-pot crack some hard-shell crabs or shrimp or put some pieces of fresh, raw meat within the pot and drop it overboard. Run the pots morning and night, and remove the eels by unstrapping the cap and dumping them into a barrel which may be carried on the boat.

A Scap-net

A scap-net for crabbing or landing fish on a hook may be made from a ring of heavy galvanized iron driven into the end of a hard-wood stick. Scap-nets may be purchased in most any general store near a bay or pond, but the ingenious boy can make one himself from a hoop and a ball of cotton twine. Hang long pieces of string over the ring and tie them fast with a square knot. Then tie one string

175

with its next neighbor all around the circle. Begin lower down and tie them again, and continue in this manner until the net resembles Fig. 23. When it is seven or eight inches deep begin to shape it in at the bottom by making the meshes or openings smaller so that it will have a rounded bottom. The ends of the string should be tied together or over a small galvanized-iron sail-ring. All the strings should be tied in square knots so that they will not become undone after the net has been used for a while.

A Hoop Drop-net

A hoop drop-net such as shown at Fig. 24 may easily be made from three galvanized-wire rings and a mesh of tied string as described for the scap-net. The hoops should be eighteen inches in diameter and separated ten inches, thus making a net twenty inches deep. A mesh is to be formed across the bottom, and at the top six small ropes are tied and the ends brought together fifteen or twenty inches above the top ring.

Place some crushed crab or any good bait in the bottom of the net and slowly lower it until the rings rest on the bottom of the bay or pond, but keep the small ropes clear from the net. Watch through the water for visitors, and when the right subject is at the bait and within the rings give a quick jerk and pull the net rapidly to the surface. If fish are to be caught in this manner the hoops should be larger and one more added to the net, making it thirty inches deep. Fish are cunning and swift, and will often dart up and over the top hoop faster than you can haul it up.

Chapter X

LAND-YACHTS AND PUSHMOBILES

A Land-yacht

A FEW years ago the only kind of yacht known to the boys were those that sailed in the water, but in this advanced time, when many unheard-of things have been made possible, the land-yacht has made its welcome appearance. Down on the Southern coasts, particularly Florida and California, where the sand packs fine and hard, the land-yacht is an important feature both for pleasure and business, and if properly handled in a good breeze it will run from ten to twenty miles an hour. No end of fun can be had with a properly constructed boat, and the ingenious boy may employ old baby-carriage or bicycle wheels for the running-gear.

A yacht of medium size can be made on the lines of Fig. 1 at a comparatively small cost for the timbers and sail-cloth, spars and hardware. The leg-of-mutton sail is used in preference to the square sail, as it has the greatest area close to the ground and is less liable to upset and much easier to handle.

To begin with, obtain some spruce joist clear-grained and free from knots. They should be two-by-four inches and

177

twelve feet long. Cut one of them eight feet long and use
it for the main cross-piece to which the front wheels are
attached. Form a V of two twelve-foot joist, and fasten
them to the cross-piece as shown in Fig. 2. About ten

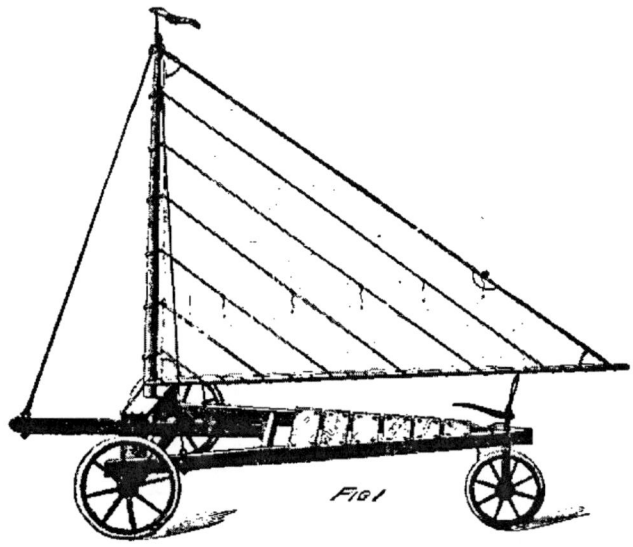

FIG I

inches of each piece should project beyond the cross-piece.
The timbers are bolted fast and at the rear end they are
bevelled and brought together, then bolted through from
side to side as shown in the plan (Fig. 2). Three feet back of
the long cross-piece a shorter timber is set in between the
V-shaped frame as shown at A. At the middle of this timber
a hole one inch and a half square is cut and into it a tenon
on the butt-end of the bowsprit fits as shown in Fig. 3.

The bowsprit is seven feet long and is bolted fast to the long cross-piece. Where the end fits into the timber A two angle-blocks are nailed fast. Seat-planking is cut and screwed or nailed fast to the V-shaped frame as shown in both Fig. 1 and Fig. 2. The boards should be ten inches wide and cut to overhang the timbers an inch or two at both ends.

If the wheels from an old baby-carriage are to be used the axle should be cut in half with a hack-saw and each part clamped under an end of the cross-timber with U-shaped clamps having the ends threaded and provided with nuts and washers as shown at Fig. 4. The rear or steering wheel is set in a fork that a blacksmith will make from strap-iron, and a round piece of the same metal, having a square-headed upper end, will do for the rudder-post as shown at Fig. 5. A short axle threaded at both ends and provided with nuts will hold the wheel in place, and when the post is passed up through a hole made in the timbers a tiller can be slipped over the square shoulder and bolted fast so that it will stay in place.

The tiller is of hard-wood two inches broad at the rear end, one inch in thickness, and tapered so that it will be about an inch square with the corners rounded where it is grasped by the hand. The handle part of it should be bound with linen cord to improve the grip. Give the deck wood-work and timbering a few coats of red, buff, or light-green paint.

The mast-step is rigged over the forward cross-timber. Two upright pieces of board twenty inches long and eight inches wide are attached to the outside edges of the frame-joist with screws. On top of these a cross-piece is made fast so that the step presents the appearance of a bench. Two pieces of board six inches wide are fastened from the corners down to the bowsprit and cross-timber to brace the step as shown at Fig. 6. An iron brace is made fast to the top of the step, behind the mast, and to the bowsprit, as may be seen in the illustration.

A hole three inches in diameter is cut at the middle of the

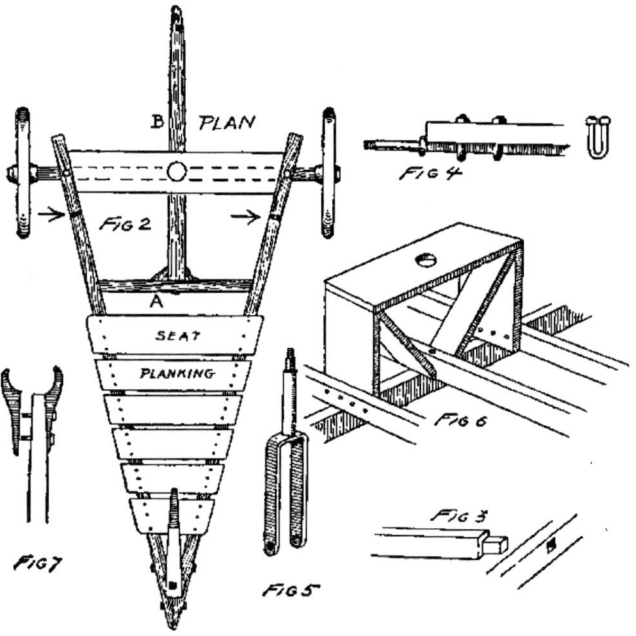

step-board, and through this the mast is slipped. A half-inch round iron is driven into the bottom of the mast after a hole has been bored with a bit. It should be long enough to project out about two inches. This steps into a hole bored in the top of the bowsprit, and with the three wire stays that are caught at the top of the mast and into the eye-bolts, shown by the arrow-heads in Fig. 2, the mast is held securely in place.

A round pole fourteen feet long may be used for the mast, but if it is impossible to find one a very good mast can be dressed from a three-inch-square spruce stick that is free from large knots or cracks. The dressing may be done with a draw-knife and plane, and near the upper end it should be tapered.

The boom is sixteen feet long and two inches in diameter, and if it is possible to get a long curtain-pole it will answer very well; otherwise it will be necessary to cut it from a two-inch-square spruce stick.

The mast end of the boom is provided with a crotch made with two jaws as shown at Fig 7. They are cut from hardwood with a draw-knife and compass-saw, and held to the boom with carriage bolts or screws and string bound round the three parts.

The sail is made of heavy, unbleached muslin that can be had at a dry-goods store for ten cents a yard. It may be sewed by hand or on a machine, and through the middle it would be well to take a lop so as to make a strengthening rib. The sail measures ten feet on the mast, fifteen feet on the boom, and eighteen feet on the leach. It is caught to the boom with stout cord and to the mast with wood or iron rings, and with a halyard and pulley at mast-head the sail may be raised and lowered at will.

In localities where there are hard roads and where the

wind has a good sweep these land-yachts have become very popular. Of course they are much safer than water-boats for there is no danger of drowning, and it is quite impossible to capsize a land-yacht if the cross-timber is long enough to give the wheels a good spread.

Wheels with rubber tires will make the running motion easier and so add to the owner's comfort.

A Sail-wagon

For level streets or sidewalks where trees do not interfere and where the walks are wide, a sail-wagon will afford much amusement.

In the drawing (Fig. 8) a sail-wagon of medium size and simple construction is shown. Obtain a pine, white-wood, or spruce plank fifteen inches wide and about one inch thick. It should be planed on one or both sides and measure eight feet long. Round the ends with a compass-saw and build a bridge for the mast, as shown in the drawing. This bridge should be twelve inches high, eighteen inches long, and eight inches wide, and should be braced underneath with angle-brackets. In the middle of the top board cut a hole three inches in diameter, and directly under it, in the plank, bore a half-inch hole for the mast-pin to step into.

One foot back from the front end arrange an axle-bar three feet long and two by three inches thick. Make another bar the same size for the rear axle but do not bolt it fast. This must be arranged on a king-bolt so that it can be turned by a post and tiller. The king-bolt and post should be in one piece, and this will have to be made by a

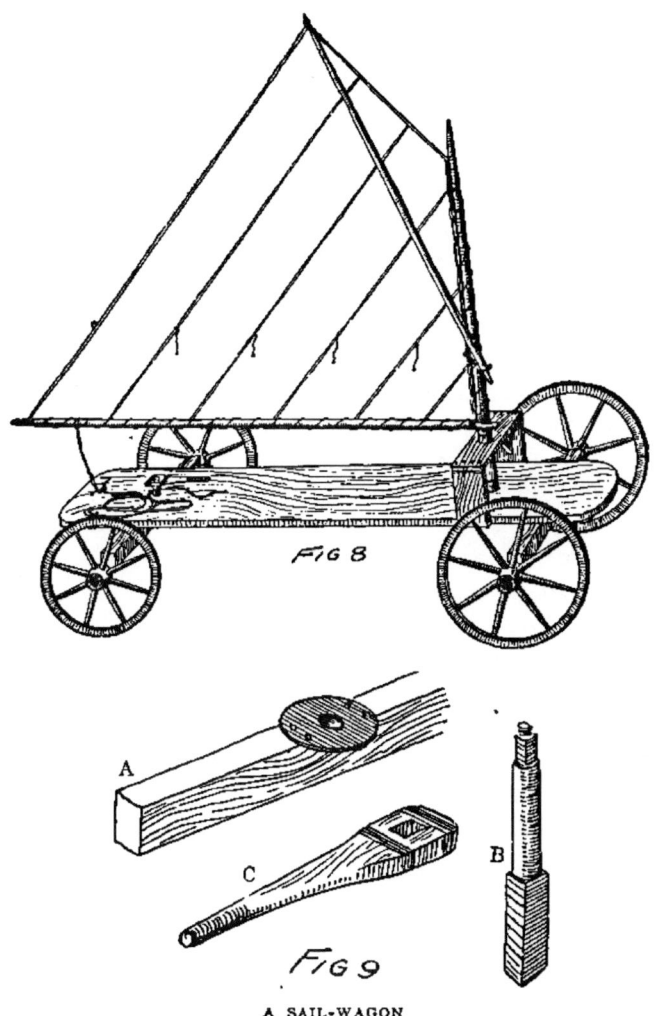

FIG 8

A · · · · C · · · · B

FIG 9

A SAIL-WAGON

blacksmith. Two round iron plates of metal one-eighth of an inch thick and five inches in diameter are provided with screw-holes at the outer edge and with round holes at the middle. One of these plates is to be attached to the middle of the axle, as shown at Fig. 9 A, and the other to the under side of the plank in the middle and about ten inches in from the end. A hole is to be bored and cut three-quarters of an inch square in the axle-tree, and the holes in both iron plates are also three-quarters of an inch in diameter. Have a blacksmith make an iron post eight inches long and three-quarters of an inch in diameter. A piece of iron should be welded at the lower end so as to make it three-quarters of an inch square for a distance of three inches. At the top form a square shoulder an inch long, and above it have a short round shank threaded to take a nut as shown in Fig. 9 B. Drive this shaft up through the square hole in the axle-tree, and to prevent it from dropping nail a piece of wood or tin over the end of it and to the under side of the tree. Slip the round post up through the plate and board so that it extends several inches above the top of the board. Make a tiller of hard-wood fifteen inches long and three inches wide at the post-end and taper it to the handle. Cut a square hole in the broad end to fit over the square shoulder on the iron post, then screw the nut on over a washer to hold the tiller in place. To prevent the tiller from splitting near the hole it would be best to bind the wood at both ends of the hole with copper wire as shown in Fig. 9 C. When the wagon is in motion a turn of the handle will operate the axle and steer the moving vehicle easily.

The wheels should be all the same size, but if they cannot

184

be had and only a pair of large and small ones are available place the smaller ones at the rear. The axle need not run the entire length of the axle-tree, but shorter pieces may be bolted fast to the ends of the trees. Give the wagon two or three coats of paint and it will then be ready for use.

From spruce or pine cut a mast five feet long and three inches in diameter, using a draw-knife and plane to shape it. Taper the stick at the top, place an iron band about the bottom, and drive a half-inch iron pin into a hole bored in the bottom so that two or three inches of it will project. The foot of the mast is to be slipped through the hole in the bridge and the pin stepped into the hole made in the long board directly under it. From two-inch spruce cut a sprit seven feet long and a boom seven feet long with a crotch formed at one end, as described in the boat chapter. The sprit acts as a gaff, and at the same time it does away with halyards and makes it possible to use a shorter and stouter stick for the mast.

From unbleached muslin make a sail three feet and six inches on the mast, six feet on the boom, three feet at the head, and seven feet on the leach. A sail of this proportion will set properly, and when the peak is jacked up with the sprit the boom will clear the boy on the deck when it swings over. To stiffen the sail bind the outer edge with thin rope or cotton line a trifle smaller than clothes-line.

A Pushmobile

The pushmobile (Fig. 10) is another interesting road or sidewalk car and one with which two boys can share considerable fun. In general appearance the pushmobile resembles something between an automobile and a buck-board, as there is a long reach between the fore and aft wheels. The body consists of a long board one inch and a quarter in thickness, eighteen or twenty inches wide, and seven feet long. Or two nine-inch planks may be fixed together with the battens that hold the axles and a shorter one under the seat. At the front of the body a keg is mounted and held fast with iron straps which go over the top of the keg and are fastened to the sides of the large board as may be seen in Fig. 10. This keg will represent the engine cover, and at either side of it and mounted on the board two tin cans arranged with glass at the front will serve as lamps. By perforating the tops and sides of these cans a candle may be used or bicycle lamps may be substituted for them. The glass is fitted to the cans by bending a piece of spring-wire in a circle and placing it within the can. Against this wire a circular piece of glass will rest, and to hold it in place another wire may be slipped within the can. If large baking-powder or coffee cans are used the greater portion of the cap may be cut away with a tin-shears, leaving a rim and flange just wide enough to hold the glass in place.

The seat is made from a box eighteen inches wide and high and arranged with back and sides which can be built up six inches above the seat as shown in Fig. 10. This seat is to be securely attached to the board with long screws driven up through the under side of the board and into the lower part of the box. The steering-shaft and wheel are arranged about one foot in front of the seat. This is a shaft of hard-wood (such as a curtain-pole or any good tough

stick) about one inch and a half square or in diameter. It
mounts on a block of wood which is screwed fast to the large
board and provided with a hole through which the shaft
will pass so that it will extend down through the large board.
A collar of wood or iron is slipped down over the shaft and
screwed fast to it so as to prevent it from slipping down too

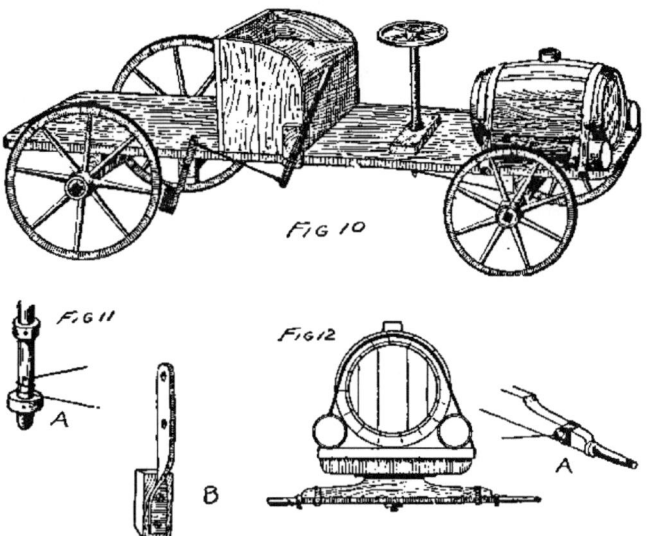

FIG 10

FIG 11

FIG 12

A

B

A

far. Another collar is provided and made fast at the bottom
to prevent the steering-cable from slipping off. The arrangement of the collars and wire is shown at Fig. 11 A. At
the top of the shaft a small wooden wheel should be slipped
on over a shank that may be cut down in size to fit the opening in the wheel; and with a screw the wheel is to be made
fast to the shaft so that it is held securely in place.

The rear wheels are attached to an axle that in turn is bolted fast to a bar of wood eighteen inches long and two by three inches in thickness. These wheels are held in a fixed position, and the bar to which they are attached is located about a foot in from the end of the long board. The front axle is bolted to a movable bar which is held to another bar by a king-bolt, so that the lower axle-bar can turn in the same way as on a wagon. The bar to which the axle and movable bar are attached is located about one foot from the front of the long board. This arrangement can be seen at Fig. 12, which is a front view showing axle and fifth wheel, as the turn-plate between the axle-tree and the body of the wagon is called. The fifth wheel is made of two pieces of tire-iron, one fastened to the under side of the fixed bar, the other to the top of the axle-tree, so that when greased the lower part will turn easily.

Flexible wire-cable or very strong twine should be used for the steering-gear. The ends are made fast to the axle-tree as shown at A in Fig. 12. Several wraps of the wire or twine are taken about the lower end of the shaft, and the wire passes through a hole to prevent it from slipping. The wire should be attached first at one end of the tree, carried to the shaft, and given several turns, then passed through the hole. Several more turns are to be made above the hole, then the loose end should be attached to the other end of the axle-tree. If a small turn-buckle can be had, make it fast to the wire and axle at one end so as to draw the wire taut and hold it in place, for the tighter the wire the better the shaft will act when turned by the wheel.

A brake is to be made fast at one side of the car as shown in Fig. 10. Have a blacksmith turn a piece of one-inch thin tire-iron for you as shown at Fig. 11 B, and bore two holes at the short end and two larger ones farther up as indicated in the drawing. With screws attach a brake-block to the short end, and with a square-headed lag-screw make this brake-bar fast to a block fastened at the under side of the long board so that the lever and brake-block will act on the tire of the wheel. The hand-bar is of iron twenty-four inches long and provided with a hole at the lower end and another one six inches above it. The upper end of the bar is drawn out on the anvil so that a wooden handle can be slipped on it, then it is bolted to a block attached to the lower front side of the seat as shown in the illustration. A stout wire connects the lower end of the hand-bar with the top of the brake-bar, so that when the handle is pulled back the wire and top end of the brake-bar is drawn forward and the block pressed against the wheel.

Several coats of paint will give this pushmobile a good appearance and it will then be ready for use.

One boy on the seat steers the machine, while another grasps the overhanging edges of the long board and pushes as he runs behind. On level sidewalks or streets a good run and push will send the car along at a good speed and the pusher can then jump on behind. When going downhill both boys can ride, and if the driver has his hands full with the wheel and shaft the boy behind can reach forward and operate the brake.

If coasting is done on very steep hills or roads it would be well to have a brake to operate on both rear wheels, for the momentum of a rapidly moving car will often drag a "dead" wheel if the other three are running easily; whereas if both back wheels are "dead" the car can be brought to a quick stop.

Chapter XI

FIRE-ENGINES AND TRUCKS

The Engine

EVERY boy is interested in fire-engines and fires, and in the absence of the real thing there is a great deal of fun to be had in playing fire. The regular steam apparatus is rather beyond a boy's constructive ability, but the engine shown in the illustration (Fig 1) can easily be made from an oil or pork barrel, a keg, a pump, and a set of old wagon wheels. A box may be used for the seat and a small force-pump may be had at a hardware store for a nominal sum. The pump should be fitted with a hose-coupling at both inlet and outlet, so that a piece of garden hose can be used for the suction and force.

The construction of the body part of the engine is shown in Fig. 2. Two rails six inches wide, seven-eighths of an inch thick, and six feet long are set wide enough apart for the barrel (representing the boiler) to fit between. These pieces are securely attached with stout screws to the barrel so that a foot of each rail will extend beyond the rear of the barrel. At both ends a rail corresponding in width and thickness is cut and fitted between the ends of the rails as shown at A A. These are to be held in position with long, steel-wire nails or with screws, which always make the best and most secure joints.

To prevent the side-rails from spreading, a cross-rib should be made fast to the under side of the side-rails about at the

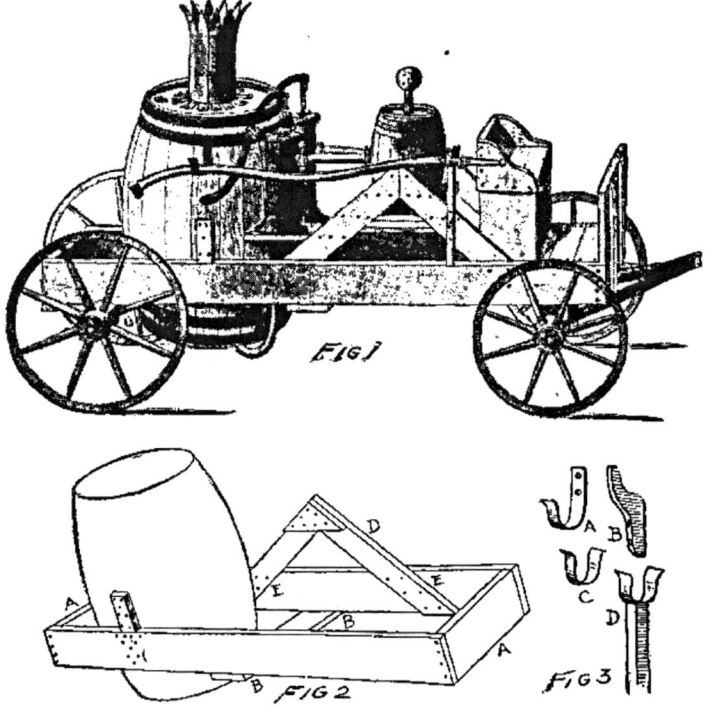

middle as shown at B B. This is a precaution taken to prevent the rails spreading and letting the heavy barrel full of water drop. In addition to the screws that are driven through the side-rails and into the barrel, it would be well to screw a batten fast at each side over the rail as shown at C. This lug will help the bearing and take the strain from the screws in the rails.

The truss which holds the keg, or imitation dry-steam chest, is made of strips four inches wide, seven-eighths of an inch thick, and built up so that the angle stands fifteen inches above the top of the side-rails as shown at D. These trusses are securely bound at the angle with screws or clinch-nails, then screwed fast to the inside of the rails as shown at E E. Cut a short piece of board and nail it fast between these truss-knees to act as a platform on which to stand the keg. Another small platform can be made between the truss and barrel on one or both sides of the apparatus to accommodate one or two pumps. The smoke-pipe at the top of the barrel is cut from an old stove-pipe and is shaped as shown in Fig. 1. With a tin-shears or snips the ears are cut at top and bottom. Those at the top are pointed and give a crown effect, but if the plain-rim top is preferred do not cut the pipe At the bottom, slits are cut in the pipe two inches in from the edge, about three-quarters of an inch apart, and with a flat-nosed pliers the ears are bent out so that they will lie flat on the barrel-top when the smoke-pipe is set in place. A piece of tin or zinc is placed on the barrel-head under the smoke-pipe, and with large tacks the pipe is then made fast.

When running to a fire some shavings, chips, or cotton on which some paraffine has been melted is put in this smoke-pipe and lit, and as the engine is drawn along the sparks and smoke will shoot out from the top of the pipe in a very realistic manner. The seat is made of a box on top of which a back and side-arms are arranged as shown in Fig. 1, and when it is complete it is attached to the side-rails and truss. The upper edges of the side-rails are decked over in front of the box so as to make a platform, and at the front end of the frame a dash-board is arranged and held in position with battens.

A small, water-tight keg is fastened to the platform between the knees of the truss by means of screws passed up through the bottom of the platform and into the under side of the keg. One or two openings are made in the keg and a hose-coupling driven into them so that the long hose may be attached when at a fire. Short lengths of hose and couplings extend from the top of the pumps to the keg, so that when the pumps are in action the water is forced into the keg and out through the openings. There will always be a cushion of air above the water which is more or less elastic, and when the water is forced in faster than it can escape through the nozzles the air-cushion will take care of the pressure automatically.

Small carriage wheels and axles support the frame, and at the front a fifth wheel is arranged so that the front wheels can be turned. Back of the barrel the frame is decked at the under side so as to make a fuel-box where more smoke and spark making materials can be stored. It would be well to fasten a lid to this compartment so that sparks dropping from the smoke-pipe will not fall on and ignite the contents. If it is possible to obtain a force-pump it can be mounted on one of the bases arranged at the side of the barrel.

The suction-hose should come from the under side of the barrel and be attached to the base of the pump. The coupling to which the long hose is attached should be arranged at the side of the keg or it can be screwed directly on the outlet of the pump. A short length of the hose—a coupling and nozzle—may be supported on hooks and a standing Y as shown in Fig. 1. The hook on the barrel is made from a piece of iron bent as shown at Fig. 3 A, with holes bored to receive screws. If the iron is too hard to work a wooden bracket can be made, as shown at B, and screwed fast to the barrel.

The Y may be made from strap-iron and a stick, as shown at C and D (Fig. 3), the iron being attached to the top of the stick which in turn is screwed fast to the truss. A pole is made fast to the forward running-gear to drag the engine with, and if several boys are to be members of the fire company a rope should be made fast to the axle at both ends or to the body frame, and the boy nearest the engine can steer it with the pole. All the wood-work should be painted red and the metal parts with asphaltum varnish, which will give them a good appearance, and as it is water-proof it will prevent the metal parts from rusting.

Trip-gongs and signal-lamps should, of course, be provided, for without these appurtenances the engine would be a flat failure.

The Hose-carriage

A hose-carriage (Fig. 4) to accompany the engine is made of wood and constructed on the same lines as the engine.

The frame is made of boards six inches wide, seven-eighths

of an inch thick, and is five feet long by two feet wide as shown at Fig. 5. A dash-board is made and fastened to the front of the frame, and between the dash-board and seat the side-rails are decked over to make a platform. The remaining part of the frame may be left open. Across the under side of the frame fasten two cross-bars to which the axles are to be made fast. Baby-carriage or small wagon wheels are to be used for the hose-carriage, and if the axles should not be long enough a blacksmith will weld in a piece at the middle so as to make them the required length.

The reel is made from a round piece of wood and two circular sides and arranged so as to revolve in a supporting frame. One side of the frame is shown in Fig. 5. It is made from wood three inches wide, seven-eighths of an inch thick, and the pieces are securely attached at the inside of the side-rails with screws and clinch-nails. The sides of the reel are made from three pieces of matched boards and are twenty inches in diameter.

Drive three pieces of board together and lay them flat. With a pin, a piece of string, and a pencil describe a circle twenty inches in diameter using the centre of the middle board as a place to drive the pin. After the circle is drawn, separate the boards, and with a compass-saw cut the wood on the lines. Then drive the boards together again and band the outer edge with a piece of box strap-iron, driving the nails in about two inches apart all around the edge.

Attach one end to the flat end of the hub. The other piece should have a square hole cut in it so that it will fit over the square shoulder cut on the other end of the axle as shown at Fig. 6 A. Attach both ends to the axle with

FIG 4

FIG 5

FIG 8

FIG 9

D

C

B

A

FIG 6

FIG 7

HOSE-CARRIAGE AND HOOK-AND-LADDER TRUCK

long, steel-wire nails, then from a piece of hard-wood cut a
crank and handle as shown at Fig. 6 B. The crank is ten
inches long and at both sides of the square hole the wood
should be bound with wire to prevent its splitting. At the
opposite end from the crank an iron pin half an inch in
diameter is to be driven through the side and into the end
of the hub through a half-inch hole bored with auger or bit
and brace. This is shown in the drawing of the complete
reel. Fig. 6 C.

On the end of the hub and close to the square crank-shaft
the hub is turned round for a distance of two inches. This
is the part that will fit in the bearing cut in the supporting
frame. To hold the reel in position at the top of the truss,
straps of iron, as shown at Fig. 6 D, are screwed fast over the
angle when the reel is in place. With a coat or two of paint
this hose-carriage will be ready for use.

The Hook-and-Ladder Truck

To complete the outfit a hook-and-ladder truck (Fig. 7)
will be necessary, on the racks of which four hooks, three
ladders, six buckets, and other paraphernalia can be accommodated.

The length of the truck will depend somewhat on the
strength of the wheels that can be had, also on the size of
the boys in the fire company; but for serviceable use for
both small and large boys a truck eight feet long will be a
very good size. The frame or body is made of boards six
inches wide, seven-eighths of an inch thick, and is eight
feet long by thirty inches wide. The frame should be braced

across the bottom, at the middle, and near both ends to prevent it from racking. Two cross-timbers for the axles are made fast under the forward and rear ends, and to the forward one the fifth-wheel bar is made fast so that the front wheels can be turned.

The ladder-rack is constructed from pieces of curtain-pole and side uprights, six inches wide at the bottom and tapered to three inches at the top. The uprights are attached to the inside of the body frame, and the bars on which the ladders rest are let into holes in these uprights and keyed as shown at Fig. 8 A. The end of the bar is cut across with a saw, and when this is passed through a hole in the upright a wedge-shaped key is driven in the cut to spread the end of the bar and expand it so that it will hold. Some glue on the wedge will cause it to stay in place after it has been driven in as far as it will go.

The ladders are made of two spruce rails three inches wide and one inch and a quarter thick. The rungs are let into holes made in the middle of the rails and keyed fast with wedges as just described for the ladder-rails. If a flat rung is preferred the rails may be cut in as shown at B in Fig. 8, and flat strips are to be laid in these laps and nailed or screwed fast. The sharp corners may be planed off so as to make the grip easier to the hands. The ladders may vary from seven to twelve feet in length and from eighteen to twenty-four inches wide, preferably the wider ones, as they are safer and will not slide sidewise as a narrower ladder is apt to do.

The dash-board and forward deck are supported on two bracket-plates made fast to the forward part of the body frame, and on the deck planking a box-seat with sides and back is to be made fast. Stout iron hooks are driven in along both sides of the body between forward and rear wheels, and on them ordinary wooden pails or buckets may be hung. Two sets of hooks arranged at the outer side of the ladder supports will hold the long handles of fire-hooks, and a scaling-ladder can be hung under the truck.

The goose-neck of a scaling-ladder should be made of tempered iron by a blacksmith, and all the wood-work should be of hickory. The plan for a scaling-ladder is shown in Fig. 9. The stick is three by one and a half inches and the rungs are three-quarters by two inches, driven through mortises cut in the stick twelve inches apart and held by a steel nail driven through the centre. The goose-neck base is divided like the front-wheel fork of a bicycle and with corresponding holes bored in each side. Bolts should be passed through them and the head of the stick so as to hold the iron straps securely. Good, strong hickory may be had from a wheelwright or wagon-builder, and care should be taken to cut the mortises accurately so that the parts will fit snugly together. Ladder-building is different from ordinary carpentry, and pains should be taken to have all the joints very tight so that they will not rack.

Chapter XII

WATER-WHEELS

ALL boys like to play about the water, and dams and water machinery afford an endless amount of amusement. Moreover, the pastime has its useful side. Once you get a wheel in operation with a shaft and pulley attached, it is then a simple matter to harness your power and make it do all sorts of things, such as sawing wood, churning milk, operating a fan on hot days, and even turning a grindstone or light wood-working machinery.

There are three kinds of wheels, the overshot, breast, and undershot. The overshot is the most powerful, for it is not only moved by the weight of water that it holds but also by the force of the onrushing water from the sluice arranged to feed it. The breast-wheel is the next in power and is used where the fall of water is not so great. The undershot wheel is employed in a rapidly running brook or stream where there is no dam or body of headwater. This form of wheel is the least powerful and the most unreliable, for the height of the watercourse is liable to change according to seasons and storms. While at one time it may be flushed up to the hub, at another the water may hardly touch the blades of the wheel.

These forms of old-style wheels have become almost obsolete now as the modern turbine has superseded it as a means of employing water as a motive power. Less than one-quarter of the surface of the old-time wheels would be actively engaged at any one time, and the waste of power was appalling as compared with the sluice-box and pen-stock of the modern turbine where every drop of water is lending its influence to the blades. A turbine, however, is rather beyond the ability of the average boy to properly construct, and so we do the best we can with the old-style wheels. For a boy's purpose they will answer quite well enough.

In the accompanying drawings several ideas for water-wheels are shown, and among them a boy should be able to find one that he can make from boards and sticks, at a slight cost, and which if properly rigged and adjusted will develop a considerable amount of power.

A Simple Paddle-wheel

The simple paddle-wheel, as shown at Fig. 1, is made from an axle three inches square, four spokes, and four boards. For a wheel of medium size that will develop about one-eighth of a horse-power the axle should be four feet long. One end is rounded for a distance of four inches as shown at A, and with bit and chisel two mortises are cut in opposite directions as shown at A. These holes are one inch and a quarter wide and three inches long. Into them the spokes are driven and held with screws or iron pins. Another pair of holes are cut thirty inches from the first and two more spokes driven in them. The spokes are thirty inches long, thus leaving thirteen and a half inches of each one projecting beyond the axle or hub.

The paddle blades are boards thirty inches long, ten inches wide, and seven-eighths of an inch thick. They are attached to the spokes with carriage-bolts and washers.

A rounded bearing two inches wide is cut in the axle beyond the spokes so as to correspond with the other end, and beyond this the axle is left square. Bearings for this wheel are made in the edge of a stout plank notched as shown at B, and held in place by iron straps as also depicted at B. Long screws or screw-bolts, commonly known as lag-screws, will hold the strap in place, and from the square end of the shaft the connection is made for power. In place of the iron strap another piece of wood may be cut and clamped down over the axle end as shown at C.

A Wagon Wheel

Another variety of water-wheel may be made from the hubs and spokes of two old wheels, preferably those from a buggy or light wagon. Fig. 2.

Remove the iron boxes from the hubs by driving them out, then cut a hole in each hub with a chisel and mallet, as shown at A, so they will be at least an inch and a half square. From hickory or other hard-wood make an axle the size of the holes and arrange the hubs on it so they will be thirty inches apart. One side of each spoke should be cut as shown at B in order that the blades may rest against a flat place instead of a rounded surface. The blades should be from thirty to thirty-six inches long and ten or twelve inches wide, and held to the spokes with carriage or tire bolts. This wheel may be swung in bearings as described in Fig. 1, and from the square end of the axle the power can be taken.

Both of these wheels may be used as over or undershot but not as breast-wheels, for a breast-wheel must have pockets to hold the water, and the overshot-wheel should have them too if all the available force and weight of water is to be employed.

A Barrel-wheel

A very simple and efficient device is shown in the drawing of a barrel-wheel (Fig. 3). This consists of an oil or pork barrel having tight ends and staves, a number of blades, and some siding-boards.

The blades are of hard-wood ten inches wide and the length of the barrel. One edge of each blade is cut to conform with the bilge of the barrel as shown at A, and with three or four long screws each blade is made fast to the barrel at the middle. The ends of the barrel are replanked so as to build their surface even with the projecting edges of the staves, then some matched boards are nailed or screwed to the heads to bind together the ends of the blades. Screws are passed through the boards and into the ends of the blades to make them secure, and in this manner a hollow wheel is made with pockets around the outside.

A square hole should be cut in each end of the barrel and into them an axle is driven. It is provided with rounded bearings and square end. When swung in a carriage and connected a powerful wheel will be the result if the force of water is sufficient to drive it.

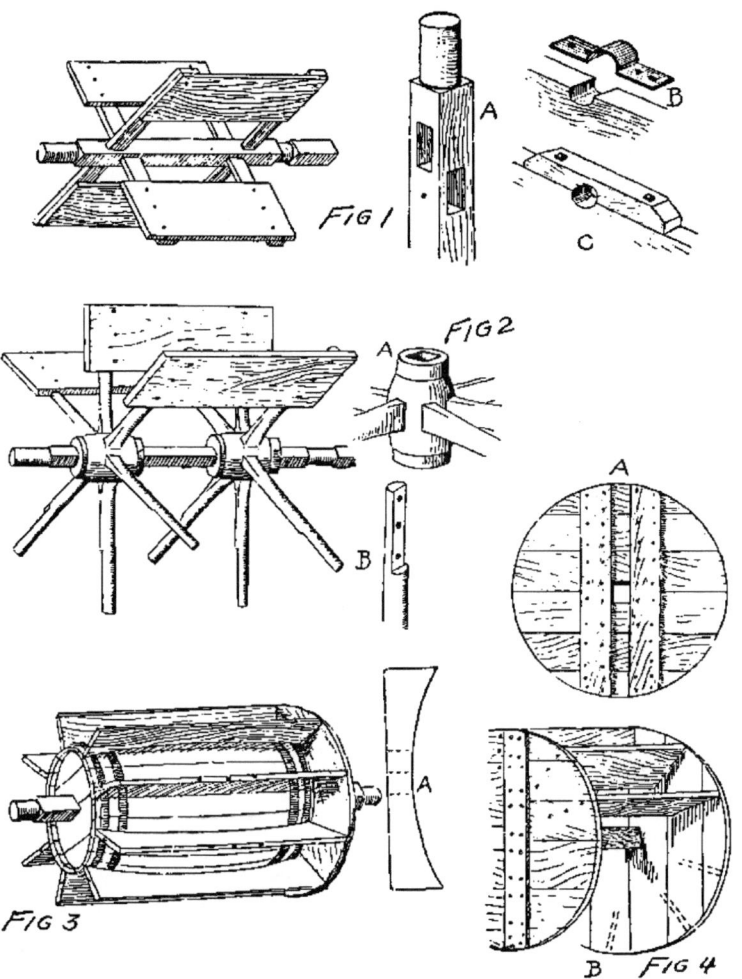

FIG 1

FIG 2

FIG 3

FIG 4

WATER-WHEELS

An Undershot-wheel

For a brook an undershot-wheel can be made with two round ends and ten or twelve blades according to the size of the wheel. For an efficient one the wheel should be thirty-six or forty-eight inches in diameter and thirty inches wide. Two ends are made from matched boards held together with battens as shown in Fig. 4 A. These are arranged on a square axle and the blades are made fast between them with long screws or steel nails. Fig. 4 B.

A Power-wheel

To utilize the power from a rapidly running brook place two tree-trunks across the brook about six feet apart as shown in Fig. 5. On top of these timbers attach two spruce beams eight or ten inches wide and two inches thick, and anchor them well with spikes and check-blocks. At the middle and on top of both timbers cut notches for the axle to fit in and provide them with metal straps to hold the axle in place. A long axle leading to the land can be supported on a short timber attached to stout stakes driven in the ground, and another bearing and strap will hold this from jumping with the rapid revolutions of the wheel. A wooden pulley may be arranged at the end of this axle, and from it the power can be taken off by means of belting or rope.

Another arrangement for this wheel will be to swing it in a cradle or frame so that one end of it may be lifted to reduce

FIG 5

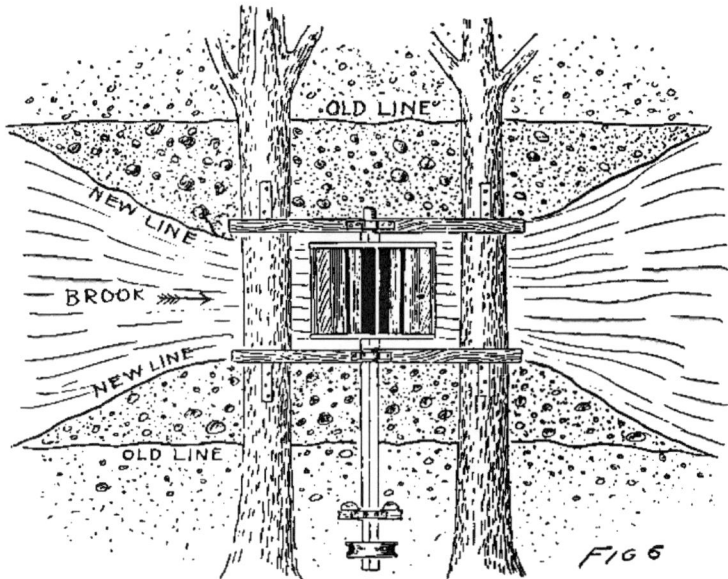

OLD LINE

NEW LINE

BROOK

NEW LINE

OLD LINE

FIG 6

POWER-WHEEL AND WHEEL-RACE

the speed or power of the wheel, the other end being securely attached to a tree-trunk with hinges.

A Wheel-race

The water from a wide, shallow brook may be directed so as to throw its full force against the blades of a wheel by digging it out at the middle and damming it at the sides as shown by the diagram of a modified brook (Fig. 6). The dams should be solidly built and if possible cribbed to prevent their washing away.

Part III

AFLOAT

Chapter XIII

BOATS

OF all the things that a boy is interested in there is nothing more fascinating than boats, whether they are to row, paddle, or sail in, and, as many of the simple kinds are quite within the ability of a boy to make, he can take a great deal of pleasure in their construction.

For the sea-shore and salt waterways the boats should be heavily constructed, and as this is usually beyond the average boy's ability, the sea-going dorys, surf-boats, and heavy sail-boats will be omitted, and those described and illustrated will be for use in fresh water, or on small enclosed salt waterways where the wind and tide are moderate.

In making a boat it is not only necessary to have it float, but to construct it in such a manner that the joints will keep closed and the boards will not rip off if run on a snag or against a rocky shore.

These are essential points in the proper construction of boats, and they might as well be learned by the amateur boat-builder when he is young, instead of constructing something for fun and having to learn the right way all over again when he is older and more serious work begins.

In this chapter a few of the simpler forms of boats are shown, and the warning must be given at the start that the young shipwright should use the greatest care in constructing a boat, not only for the natural pride they will take in making a good one, but for the still more important reason that the safety of all on board is dependent upon his skill and conscientious work.

Punt and Scow

A punt with a flat bottom is about the easiest and safest boat for a boy to make and own, for it is straight in construction and difficult to upset if not overloaded. As both ends are the same it can be rowed or poled forward or backward, and the overhanging ends allow plenty of seating room.

The punt shown in Fig. 4 is fifteen feet long, nineteen inches deep, and four feet wide. The ends cut under twenty inches, and at one end a skag and rudder can be arranged as shown in Fig. 2.

The sides are made of two boards, one of six and the other of a twelve-inch width, and the added thickness of the bottom boards make the total depth of the sides nineteen inches. The wider boards are the lower ones, and they are fastened together near both ends and at the middle with battens as shown in Fig. 4. The middle battens are six inches wide, and into the upper ends of them the rowlock pins are driven. The bottom planking should not be more than four or five inches wide, and it is securely nailed to the edges of the sides and to an inner keel-strip running the entire length of the bottom as shown in Fig. 3.

The wood should be very dry so that it will not shrink

Fig. 1

Fig. 4

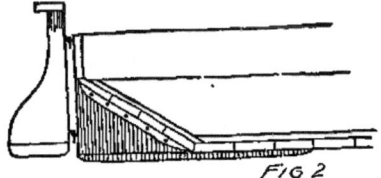

FIG 2

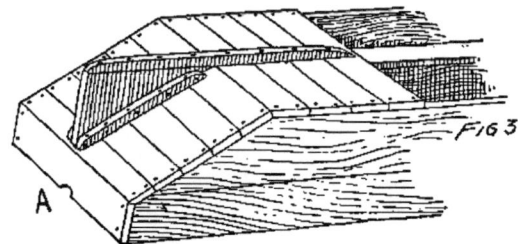

FIG 3

A

PUNT AND SCOW

afterwards and open the seams. Along the edges, and before the planking is laid or nailed on, smear white-lead, and lay one or two thicknesses of lamp-wicking on the lead, so that when the ends of the planking are driven down it makes a water-tight joint. Where the planks butt up against the other planking, the joints are to be generously smeared with white-lead and laid with a string of the lamp-wicking. Begin at one end and work towards the other, having first attached the end planks. Fig. 3 A.

The method of attaching the skag is also shown in Fig. 3, and if the punt shows a tendency to swing around in the water and not mind the oars or rudder, a keel three inches wide may be attached on the bottom of the punt to run from the forward end of the straight bottom back to the end of the skag.

The bottom planking is to be attached at both sides and to the inner keel-strip with galvanized nails. Do not use ordinary nails as they will rust in a short time, and the only ones that are of use are the regular galvanized boat nails that can be had at most hardware stores, and always at a ship-chandler's or from a boat-builder.

A rudder can be made and hung at one end of the boat as shown in Fig. 2.

A scow (Fig. 1) will be found the easiest of all boats to construct, but at the same time the hardest to row, since both the ends are blunt and vertical. A scow is for use in shallow water and is poled generally instead of being rowed. It is built in a similar manner to the punt, but the ends are not cut under. A good size to make the scow for general use will be fourteen feet long, eighteen inches deep, and four feet wide. It may be provided with two or three seats, and when complete both the punt and scow should receive two or three good coats of paint.

A Sharpy

It is not a difficult matter to make a sharpy like the one shown in Fig. 5, but care must be taken in its construction to insure good unions and tight joints.

Cedar, white-wood, pine, or cypress are the best woods of which to build small boats, and wide boards can be had at almost any lumber-yard. White cedar is somewhat more difficult to get than the other woods, but if possible it should be used.

To make this sharpy the proper size for a boy's use, obtain two boards fifteen or sixteen inches wide, fourteen feet long, and seven-eighths of an inch thick, planed on both sides and as free from knots as possible. If the boards cannot be had fifteen inches wide, then batten two boards together with strips just as plain board doors are made. Before they are fastened, however, smear the joint edges with white-lead and embed a string of lamp-wicking through the middle. Use plenty of white-lead, and after the boards are pressed together and fastened the surplus lead can be scraped from both sides of the joint and saved for other joints.

From a piece of hard-wood cut a stem eighteen inches long and four inches wide, with bevelled planes, as shown in Fig. 6. A section or end view of this post will appear like Fig. 6 A. Against the cut-in sides of this post the bow ends of the side boards are to be attached with screws or galvanized boat nails.

The long side boards are to be cut at bow and stern as shown at Fig. 7 A and B. The bow recedes three inches and the stern is cut under thirty-four inches. Attach the bow ends of the boards to the stem-piece or post so that the top of the sides will be seven-eighths of an inch below the flat top of the post. If properly done you will then have a V-shaped affair resembling a snow-plough, which must be bent and formed in the shape of a boat.

From a board seven-eighths of an inch thick cut a spreader ten inches wide, forty-eight inches long at one side, and forty-two inches at the other, as shown in Fig. 8. Arrange this between the boards about midway from bow to stern, so that the bottom of the spreader is flush with the bottom of the sides; then draw in the rear ends of the boards and tie them temporarily with a piece of rope.

Drive a nail into the edge of each board near the end, to prevent the rope slipping off, for if it should do so the boards would fly apart and might break away from the stem-piece.

In order to draw in the ends to the proper position, insert a short stick between the ropes and twist it around until the rope is wound up; then if the end is not in far enough, slip another rope around the ends of the boards, and after releasing the first rope insert the stick and continue the twisting until the ends of the side boards are twenty-one inches apart. Before this bending process is begun, it would be well to pour a kettleful of boiling water over each side board to limber them, for dry boards are

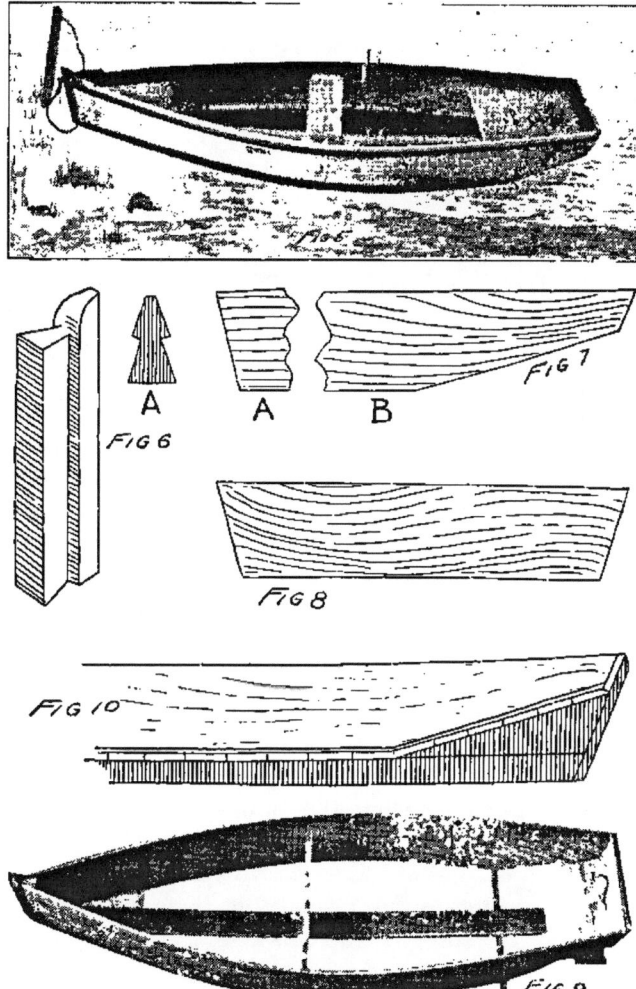

FIG 6

FIG 7

A

A   B

FIG 8

FIG 10

FIG 9

A SHARPY

stiff and will not bend easily without checking or cracking. If it is possible to steam the boards they will yield still better to the bending process.

The stern-plank is cut in the same shape as the spreader, but it is curved or crowned at the top, where it is twenty-three inches long, while at the bottom it measures twenty inches. It is six inches wide at the ends and nine inches at the middle, and is attached to the ends of the sides with boat nails while the tension-rope is still in place.

An inner keel is then cut six inches wide and pointed at the bow end, where it is attached to the lower edges of the sides at the bow and flush with them. The planking or bottom boards should fit snugly to it and to the edges of the sides.

A lap six inches long and seven-eighths of an inch deep is cut in the bottom of the spreader at the middle. In this the inner keel will fit, and after the first two or three bottom boards are nailed on at the bow end the frame of the sharpy will appear as shown in Fig. 9. The spreader and stern-plank will give the sides a flare which will have a tendency also to curve the bottom of the boat slightly from bow to stern. The bottom planks are four inches wide, of clear wood, and must not have tongue and grooved edges, but should be plain so that the white-lead and lamp-wicking will make a tight joint when the planks are driven up snug to each other.

Drive all nails carefully so as not to split the planking or sides, and as a precaution a small bit or gimlet should be used to make the start for the nail-hole.

A seat ten inches wide is fastened at the middle of the boat, over the spreader, and seats may also be arranged at the bow and stern, where they rest on cleats that are screwed fast to the sides.

A short keel or skag is fastened to the under side of the sharpy and extends from about under the middle seat aft to the stern-post. A V-shaped p ece is let in where the stern is cut under as shown in Fig. 10. This keel prevents the sharpy from turning about quickly and serves to steady her when rowing, as well as making a deeper stern-post to which a rudder may be hung as shown in Fig. 2. Six inches to the rear of the middle seat plates of wood six inches wide are attached to the sides of the sharpy, as shown in the illustration (Fig. 5), and on the tops of these oar-locks or pins are inserted after the usual fashion.

At the outside of the sides and an inch below the top edge a gunwale-strip is made fast, and with a ring in the bow for a painter and a pair of oars the sharpy is ready for use.

Of course it should be thoroughly painted. Three or four successive coats of paint should be applied to a boat the first time it is painted, and before using, it should be launched, half filled with water, and allowed to stand for a few days so that the joints will swell and close properly. A mast six or eight feet high and a leg-of-mutton sail will enable a boy to sail before the wind in a quiet breeze, but rough - weather sailing should not be attempted in this style of open boat.

A Dory

A dory (Fig. 11), is somewhat similar to a sharpy but has higher sides and a narrower bottom, therefore it draws more water than a wide, flat-bottomed sharpy.

A boy can make a dory from twelve to sixteen feet long, but a fourteen-foot dory will be quite large enough to hold from four to six boys comfortably and safely. The sides should be twenty-four inches high and the bottom twenty four inches across amidships.

The bottom is made from four six-inch planks battened across as shown in Fig. 12. The joints are leveled before

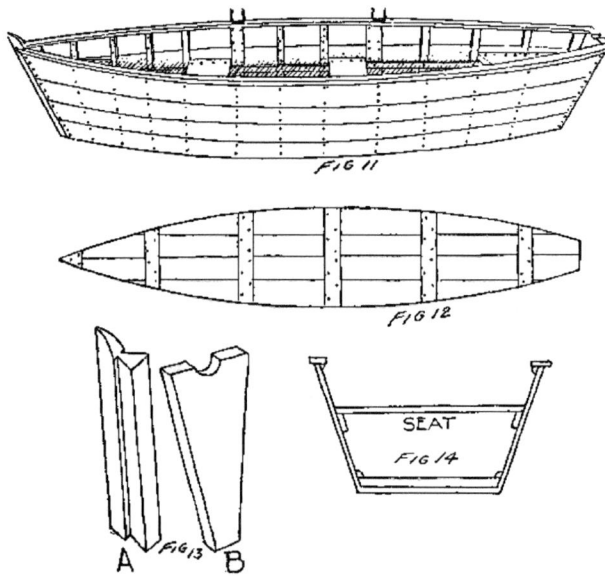

FIG 11

FIG 12

SEAT

FIG 14

A   FIG 13   B

the boards are brought together, and the fastenings are of galvanized nails clinched at the inside. The battens, of course, are on the inside, but the nail-heads are on the outside or bottom of the boat.

A stem and stern-piece (Fig. 13 A and B) are cut from

hard - wood, and to these the wooden sides are made fast at both ends. The bow and stern of a dory have more of a rake than those of a sharpy as may be seen in Fig. 11. The top of the bow extends out beyond the bottom at least from fifteen to twenty inches, while the stern overhangs the keel about twelve inches. The sides flare out nine inches at both sides amidships, so that the total width of beam is forty-two inches for a dory fourteen feet long.

Planks sixteen feet long are necessary with which to make this dory, for when they are sprung out at the sides they take up on the length. They can be six inches wide, and are made fast to ribs along the inside of the boat and attached with galvanized boat nails.

In Fig. 14 an amidships section of the dory is shown and the position of the seat is located. Along the top of the sides, to cap them and the upper ends of the ribs, rails two inches wide and three-quarters of an inch thick are made fast with boat nails. These rails should be of hard-wood, and they should be sprung into place and securely fastened.

A dory of this description makes an ideal fishing - boat where the water is rough, since it can be rowed either forward or backward.

A Sailing Sharpy

A rowing sharpy can be converted into a sail-boat by partially decking it over, making a mast-step, and providing it with a lee-board if a centre-board cannot be arranged in the middle of the hull. Fig. 18.

The half-deck will keep out the water that might splash

FIG 18

FIG 15

A SAILING SHARPY

over the sides or come over the bow and stern, and the row-boat features need not be altered nor the seats removed, as the rib and brace work for the deck can easily be fitted and fastened over the seats, and so give additional strength to the deck.

Just behind the front seat and at the forward edge of the back seat cross-ribs are made fast to the sides of the sharpy. Between these, and eight inches from the sides of the boat, additional braces are sprung into place and securely attached at the ends, and provided with short cross-braces as shown in Fig. 15. The deck planking is nailed to these ribs and the seats under them give a substantial support to both the ribs and deck. The opening or cockpit will be six feet long and varying in width, as the side decks are eight inches wide and follow the line of the boat's sides. Amidships it should measure about twenty-eight inches.

The braces and ribs are made of three-quarter-inch spruce boards five or six inches wide, and to bend them in the segment of a circle (as they will have to be for the side-ribs) pour hot water over two of them and place the ends on boxes with heavy stones at the middle to bend them down to the required curve. Allow them to remain in this position for several hours to dry in the sun; they may then be cut and fitted to the boat. The decking is done with narrow strips of pine, cypress, or cedar one inch and a half wide and three-quarters of an inch in thickness. They are bent to conform to the side lines of the boat, and if they are fitted nicely and leaded the deck should be water-tight after it receives varnish or paint.

If straight boards are employed in place of the narrow

planking the deck can be covered with canvas and first given a coat of oil, then several successive thin coats of paint. The canvas should be tacked down over the outer edge of the boat and to the inner edge of the cockpit. A gunwale-strip an inch square is to be nailed along the top edge on both sides of the boat, and one inch below the top of the deck nail a guard rail along each side.

To finish the cockpit arrange a combing in place to project four inches above the deck, and make the boards fast to the inner side of the ribs with screws as shown in the illustration of the hull of sailing sharpy. Fig. 15.

Ten inches back from the bow-post bore a hole two inches and a half in diameter so that a mast will fit securely in place. The hole should extend through the deck and front seat, and a step-block with a hole in it to receive the foot of the mast must be nailed fast to the bottom of the boat. The hole in this block is oblong, and the foot of the mast should be cut on two sides so as to fit in the block as shown in Fig. 16.

Spruce or clear pine sticks are to be dressed and planed for the mast and boom, the mast measuring fourteen feet high by two inches and a half at the base, and the boom thirteen feet long by two inches in diameter, both tapering near the end.

The rudder is eighteen inches long, including the post, and ten inches high. It is fastened to a post of hard-wood three inches wide and seven-eighths of an inch thick. At the top of this an iron strap is fastened to hold the tiller as shown in Fig. 17 A. The rudder is hung to the stern of the boat with pins and sockets, as shown in Fig. 17 B, so that if it becomes necessary the rudder may be unshipped by lifting it out of the sockets or eyes. The rudder is fastened to the post with galvanized-iron pins ten inches long and three-eighths of an inch in diameter driven through snug holes bored in the wood as shown by the dotted lines in Fig. 17 B.

It is impossible to hold a boat on the wind without a centre-board, but as this sharpy has none a lee-board will be required to keep her from drifting leeward. Fig. 18.

This board can be made five feet long, thirty inches wide, and hung over the lee side when running on the wind, where ropes and cleats will hold it in place. The board may be made of three planks banded together at the rear end with a batten, and at the forward end it is strapped across with bands of iron as shown in Fig. 18.

With a sail of twilled or heavy unbleached muslin this boat may be driven through the water at five or six miles an hour, and two boys can have a great deal of fun out of her. Care should be exercised in handling the boat; and be sure to reef the sail in case of a strong breeze.

A Centre-board Sharpy

When making a sharpy to sail in, a trunk and centre-board should be built when the keel is laid so that the cumbersome and unhandy lee-board may be done away with. The centre-board is housed in the trunk, through which it can be raised or lowered as occasion requires.

The arrangement of the trunk in the boat is shown in Fig. 19, and it is located so that the front of the trunk is three feet from the bow. For a centre-board one inch and a quarter in thickness the trunk should be one inch and three-quarters wide between sides, five feet long, and eighteen inches high. It is made of tongue-and-grooved boards one inch and one-eighth in thickness, and these are attached by stout screws to posts one inch and three-quarters square at bow and stern. The trunk is mounted on the keel, set in white-lead, and securely fastened with screws. A slot is cut in the keel the same size as the inside opening of the trunk— that is, two inches wide and about five feet long. The bottom planking is butted against the sides of the trunk at the middle of the boat as shown in Fig. 20.

An inner keel is laid over the bottom planking through the centre of the boat from stem to stern, and where it fits around the trunk it is cut out. Both the inner and outer keels are six inches wide and the exposed edges are bevelled with a plane. A sectional or end view of the trunk and its location in the keels is shown in Fig. 20, where the shading and lettering will designate each part.

The centre-board is four feet and nine inches long, thirty inches wide at the back, and twenty-four inches at the front. It is attached to the trunk with a hard-wood pin located near the forward lower end, and when it is drawn up it will appear as shown in Fig. 21 A, but when lowered it will look like Fig. 21 B.

The centre-board is made of hard-wood, several boards of which are pinned together with galvanized-iron rods three-eighths of an inch in diameter and driven through from edge to edge of the boards in snug holes made with a long bit or auger. The rods are riveted at both ends over washers to prevent the boards from working apart.

It would be better to let a boat-builder or carpenter make

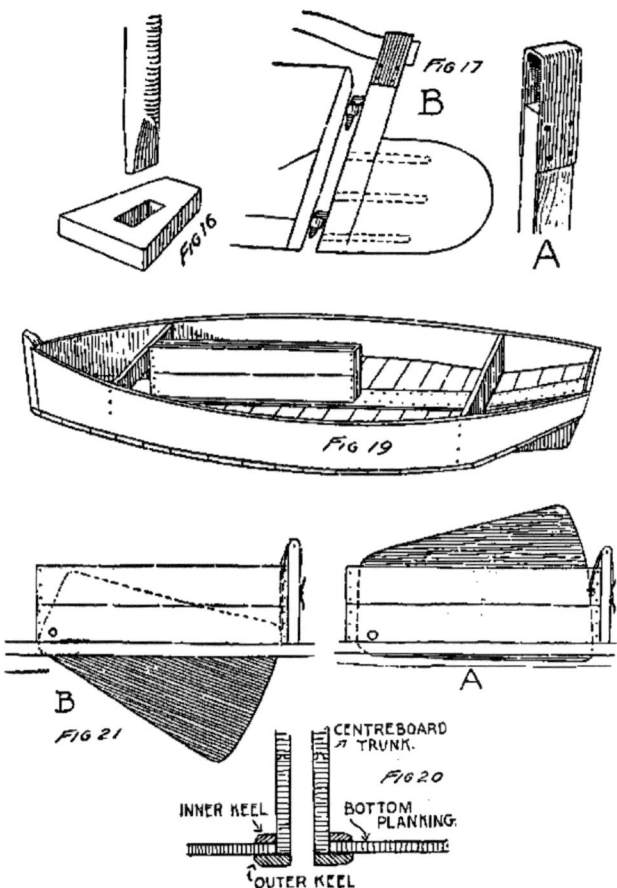

FIG 17

FIG 16

B

A

FIG 19

B

FIG 21

A

CENTREBOARD
TRUNK.

FIG 20

INNER KEEL

BOTTOM
PLANKING.

OUTER KEEL

A CENTRE-BOARD SHARPY

this board the proper size and shape to fit the trunk, for it is the most difficult thing to construct about a boat and somewhat beyond the ability of many boys. A large galvanized eye and a rope made fast below the middle of the board at the rear edge will provide the means for raising and lowering the centre-board.

The deck ribs and the planking are put in the same as described for the sailing sharpy.

A Proa

In the South Sea Islands the natives dig out the trunk of a tree, rig a lateen sail on a single stick, and arrange a counter-balance on the end of two poles in the form of a catamaran. With this rude contrivance they can outsail anything in the shape of a small boat such as our types of cat-boats and sharpies.

These queer craft are called proas, and a modified type that a boy can make is shown in the illustration Fig. 22.

This is a perfectly safe boat, and as it lies close on the water a great deal of fun can be had with one in comparatively smooth waterways.

To make the hull get two ten-inch planks sixteen feet long and spring them five feet from either end so that they come together at both ends and are separated fifteen inches along the middle for five or six feet as shown in Fig. 23. Between the sides place four or five spreaders, two of which should be stout enough to receive the bolts that will hold the two cross-braces or outriggers. Set a step-block for the mast, then

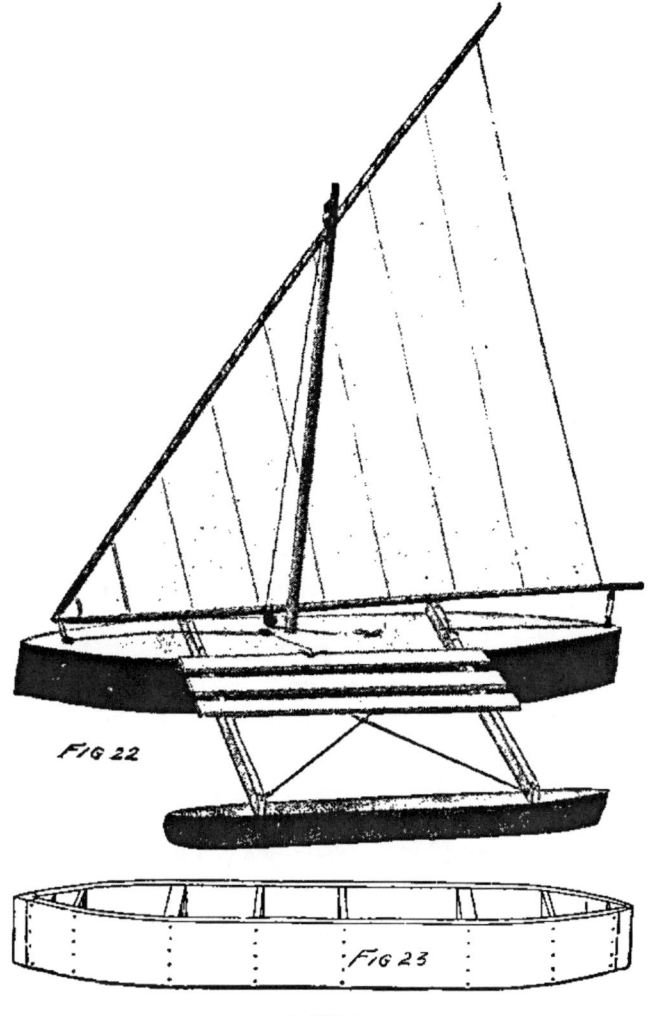

FIG 22

FIG 23

A PROA

plank the deck and bottom, using plenty of white-lead and lamp-wicking between the joints.

The cross-braces or outriggers are of two-by-four-inch clear spruce six feet long, and their outer ends are bolted to a solid spruce timber twelve feet long, four inches wide, and ten inches deep. They should be sharpened at both ends with an adze, draw-knife, or a chisel and plane.

A mast twelve feet long and three inches in diameter is stepped seven feet from the bow, and to it a lateen rig is lashed fast having the gaff eighteen feet long and the boom fifteen feet in length.

A block and tackle at the bow will pay off the angle and another at the stern will regulate the position of the sail.

Cross-wires for braces may extend under the short decking to steady the outrigger and keep it from racking the braces, and three or four narrow planks can be laid across the braces close to the large boat on which the boy and a friend or two may sit when sailing.

A rudder may be attached to the stern of the large boat, as shown in Fig. 17, or an oar can be used to steer with.

Paint the boats any desired color, and for the first time give them at least three or four thin coats not less than two days apart, so that one will dry thoroughly before the next one is laid on. Never put thick or gummy paint on a boat; thin it down and apply two coats rather than one thick one.

A Lark

Perhaps the safest kind of a sailing-craft next to a catamaran is a lark with a broad beam and flat at both bow and stern. There are various forms of the half-rater, but the one shown in Fig. 24 is easy to construct and requires less careful fitting and joining than the hulls with pointed bows and long, overhanging sterns.

In general construction this hull is similar to the punt, and when putting it together the description for the building of the punt must be borne in mind.

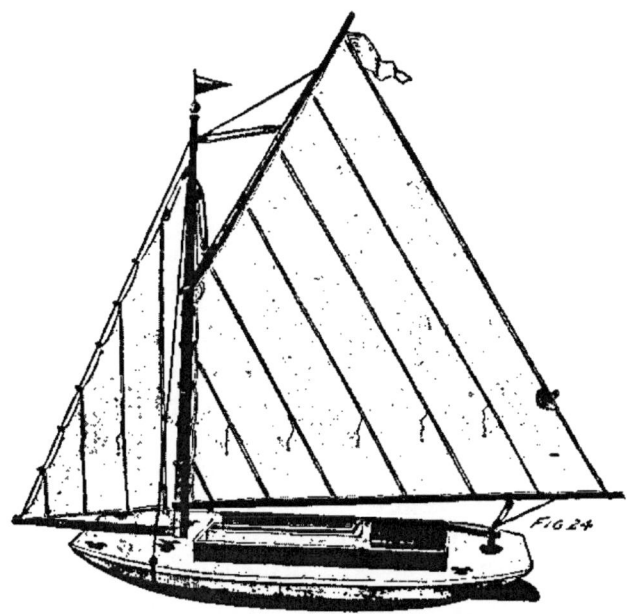

Obtain two clear cedar planks sixteen feet long and from fourteen to sixteen inches wide. Four feet from either end begin to round the lower edges of these side boards. Cut two spreaders five feet and six inches long and make them fast four feet from the ends of the sides as shown at Fig. 25. Between these spreaders attach an inner keel in the forward end of which an opening has been made. The keel is of hard-wood eight inches wide and the opening is three inches and a half in width and four feet and eight inches long.

A centre-board trunk is made and fitted into this opening as described for the sailing sharpy. Then braces are fastened between the sides and trunk as shown at Fig. 26.

Two bevelled hard-wood bow and stern pieces are cut as shown at Fig. 27. The ends of the boards are sprung in and attached to the ends of these pieces, and between them and the spreaders two more boards are fastened as indicated by the lines of nail-heads in Fig. 26. At the bow just ahead of the forward long cross-piece or spreader step the mast, and at the stern make the rudder-post trunk, taking care to use plenty of white-lead and lamp-wick so as to render the joints water-tight. Put a line of braces through the middle of the frame, then begin at the bow and plank the bottom with boards not more than three or four inches wide.

With the planking on and the braces, spreaders, and trunk in position the frame will appear as shown in Fig. 28. The deck planking is of strips seven-eighths of an inch thick and three inches wide. Begin at the middle of the boat by laying down a strip six inches wide by one inch and a quarter in thickness. Drive the deck planking close to this and smear the points with white-lead in which the lamp-wicking is embedded. Make all the fastenings with galvanized boat nails and drive the heads well into the wood with a nail-punch so they can be puttied and covered from the action of the water. An outer flat keel is laid along the bottom

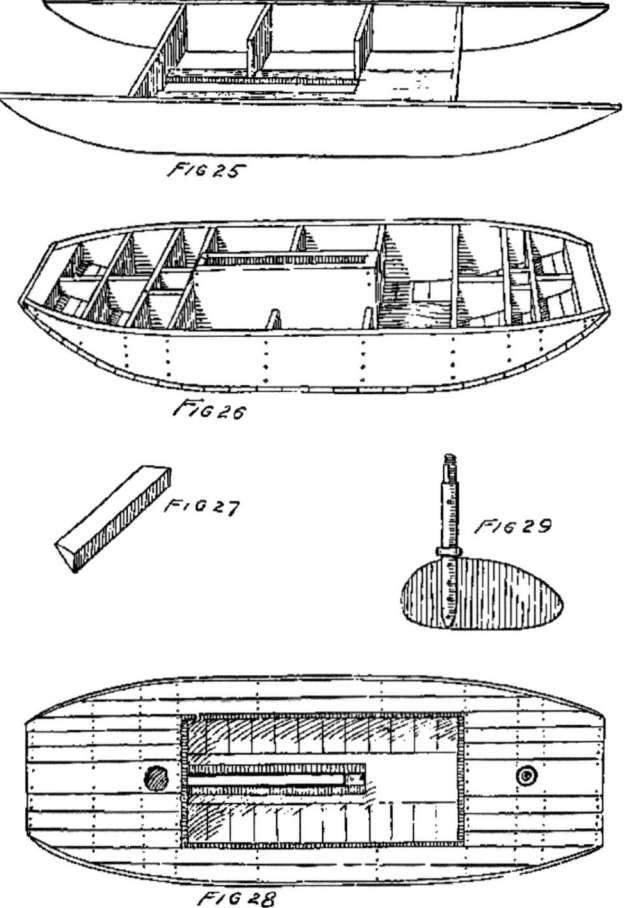

FIG 25

FIG 26

FIG 27

FIG 29

FIG 28

A LARK

of the hull from the forward part of the cockpit or about under the mast. This leads aft to where the stern begins to round up and there it is stopped.

This keel is attached with galvanized or brass screws, and a generous number are driven through the keel into the bottom edges of the centre-board trunk.

The rudder is made from galvanized sheet-iron as shown at Fig. 29, and is let into a one-and-a-quarter-inch round iron rudder-post and riveted fast. Just above the rudder-blade a collar of iron is welded to the post and this bears against the bottom of the boat. To prevent the rudder from dropping down a pin is passed through a hole in the post close to the deck and a large washer made fast to the deck will prevent the pin from chafing the wood.

Have the top of the post made with a square shank so that a tiller may fit over it and be held in position by a nut.

The rudder-blade should be twenty-six inches long and twelve inches wide.

The mast is fifteen feet long, cut from a four-inch spruce stick with draw-knife and plane. The boom is fifteen feet long, cut from a two-and-one-half-inch spruce stick, and the gaff is eleven feet long.

Extending out from the mast and attached to the deck is a short bowsprit five feet and six inches long. This is of two-by-three-inch spruce with the sharp corners rounded off beyond the end of the boat.

A wire forestay and two shrouds lead from mast-head to bowsprit and to both sides of the boat as shown in Fig. 24.

The main-sheet is seven feet on the mast, ten feet on the gaff, fourteen feet at the foot or on the boom, and eighteen feet on the leach. The jib is eleven feet on the forestay, five feet at the foot, and ten feet on the leach. The blocks are all of galvanized iron or wood, and three-eighth-inch Manila-rope should be used for the halyards and sheets.

This lark will ride well on the water, and if properly rigged it should be a very speedy boat.

A Power-boat

A novel feature for the propulsion of a flat-bottom boat or punt is shown in Fig. 30. Two small paddle-wheels attached to one shaft are hung out over the stern, and by means of a sprocket on the shaft connected to another and larger one on the seat frame the wheels are turned by the boys who mount the seats and work the pedals.

The punt is fifteen feet long on the deck line and six feet wide. The side boards are twelve inches wide, and with the thickness of the deck and bottom planking it will make the total depth about fourteen inches. Through the middle a strengthening rib is run the same size and thickness as the outer sides as shown in Fig. 31. This gives an additional rib to nail the sheathing boards to and also an anchorage to which the uprights forming the seat frame can be made fast with bolts.

The outriggers that suspend the wheels are of spruce two inches thick and three inches wide. They are bolted to the deck and at the outer end U-notches are cut for the axle of the wheels to fit into and capped with iron straps such as shown in Fig. 32. A blacksmith will make these for you from strap-iron an eighth of an inch thick and two inches wide. They should be bolted on when the wheels are in position, for they not only have to support the weight of the wheels but also stand the action of the water against them.

The wheels are each twenty-four inches in diameter and

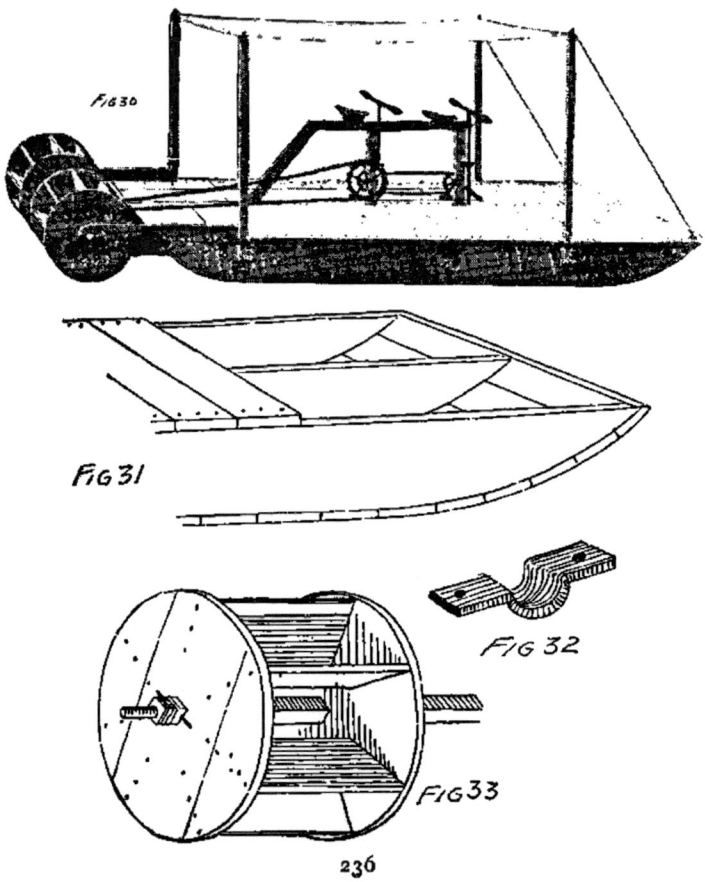

Fig 30

Fig 31

Fig 32

Fig 33

two feet long, and are made from wood seven-eighths of an inch in thickness. Seven blades eight inches wide are screwed fast to the sides or held in place with long, galvanized boat nails.

The axle is of spruce two inches square, and the wheel sides are provided with square holes through which the axle is driven as shown in Fig. 33. The ends of the axle are banded with iron, or copper wire may be wound round them to prevent their splitting. Into the ends half-inch round iron pins are driven which revolve in the bearings.

The seat-frame is thirty inches high and made from spruce rails three inches wide and one inch and a half in thickness. On the middle upright a large and small gear wheel are arranged on an axle with the cranks and pedals, and on the front post a small wheel is attached so that tandem power may be used on the paddle-wheels or one boy alone can work the boat. A rod and handle-bars may be arranged for the rear boy to grasp, and with a socket and set-screw it can be raised or lowered at will.

The forward bars have a cross-piece of iron at the foot of the vertical rod. This is two feet long, and from the ends of it running aft wires connect with the ends of a tiller for operating the rudder.

The rudder is hung between the wheels on a skag which is the rear extension of a short keel that should be nailed fast to hold the punt steady on the water.

Four canopy poles may be arranged to fit into sockets at the sides, and an awning six by ten feet can be supported over the machinery of the boat to keep off sun and rain.

This is a genuine boy-power boat, and as the wheels are

substantially large and strong it can be driven over the water at quite a good speed. While it takes two boys to properly run it, that is not the boat's capacity, for she will easily carry from four to six boys, their lunch-baskets, or a one-day camping outfit for a visit up the river or lake.

Chapter XIV

CATAMARANS

A Rowing Catamaran

FOR safety on the water, as nearly as safety can be assured, there is nothing to compare with a catamaran, for they are practically "non-capsizable," and if not damaged to the leaking-point one or the other of the two boats will float and hold up several persons. Fig. 1 gives a good idea for a rowing catamaran that any boy can make from some boards and light timbers. It is provided with a seat and oar-locks so that the occupant may be seated above the water far enough to row easily.

The boats are fourteen feet long, eighteen inches wide, and fourteen inches deep, including the bottom and deck.

Pine, white-wood, cedar, or cypress, three-quarters of an inch thick and planed on both sides, will be necessary from which to construct the boats. At the bow the ends of the sides are attached to a stern-piece of hard-wood as shown in Fig. 2. Having poured boiling water on the forward ends, they may be drawn around a spreader sixteen inches long and twelve inches wide provided with two U-cuts as shown in Fig. 3. These are placed at the bottom, so that any water may be run to one end of a boat where it can be pumped out.

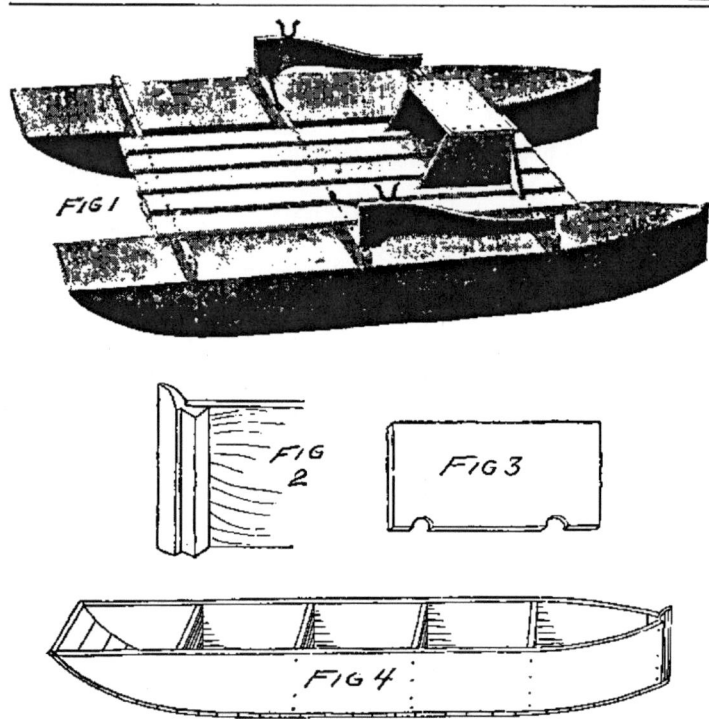

The first spreader is placed three feet from the bow, and three or four more of them should be fastened between the sides as shown in Fig. 4, the last one being three feet from the stern where the sides begin to curve up to the upper edge of the stern and to the deck.

The bottom is of three-inch pine or white-wood boards seven-eighths of an inch thick and well leaded in the joints and along the edges where the bottom and top boards join the sides. Before the top or deck is placed on, the interior of the boats should have two or three good coats of paint.

Three cross-stringers of spruce two and one-half by four inches and six feet long are securely attached to the boats, and on these the deck of four-inch boards is made fast as the illustration will show. Between the middle and forward stringer, at the ends, two boards are attached on which the row-locks may be fastened. These boards are eight or nine inches wide and cut away at the front so that they are not more than two or three inches wide.

The high ends are braced with round iron braces as shown in the illustration, and where the oar-locks are mounted a short plate of wood is screwed fast to the inside of each piece.

Near the front cross-piece a seat is built and braced with a board. With another boy at the stern sitting on the deck this catamaran will be well balanced and will prove very seaworthy, as well as a light boat to row.

A Sailing Catamaran

It is almost impossible to upset a sailing catamaran even in a gale, and for boys a boat of this kind affords a great deal of comparatively safe pleasure.

A catamaran is about the easiest sort of a boat to make, and no matter in what locality one lives there is always material at hand from which to make one as the wood is similar to that used for house construction.

Fig. 5 shows a side elevation of a safe catamaran, and in Fig. 6 the deck plan is shown. In Fig. 7 an elevation view

of the stern shows the arrangement of the boats, deck timbers, and rudders.

The boats are fifteen feet long, eighteen inches wide at the
middle, and two feet deep uniformly from bow to stern except for a short distance at the bow where the keel rounds up.

They are in the form of a V, and at the ends the angle becomes more acute, so that at the stem and stern the lines are
vertical.

Four feet from both ends the deck line begins to curve as
shown in Fig. 6, and in Fig. 8 the cross-braces are shown.
They are cut in at the bottom to slip over the keel and to
them the sheathing planks are made fast.

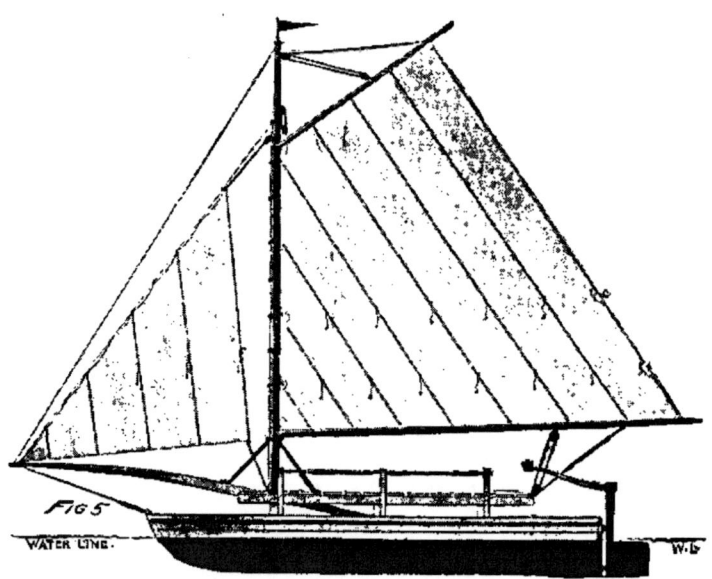

FIG 5

WATER LINE.

W.L

242

In Fig. 8 the curved stem-piece and one side of planking is shown, and it indicates also where the curved stem-piece is joined to the keel, which extends in a straight line to the stern of the boats.

The keel is of hard-wood one inch and a quarter thick and six inches wide. The cross-braces or spreaders are of pine or other soft wood seven-eighths of an inch thick and made up of three pieces of wood with the grain running vertically.

The sheathing is of pine, cedar, or cypress three-quarters of an inch thick, planed on both sides, and three or four inches wide. Each board should be given a priming coat of paint before it is nailed to the braces, and where the planks are edged together white-lead and lamp-wick should be employed for calking. Galvanized boat nails are to be used for all the fastenings, but screws may be employed where it is necessary to have a very secure joint.

The cross-pieces that fasten the boats together are bolted fast by means of long bolts that pass through the timbers and deck and into stout pieces of wood that are nailed fast to the upper part of the spreaders as shown at A in Fig. 8. The boats are decked over with the three-quarter-inch planking, and to insure an absolutely tight deck the wood may be treated to a thick coat of paint and covered with canvas which is pressed down well into the paint and the edges tacked down over the sides of the boats. The canvas is then given a coat or two of paint and allowed to dry thoroughly, after which it can be sand-papered and finished with the desired shade of paint.

Three spruce timbers eight feet long, three inches thick, and six inches wide are bored with holes at the ends where the bolts pass through them and into the boats. Running parallel to the boats three timbers are laid across the brace-timbers and on top of these the deck planking is nailed. These pieces are two and one-half by four inches, and ten feet long, and are bolted down with long slim bolts.

The decking is formed of slats three-quarters of an inch thick and four inches wide nailed down to these stringers. Spaces half an inch wide are left between each one.

The bowsprit is of three-by-four-inch spruce left with its square corners for half its length but dressed round at the outer end. It is caught under the middle cross-brace where the end is bolted, and extending over the front piece it projects four or five feet beyond the bow ends of the boats. With wire-cable the bowsprit end is stayed to the bow of each boat, where turn-buckles can be caught into eyes in the stem-posts.

The mast is of spruce dressed from a four-inch spruce stick and slightly tapered at the top. It is fifteen feet long and stepped at the middle of the front cross-piece and on top of the bowsprit where it is held in place with a collar and iron braces as shown in the illustration. Fig. 5.

Standing rigging of wire-cable stays the mast from the top to both ends of the front cross-piece as indicated by the dotted line in Fig. 7.

Three short posts are made fast to the cross-pieces close to the decking, and holes bored in the tops of them will hold a safety-rope around the deck.

The rudder-posts are of hard-wood one inch and a quarter thick and two inches and a half in width. They are three

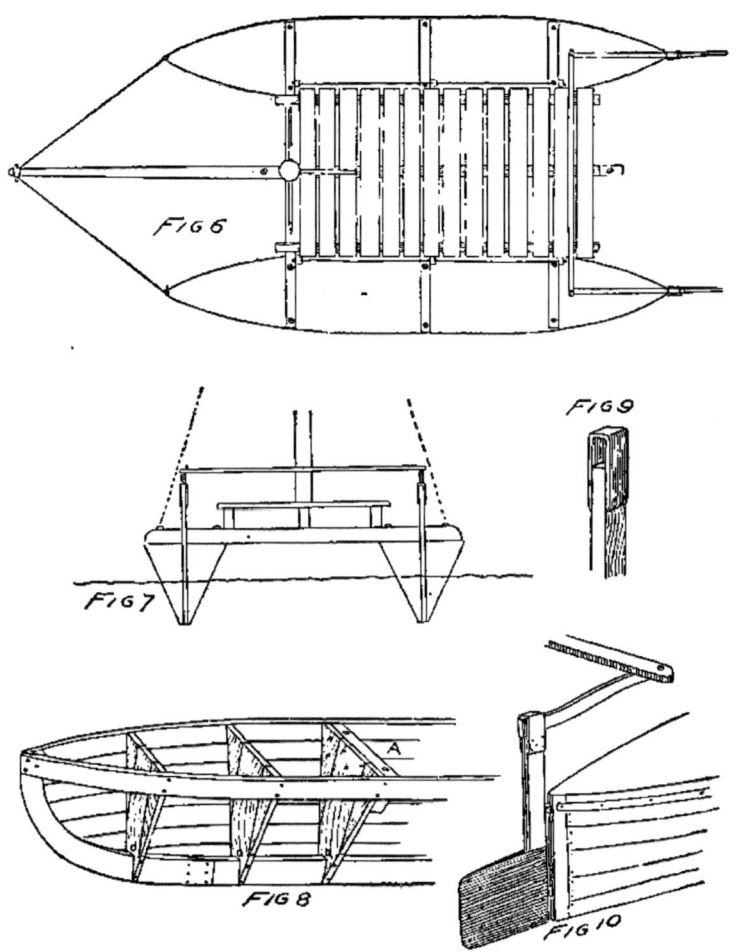

FIG 6

FIG 7

FIG 9

FIG 8

FIG 10

A SAILING CATAMARAN

feet long and to the upper end of each a strap of metal is arranged to receive the tiller as shown in Fig. 9.

The tillers are of hard-wood three feet long and their inner ends are connected with a hard-wood stick by means of which the steering is done and both rudders operated at the same time.

The rudders, made from two sheets of galvanized iron, are riveted fast to the rudder-posts and are twelve inches high and fifteen inches long. Pins on the posts fit into eyes attached to the stern-post of the boats, and in Fig. 10 the arrangement of rudders, tillers, and connecting-rod is shown.

The main-sail is of twilled cotton that can be had at a dry-goods store for about ten cents a yard, and a rib should be sewed through the middle of each breadth to strengthen the cloth. The sail is nine feet and six inches on the mast, six feet on the gaff, thirteen feet on the boom, and fifteen feet on the leach. The jib, also of twilled cotton, is eleven feet and six inches on the forestay, eight feet across the foot, and eight feet and six inches on the leach. The blocks can be of galvanized iron but patent sheave-wood blocks are preferable.

For the halyards Manila-rope three-eighths of an inch in diameter will be the right size, and a half-inch anchor-rope will be stout enough, since a catamaran does not tug as heavily on an anchor as does a boat.

The wood-work of the boat and deck should be painted and the spars varnished. A pretty effect will be to paint the boat a rich olive green, with buff decks, and all the cross-pieces and deck planking in ivory white.

The ordinary sailing rules will apply to the handling of a

catamaran. With these wedge-shaped boats you can sail quite close to the wind, but if round-bottomed and shallower boats are used they will have to be provided with centre-boards.

A Side-wheel Catamaran

The rowing catamaran can easily be converted into a side-wheel boat by removing the middle slat of the deck and making an opening through which a chain will lead to a cog or sprocket wheel on an axle.

At the outer side of each boat, between the middle and rear cross-braces, fasten two pieces of wood two inches wide and three inches high. Six or eight inches from the rear end make two U-cuts for a five-eighth-inch axle to fit into. At a blacksmith's obtain two old carriage or buggy wheels, and cut the spokes so that they will be fourteen inches long from the hub. Dress one side of each spoke flat, so that a paddle may be attached to it with screws. The paddles are of hardwood, eight inches wide at the outer end, six at the inner end, and six inches deep.

Have a blacksmith heat the ends of an axle and pound them square, then slip one hub over the iron, and with hardwood wedges make it fast. The other wheel can be slipped on when the axle is in place and attached in a similar manner. It would be best to remove the old iron boxes from the hubs, so that a few screws can be driven through the hub and into the wedges to help in holding them securely in place.

In Fig. 11, which is a stern view of the rowing catamaran, one of the paddle-wheels is shown in place, and it also shows the location of the axle, the sprocket-wheel, and the chain

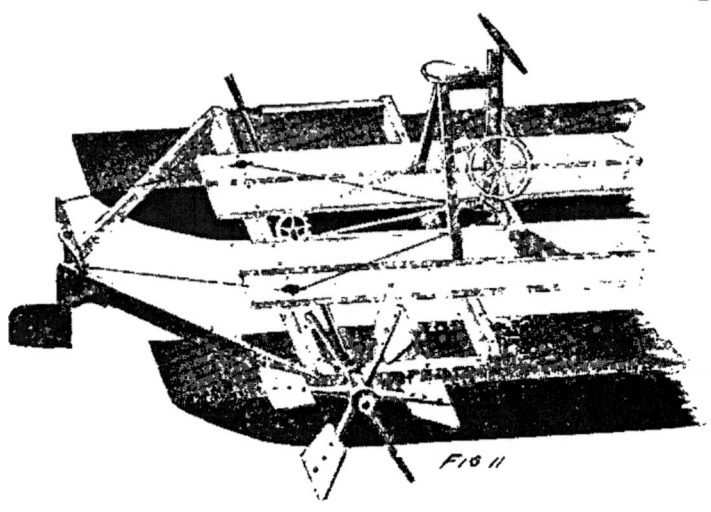

FIG II

that leads to the large sprocket-wheel by means of which the axle is turned.

An old bicycle chain and sprockets, together with the axle, cranks, and pedals, can be arranged on a frame, so that a saddle may be mounted the proper distance above the pedals. This arrangement is clearly shown in the illustration, which shows also the outrigger timbers at the stern, to which a sheet-iron rudder may be made fast. It is operated by a handle and bar, which turns the rudder by means of flexible wire-rope run through two deck-pulleys at the outer rear ends of the deck planking. The iron rod is held in place to the forward upright of the seat-frame with metal straps. At its lower end a wooden wheel having a groove is made fast, around which a wrap or two of the wire-cable is taken to hold the rudder steady.

Chapter XV

ICE-BOATS

A Sloop-rigged Ice-yacht

FOR travelling over the ice there is nothing to beat an ice-yacht, and some that have been constructed on the Hudson River are of gigantic size and power. Boats of this kind, and having the speed of an express-train, are dangerous for boys to play with, but the ordinary ice-boat that will go from ten to twenty miles an hour is within the ability of any well-grown boy to make and safely handle.

It is quite a simple matter to make a good ice-boat, for it is but a framework properly put together and bolted, on top of which a deck is nailed, with a mast-step arranged at the front.

Fig. 1 shows the elevation view of a moderately sized sloop-yacht; and in Fig. 2 the deck plan is shown, the joints and deck boards being clearly indicated. The triangular body of the boat is ten feet long and eight feet wide, and the bowsprit projects out six feet beyond the timber A in Fig. 2.

The frame is made of clear spruce timbers six inches wide and two inches thick. The timber A is eight feet long, B B are eleven feet long, C is five feet long, and D D are each three feet long.

At the front corners and at the back the timbers are bevelled, as shown in the plan drawing, and they are joined with long bolts as indicated by the dotted lines. Timbers C and D D are set in place and securely fastened with long, steel-

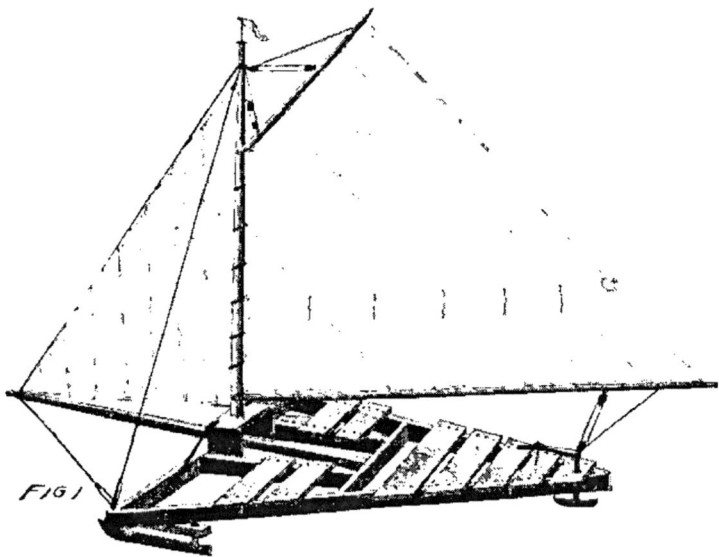

FIG 1

wire spikes. The bowsprit E is mounted against timber C and laid over timber A, to which it is bolted fast. A half-inch iron pin is driven in the butt end of the bowsprit, and it fits into a hole made in timber C.

The bowsprit is cut from spruce two inches and a half by four inches, and tapered at the outer end, where a withe having three eyes is driven on. The top eye receives the forestay and the side ones the bobstay cables that run to the corners of the boat, where they are drawn taut with turn-buckles. The shoe-blocks F F are twenty-four inches long and three inches square, and are bolted to the timbers A and B as shown.

At the stern a triangular block is mounted between the ends of the timbers B B, through which the rudder-post will pass. The decking planks G are then attached to the frame with screws or steel nails.

The mast-step is made by attaching two twelve-inch pieces of plank eighteen inches long and an inch and a quarter thick to the inside sides of timbers D D. Across the top of them attach another plank, and in the middle of it cut a hole three inches and a half in diameter, or large enough to receive the mast. In the bowsprit, directly under the large hole, make a small one to receive a three-quarter-inch pin. This iron pin is to be driven in the bottom of the mast so that six inches of it projects beyond the bottom of the stick. These will form the mast-step, and when the mast is in place and held by the forestay and shrouds it cannot jump out. Iron stanchion-rods are attached to the top of the mast-plate and to the inside of timber A as shown in the illustration.

The shoes are of tire, steel and will have to be made by a blacksmith. The front ones are thirty inches long, curved up at the front, as shown in Fig. 3 A, and bevelled at the bottom so as to form a gripping or cutting edge. When mounted the lower edge is at the outside of the boat. Shanks with bolt-tops and collars pass through the holes made in the shoe-blocks F F, and are securely held with nuts screwed down on washers so as not to cut the wood.

The rudder (Fig. 3 B) is a chisel-edged piece of steel twelve inches long turned up at both ends and mounted at the foot of a shank C, which is provided with a collar, a square shoulder for the tiller D to fit on, and a threaded top so that a nut will hold the tiller in place. The shoes can only be made of steel or iron, as wooden ones are useless.

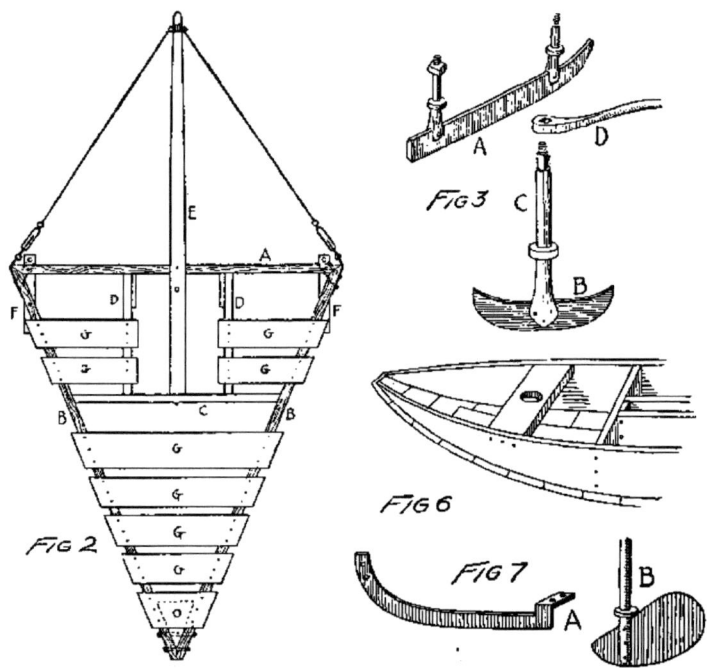

The mast is twelve feet high and three inches and a half or four inches in diameter, slightly tapered near the top. The gaff is six feet long and the boom twelve feet in length.

The main-sail measures eight feet on the mast, five feet on the gaff, eleven on the boom, and the leach is thirteen feet long. The jib is ten feet on the forestay, six feet at the foot, and eight feet on the leach. This sail area will present a good surface to the wind, and with an ordinary breeze the boat should make from eight to twelve miles an hour with two or three boys on the deck.

The rigging is done in the same manner in which boats are fitted out. The spars should be varnished and the boat can be painted or varnished, as a matter of choice. All white wood-work with black metal parts, or a red frame with cream-colored deck and black metal parts, are pleasing combinations, but a boy's own ideas can be carried out with the paint-pot and brush.

A Twin-mast Ice-boat

The twin-mast ice-boat shown in Fig. 4 is the same size as the other one, and built in the same manner except that timbers D D in Fig. 2 are omitted and a smaller deck is laid at the stern.

One foot back from the corners three-inch masts are stepped in holes made in timbers B B to receive half-inch iron pins driven in the foot of the masts. The sticks are eleven feet long and lashed together at the top or bolted with several long, thin bolts as shown in the illustration. They pitch forward at a slight angle, or so that the forestay is eleven feet long.

The gaff is sixteen feet long and the boom eighteen feet in length, and the leach of the sail is fourteen feet.

The gaff is hauled up into the crotch formed by the masts, and a set of blocks and tackle at the bottom of the sail on the boom and the deck will haul the sail into the proper position. It then swings free between the masts, and the jib and main-sail form one large sheet, so that when the main-

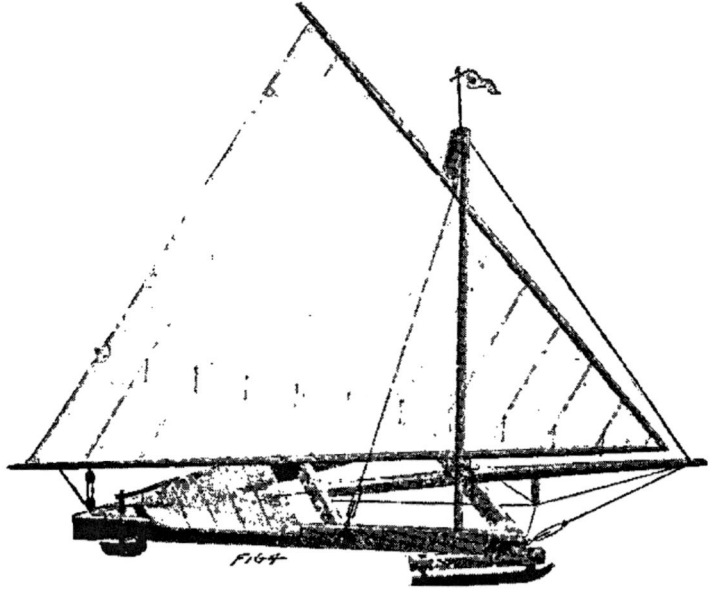

sheet goes to one side or the other the jib always takes the opposite position and the wind is playing on the entire sail at all times.

This is a very easy rig to handle as it relieves the steersman from the bother of the jib-sheets which are annoying in a stiff breeze.

Scoots and Scooters

Scoots and scooters are the latest wrinkle in ice-boats. Down on the Great South Bay, on the southern side of Long Island, they speak of them in fun as "ice-water boats." The advantage in a boat of this kind lies in their ability to sail on poor ice or to go across water that is partly open and frozen as many of the bays along the coast are at times.

The scoot shown in Fig. 5 is in the form of a sharpy, but the bottom curves up at the bow so that if it is sailing on the water and comes to the edge of an ice-floe that is not too high out of the water the wind will blow the boat up on the ice and it will sail along on its runners at double its previous speed. In the same manner when it comes to open water it will slip off the ice quite comfortably and become again a marine craft.

The model and descriptions of a centre-board sharpy may be taken for the construction of the boat, except that there is no stem or bow-post and the bottom rounds up the same as the side boards curve in. The bow is therefore nearly a point. This construction is shown in Fig. 6 (page 252), which is a view of the sides and bottom only, the deck planking being fastened down afterwards.

The boat should be calked with white-lead and lamp-wicking and as carefully made as a water-boat, for it must be absolutely tight and water-proof. The deck may be covered with canvas and painted, or it may be of varnished or painted wood.

The hull should be from twelve to fifteen feet long and from four to five feet wide across the widest part. It is

FIG 5

fifteen inches deep, and is provided with a centre-board and trunk the same as described for the sailing sharpy on page 221.

The mast is twelve feet long or about ten feet above the deck; the gaff is seven feet and the boom eleven feet long. The bowsprit is four feet long and is bolted to the forward deck, and from the end of it to the top of the mast a light, wire-cable forestay is made fast for the jib to run on.

The sails are made of twilled drill or very heavy unbleached muslin, and in the main-sheet one or two sets of reef-points will be necessary. The main-sail measures seven feet on the mast, six feet and six inches on the gaff, ten feet and six inches on the boom, and thirteen feet on the leach. The jib measures seven feet on the forestay, four feet across the foot, and six feet on the leach. The sail-cloth should be ribbed to strengthen it and a light rope run around all the edges of both sails.

The shoes are made of light, broad tire iron or steel twenty-four inches long and shaped so that the front part will bolt fast to the outside of the scooter sides and the rear ends will lie against the bottom of the boat where they can be bolted fast. The shape of these shoes is shown in Fig. 7 A (page 252), and any blacksmith will make them for you at a nominal cost. The rudder is of stout sheet-iron mounted in the end of a shank as shown at Fig. 7 B (page 252). Its fan-tail permits it to swing the boat in the water and its lower edge will guide it on the ice.

The rudder-post should be attached to the skag which is arranged at the under side and rear of the boat, and with a short iron tiller fastened as shown in Fig. 3 C and D the rudder may be swung.

When sailing on the ice the centre-board should be hauled up as high as it will go, for it is of use only when the boat is in the water.

A scoot is a cranky boat on the ice as the runners or fore-shoes are closer together than on an ice-boat with a triangular frame. Going before the wind it is all right, but when sailing on or up into a stiff wind it will keep a boy moving to hold his balance and steady the boat.

The shovel-nosed scooter shown in Fig. 8 is an easier boat to handle as it is broader than the sharpy, but it is not quite so fast, being slightly heavier.

It is twelve feet long over all with a five-foot beam and

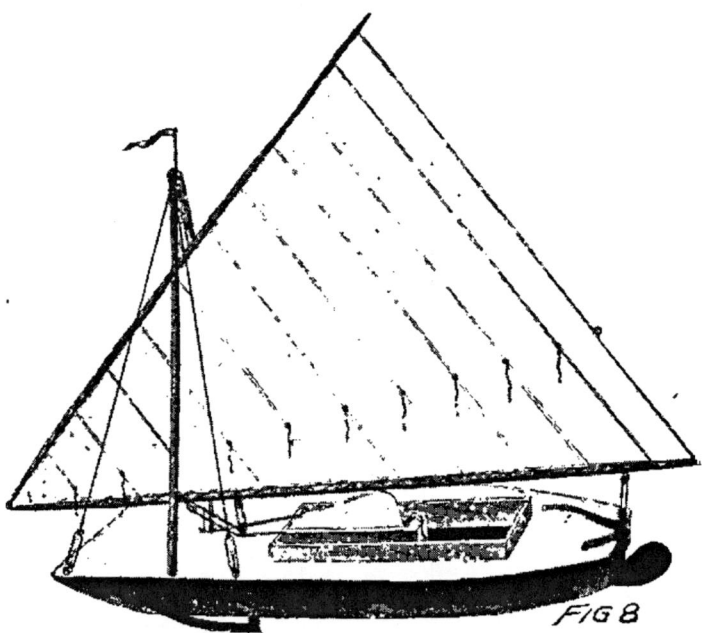

FIG 8

fourteen inches high including deck and bottom. The side boards are twelve inches wide, curved up at the bow, and bent in at the stern as shown in the illustration.

Twin masts are stepped two feet from the bow and lashed together nine feet above the deck. The rigging is the same as for the twin-mast ice-boat, and the sail measures twelve feet on the gaff, fourteen feet on the boom, with the leach eleven feet in length.

A small centre-board mounted in a trunk will be necessary for water sailing, and with several coats of paint the scooter will be ready for use.

A Wind-runner

An interesting boat for a boy to sail is a wind-runner like the one shown in Fig. 9.

Two spruce planks twelve feet long and ten inches wide are attached to three battens and separated four inches. The

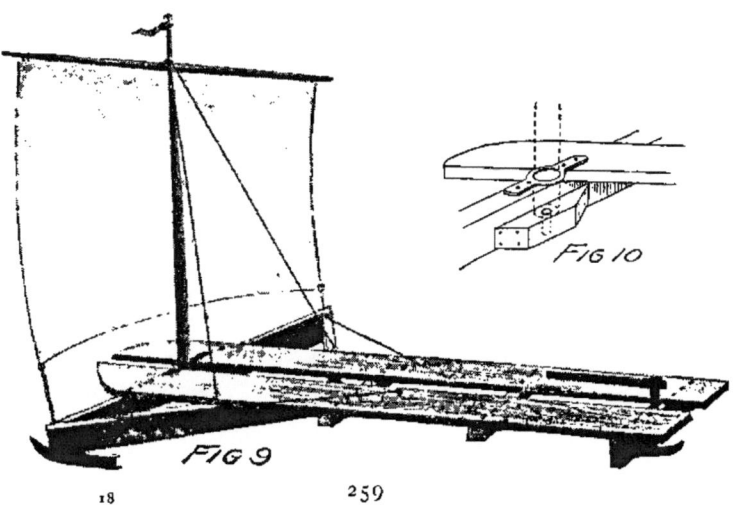

FIG 10

FIG 9

stern batten is four inches high and two inches wide, and through a hole made in the middle the shank of the rudder-post extends, from the top of which the tiller works.

The front ends of the planks are rounded and mounted on a triangular framework six feet across at the front and extending back about five feet from the ends of the planks.

A mast three inches in diameter and nine feet high is stepped through a collar and into a block attached to the back of the front cross-piece as shown in Fig. 10. An iron pin at the bottom of the mast drops into a hole made in the block and the backstays hold the mast in place.

A yard-arm eight feet long supports a square sail six feet wide, which is caught at the lower ends to the outer ends of the triangle frame.

The shoes attached to the triangle frame with bolts are fifteen inches long and the rudder-blade is ten inches long.

This is a rapid sailer before the wind, and with a little manœuvring the runner can be made to sail on the wind, though it will not run nearly as close to the wind as the ice-boats or scoots. Paint or varnish will give the wood-work a good finish, and under a stiff breeze this wind-runner will carry four or five boys.

Chapter XVI

HOUSE-BOATS AND RAFTS

A House-punt

A HOUSE-PUNT of very simple construction is shown in Fig. 1. The punt is from sixteen to twenty-four feet long according to the size desired, but for a party of four boys it should be twenty-four feet long, eight feet wide, and two feet deep with a cabin eight feet high.

The sides and middle rib should be of pine, spruce, or white-wood one inch and a quarter thick, free from sappy places and knots. If the boards cannot be had as long as twenty-four feet nor as wide as two feet, use two boards twelve inches wide and make one joint at the middle of the lower board and two in the upper board as shown in the drawing of the side elevation (Fig. 2). Six inches down from the top at either end and thirty inches in at the bottom cut the sides as shown so that the punt will have a shovel-nose at both ends and can be poled or sailed in either direction. Make a third or middle rib the same size as the side board. This is to be placed at the middle of the punt so as to receive the sheathing and deck planking. The arrangement of this middle rib and the side boards is shown in Fig. 3 and at A in Fig. 3. A batten is shown to which the upper and lower boards of a side are nailed fast. If the two boards are used it will be necessary to arrange these battens along the inside of each side about eighteen inches apart. They should be of tough wood five or six inches wide, an inch and a quarter thick, and two feet long.

Galvanized boat nails should be used, and when driven in from the outside they should be clinched at the inside. Good boat nails are of malleable iron stiff enough to go through hard-wood but ductile enough to be turned over at the ends with a light hammer and quick, sharp blows.

The sheathing and deck planking should be not less than four inches and not more than six inches in width, and before it is put on it should be well sun-dried to take out all moisture. It should then be given two good coats of paint on both sides to make it water-proof.

Lay the sides and middle rib bottom up and begin to sheath from one end. Lumber sixteen feet long should be used, and this, when cut in half, will make two pieces from each length. If matched boards are used smear the edges with white-lead before the boards are driven together, but if straight-edge lumber is employed it will be necessary to lead and wick the joints. This is done by taking a piece of round iron one-quarter of an inch in diameter and eight inches long and bending it as shown at Fig. 4 A. Lay this on the flat edge of each board at the middle and heat the iron so as to form a groove as shown at Fig. 4 B. The wood, having been beaten in, forms a gully in which a string of lamp-wick can be laid as shown in Fig. 4 C. The groove must not be cut with a chisel for then its effect would be lost. The object of this treatment is that when the punt is in the water the

262

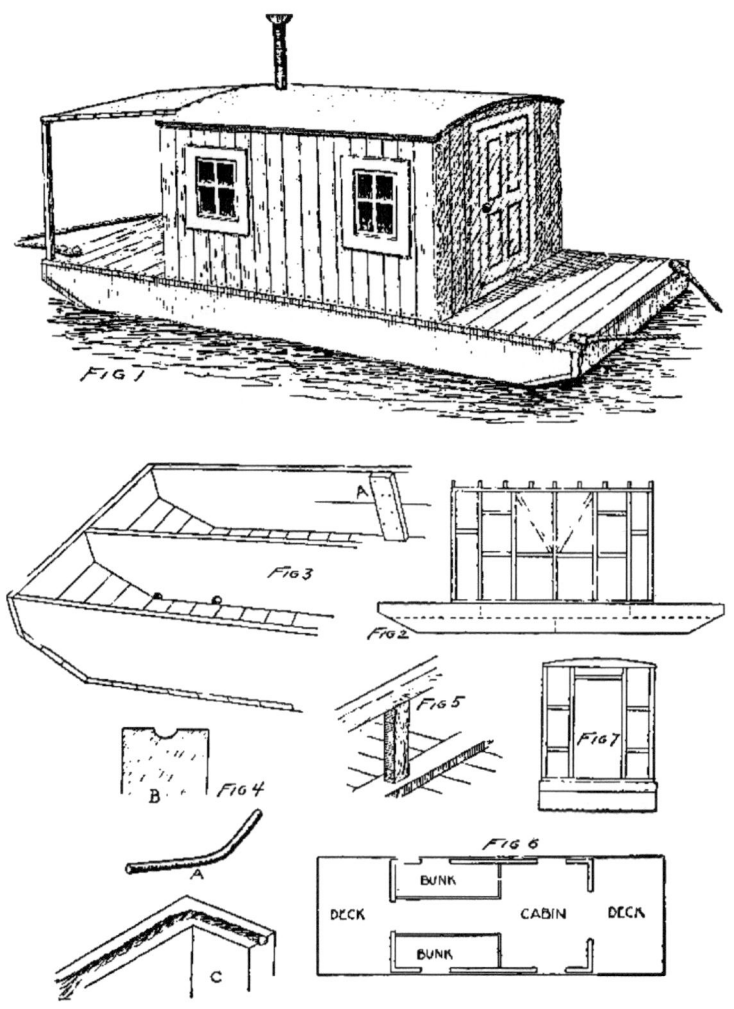

FIG 1

FIG 3

A

FIG 2

FIG 5

FIG 4

B

FIG 7

A

FIG 6

BUNK

DECK   CABIN   DECK

BUNK

C

A HOUSE-PUNT

joint swells forcing out the wood against the lamp-wick and making a water-tight joint. The edges of the wood and the wicking must be well smeared with white-lead in order to properly calk the joint.

Between the middle rib and each side an inner keel should be arranged so that each plank can be nailed fast to it. This will act as an additional brace to hold the sheathing planks in place and make the bottom more rigid. This inner keel should extend from end to end of the punt, and short pieces may be laid inside the bevelled ends to lend added strength.

At each end a spruce plank eight inches wide is made fast with long boat nails, first leading all the joints to make them water-tight. The deck planks are laid on the same as the sheathing, and to brace them from underneath, in the space between the middle rib and the sides, two-by-three-inch spruce rails are propped on short sticks which are nailed to the inner keel and to the rails as shown at Fig. 5. These under props should be arranged about eighteen inches apart, the entire length of the punt. Groove the upper edges of the end and side planks with the iron, then lay the lamp-wicking in, lead, and nail down the planking, taking care to put the nails in straight and true. When the punt is finished give it several good coats of copper paint on the bottom and sides and several coats of good marine paint on the deck.

To construct the cabin lay down the sill-joist of two-by-three-inch spruce, making the plan fourteen feet long and seven feet and eight inches wide (Fig. 6). To this nail the uprights and bracing timbers, forming the sides and ends as shown in the drawings of the side and end elevation

(Fig. 7). The door spaces at the ends should be three feet wide and seven feet high, so that when trimmed and the doors hung the actual size will be two feet and eight inches wide by six feet and ten inches high.

The window openings are two feet wide by two feet and six inches high, and between all the uprights braces are nailed fast to prevent the frame from racking. The arrangement of framing timbers is quite clearly shown in the drawings, and in the deck plan (Fig. 6) the arrangement of the bunks is indicated. Across the top of the framework one-and-a-half-by-six-inch beams are laid having their upper edge crowned as shown in the end elevation (Fig. 7). Over these the roofing boards are laid lengthwise, and on top of them canvas is drawn and tacked down all around the edges with copper tacks.

The roofing boards may be of three-quarter-inch stuff planed on both sides and from two to four inches wide, whichever is the easiest to obtain. The boards should extend over the ends and sides for two or three inches so that a finishing moulding can be made fast under the boards. Give the top of the boards two good coats of paint, then stretch oiled canvas over the top and tack it fast. Several coats of paint will finish the canvas and make it hard enough to walk on, for in pleasant weather this upper deck will make a pleasant place to spend many hours under the shade of a canopy. The cabin sheathing is of narrow matched boards planed on both sides and as free from knots and sappy places as it is possible to get them. The boards must be thoroughly sun-dried before they are laid on and nailed fast, and it would be well also to paint the matched edges so that moisture may not get in and swell them. The inside and outside of the cabin is to be painted to protect the wood from moisture, and if painted a light tint of any color, or white, it will be cooler in summer when the sun is shining than if coated with a dark color. Dark colors absorb light and heat while light ones reflect or shed them.

The window-sashes should be arranged on hinges so that they may be swung in and back against the inside of the cabin and hooked. Or, by cutting away a part of the upright, the sash may be arranged to slide. Wire screening may be tacked over the window-frame at the outer side to keep out flies and mosquitoes, and screen doors can be made also for the front and rear doorways—to swing in, as the wooden doors swing out.

Over the rear deck a canopy is arranged on poles. This is similar to a tent fly for camping, and will shed the sun and rain from the deck when the cook is preparing meals.

A small cook-stove may be arranged inside the cabin, but if it is not convenient to carry coal in a box on the deck an oil-stove will answer every purpose.

Two bunks may be built in on each side, one above the other, and four wire springs may be arranged to rest on battens driven across the bunks at the head and foot. A small hatch should be cut in the rear deck and another one through the cabin floor so that a few things may be stored in the hold. The aft hatch should be provided with a suction-pump so that any water that leaks in can be readily pumped out.

Rings, cleats, and ropes should be provided for the punt, and two anchors would be better than one, especially when near the shore or in shallow water, to hold the punt from swinging, which it is sure to do if there is any wind or waves. Always anchor it so that the wind is blowing on one end and not broadside as it is a strain on the anchors and ropes to hold a boat broadside on.

By erecting a spar fifteen or twenty feet high and four or five inches in diameter, a square-sail can be rigged on yard-arms so that the house-punt can be sailed before the wind. A long oar will be necessary to steer with, or a portable rudder may be made and hung to the stern with pins and ropes.

A house-punt of this description will be a very great source of enjoyment to several boys in the summer-time, and in the winter when not in use the punt can be hauled out on shore, the windows boarded up, and old canvas drawn over the decks to protect them from the sun.

A House-raft

Almost any boy can build a fairly good boat, even if it is a flat-bottomed sharpy. But to build a raft of the proper size, and on it a house that may be comfortably occupied, will require the aid of a good carpenter who understands construction, and under whose direction several boys can work to good advantage.

For a party of four or five young fellows, a very convenient and commodious house-raft at anchor is shown in Fig. 8. The raft is about thirty-eight feet long and twelve feet wide, while the house is twenty-three feet long and twelve feet wide by nine feet high from raft deck to top of house.

These dimensions will, if necessary, permit the raft to be taken through any canal, and without mast and deck-rails it will pass under the road bridges that span the canals.

If the house-raft is to be used on canals only, it will be better not to have the mast, and the deck-rail may be arranged so that it can be removed quickly before passing under a low bridge.

The mast is for use on lakes, bays, or rivers only, where a large square-sail can be hoisted on a yard-arm, and by means of which the raft may be made to sail before the wind slowly, so that its position may be changed from time to time.

The construction of a house-raft is quite simple, and will not require the services of a boat-builder, as the carpenter can build both the raft and the house on it. To begin with, it will be necessary to obtain four straight logs thirty-eight feet long, as sound as possible, and not wind-racked. Two of these logs are to be laid with the butt end at the stern, and the other two with butts at the bow, thus giving equal spaces between each along the entire length of the raft.

Across the ends of these logs nail a temporary strip to keep them the proper distance apart; then at right angles lay four-by-twelve-inch timbers on edge about two feet apart, and spike them securely to the logs. This part of the work should be done in shallow water, where the logs can be near enough to shore for the workers to stand on bottom.

When laying these cross-timbers it is always well to place the first ones about five feet apart, and stand a straight timber across from one to the other parallel to the logs, so that as each succeeding timber is laid it can be levelled by either

Fig. 8

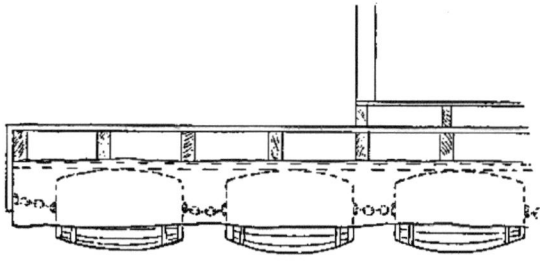

Fig. 9

Fig. 10

A HOUSE-RAFT

cutting slightly into the log or building up the bearing, as it may require.

Having timbered the logs the entire length, begin to plank or deck the raft with one-inch-and-a-quarter spruce boards six inches wide, laying the strips from bow to stern.

Fig. 9 will show the position of the logs with cross-timbers above, on top of which the planking may be seen. To the under side of the cross-beams and midway between the logs, planks should be fastened that will run the entire length of the raft. These are to form a bearing against which the upper bilge of the barrels will rest. Fig. 9 shows the heads of three barrels, each the end one of a number that are chained together and run all along under the raft to give it sufficient buoyancy to counteract the displacement that would be caused by the weight of the house and occupants.

Fig. 10 is a side view of those same barrels, showing the position they occupy and the distance from one to the other. Oil-barrels are the best for this purpose, and after being well bunged they should be treated to several good coats of copper paint before being drawn under the raft. It would be well to leave a gallon of oil in each barrel, as it keeps the glue sizing in good condition, and prevents it from yielding to the dampness caused by the water, the pressure of which might in time find its way through small cracks or openings.

A few yards of wrought-iron chain sufficiently heavy for the purpose can be obtained and cut into short lengths, and each end should be fitted with an eye-plate with four holes in it, which plates are to be fastened to the ends of the barrels with short, fat screws, having first thoroughly smeared the back of each with white-lead. The barrels should be arranged about one foot apart, and if the logs are from twenty-four to thirty inches in diameter at the butt end there should be just enough space to accommodate the three rows of barrels between the four logs as shown in Fig. 9.

Across the logs at the bow and stern attach the planking, to extend down a foot below the water-line, and with short uprights against which to nail, fasten weather-boards along the sides of the raft to cover the logs and come up flush with the deck line.

Seven feet in from the ends of the raft lay cross-stringers, three by six inches, at distances of eighteen inches apart, on which to place the floor of the house. This flooring may be of narrow spruce boards, planed on one side and having matched edges.

The uprights for the house construction are placed on the flooring beams and sills, and securely pinned to them, and the cross-beams at top of house should be placed the same distance apart as the floor beams to sustain the weight above, as the top of the house or upper deck will be the open-air living-room. The side elevation (Fig. 11) shows the position of windows that will be placed on both sides of the house, and another illustration (Fig. 12 A and B) shows both front and rear elevations of the house, as well as the location of companionway and deck-rails.

The deck plan (Fig. 13) shows the arrangement of the house and how it is divided into the several compartments.

In the front, the dining and living saloon is a room measuring about eight feet in width and eleven feet in length. At one end a couch is placed which, if necessary, can be used as a bed; and close to it are two large windows—one overlook-

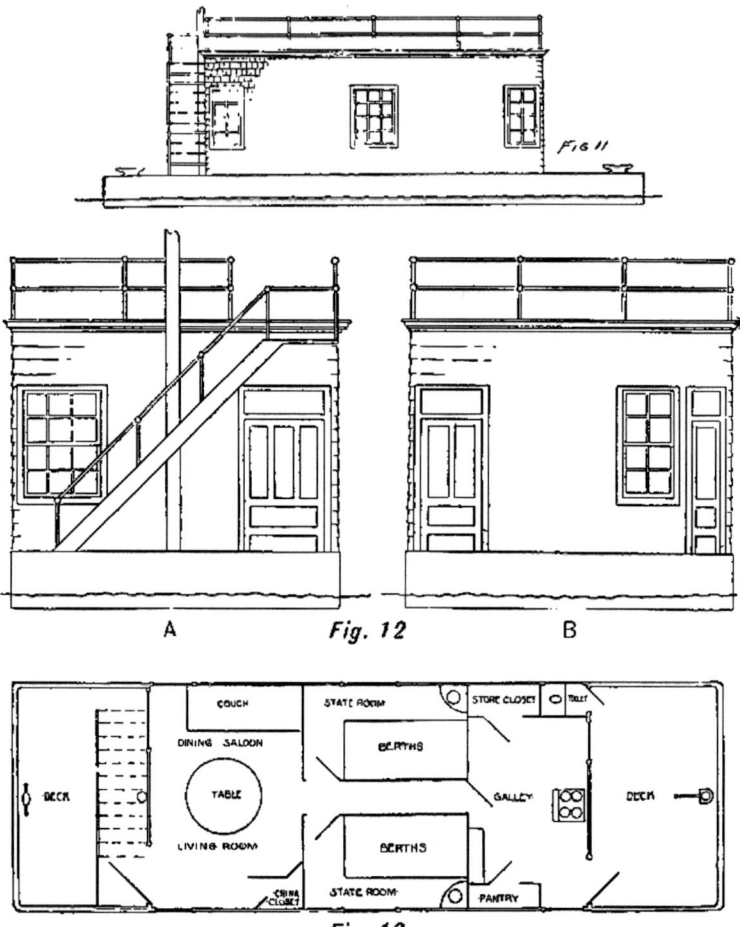

Fig. 11

A   *Fig. 12*   B

Fig. 13

DETAILS OF A HOUSE-RAFT

ing the fore-deck, the other giving a view from the side of the house. At the other end of the room a neat china-cupboard is built into the corner, and in the opposite corner the front door and a window are placed. One of the illustrations is an interior view of this cabin, showing how comfortable and attractive it can be made to appear. As it is a sort of general mess-room and living-cabin, it can be decorated and kept as such in a ship-shape manner.

Fishing-rods, guns, and nets against the wall will take up little space, while in the locker under the cupboard a variety of sporting paraphernalia can be stored.

Leading aft from this saloon, a passageway opens into the galley, a room six feet and six inches wide by eleven feet long, where all the cooking-utensils and stores are kept.

This galley should be painted a light gray or ivory white, with several coats of paint mixed for outside use, so the wood-work can all be wiped down with a damp cloth when necessary. White is always the best color for a kitchen or galley, and it has the appearance of cleanliness that no other color will give; it will be found to keep a room much cooler also, and for that reason it is recommended. A rug or rag carpet will be an acceptable covering for the floor, which should be treated to several coats of yellow-ochre paint.

Between the dining-saloon and the galley two state-rooms are placed, so the passageway runs between them, and from which the doors open that lead into them. These rooms are each about eight feet and six inches long by nearly five feet wide, and two berths, each three feet wide, are built in the rooms. Both rooms have large windows, and spaces for corner wash-stands; and as the doors open against the ends of the berths, there is no lost space nor wasted room.

Rows of hooks will accommodate clothing, and the lower berth should be at least twenty-two inches up from the floor to allow room to slide a trunk or two under it. These rooms can be ceiled and papered, or painted, as a matter of choice, but a few coats of varnish will render the wood-work in good shape and proof against dampness.

All the windows and doors in this boat can be of stock sizes, so that the cost of special sizes can be avoided. The sheathing may be of cedar shingles or of clapboards, as the cost is about the same. The clapboards should be painted, and will look better than shingles, although a very artistic effect is had by staining the shingles and painting the door and window casings in shades to match, preferably in the brown and olive-green shades.

The flooring of the upper deck should be of regular flooring boards with matched edges and planed on one side. Over this flooring canvas should be stretched and tacked, and afterwards given two or three coats of oil and varnish to make it water-proof, and finally treated to a coat or two of lead-colored paint. The seams should all be well laid down, and fastened with copper or tinned tacks, driven about two inches apart. It would be well to give the boards two good thick coats of paint before the canvas is applied, so that when the oil soaks through the canvas it will soften the paint somewhat, and help to hold the canvas in its proper place.

Leading from the fore-deck to the upper deck a stair or companionway is built, and anchored securely in place to the front of the house. The platform at the head of the staircase is braced over the front doorway by means of two iron rods that act as brackets, and which are screwed securely both to the under side of the platform and to the door-casing. This can be an open stairway composed of two side ways and eleven treads, the ends of the treads being anchored in grooves cut in the ways, and securely fastened with screws.

The rail around the deck is of common iron gas-pipe held in place by sockets and uprights. If the piping cannot be had, then hickory or hard-wood poles one inch and a half in diameter may be employed and held in place by uprights three inches wide and thirty inches high, through which two holes have been bored to receive the poles.

Around the fore and after decks a stringer three by six inches can be spiked down, and to the sides near the bow and stern large cleats should be bolted fast, by which the raft can be moored. Amidships at the bow a large post may be fastened, around which to attach a tow-line if necessary, and at the stern a rudder is arranged, with the post projecting up through the deck for a distance of a foot or eighteen inches. A mortise should be cut in the top of this post, into which the end of a tiller can be inserted when steering the craft, either when in tow or under sail.

A mast twenty-five or thirty feet long can be stepped amidships against the front of the house, and strapped fast to the upper deck with a horseshoe band. A step-block can be fastened to the deck into which the tenoned end of the mast will fit.

A yard-arm about twenty feet long, or longer if desired, can be arranged to hoist nearly to the top of the mast, and from which a large square-sail may be rigged so the lower corners will fasten to outriggers four or five feet long that can be temporarily braced at the sides of the boat when sail is set. This pole affords a good place from which to fly club or college colors, and from which to suspend lines of colored and Japanese lanterns to illuminate at night. This mast should be six inches in diameter at the base, and gradually taper near the top, and if a sail is to be used frequently, it would be a good plan to bobstay and shroud the stick with some standing rigging, so as to relieve it from the entire strain of a large sail.

The top of the house affords a living-room twenty-three feet long and twelve feet wide, and in that space a number of chairs, a table, hammocks, and benches can be accommodated.

For lake, river, and bay use this deck can be covered by a large awning, supported at the centre by a ridge-pole, and at the sides by upright posts that hold a stout wire in place, over which the striped awning canvas is caught. Drop-curtains at the sides will be convenient to ward off the bright sunlight, and this deck-room will be found the most delightful place to spend the pleasant days and evenings.

Along the inland waterways a raft of this description is a most desirable craft, as it can be towed from place to place, and for pleasure purposes its value cannot be overestimated, as it is a base for hunting and fishing as well as a retreat from village life; and the pleasure and comfort that can be had from a raft like this can well be appreciated when once tried.

To build a house-raft on these plans is not a difficult nor an expensive piece of work, and outside of the cost of the lumber, timber, barrels, and logs the amount is limited, unless finish is contemplated. With materials at hand and the help of three or four good workers, it should not require more than a week to construct this raft and house, and if fitted and painted in the manner described the cost should not exceed from two hundred to three hundred dollars, including all labor and material, according to the locality in which it is constructed.

A Float

In the spring, when every one who owns a boat of any sort is painting and repairing his craft, boat-houses, and floats, a few suggestions in regard to the floats will be found of practical value.

My chum and I own two canoes and a row-boat. The first year we built a boat-house, which exhausted our funds, and we were obliged to wait till the next spring before we could consider the expense of making a float. Most floats are constructed of spars on logs, with a mooring on top.

As we prepared to make the float ourselves, we wanted to find the easiest and cheapest way of doing so. The spars were costly, and, besides, are clumsy, and for a float of adequate size they would have to be so large that we could not move them alone.

As we lived in the city we could not get logs, or, if we could, we should have had a big bill for cartage. It was while we were painting the boat-house one afternoon that we saw an empty barrel go floating by. My chum said he had an idea that we could make a float after all. We went to one of the grocery stores and got four new flour-barrels, with the heads, at a cost of twenty-five cents apiece.

We took them, two by two, over to the boat-house, and then went to a near-by lumber-yard and got three two-by-three sixteen-foot joists, which cost us fifty-five cents, and one hundred square feet of boards such as are sold at thirty dollars a thousand feet. Some nails and our tools, and we were ready to begin work.

First we laid two barrels end to end about two feet apart; then about twelve feet from them we laid the other two in the same way. Then we took two of the joists and laid them on each side of the barrels on edge. Taking the other, we cut it in two pieces six feet long, which left a waste space of four feet in length. We then nailed the two sixteen-foot pieces and the two six-foot pieces together in the form of a rectangle as in Fig. 14.

Then, having propped the barrels to keep them in place,

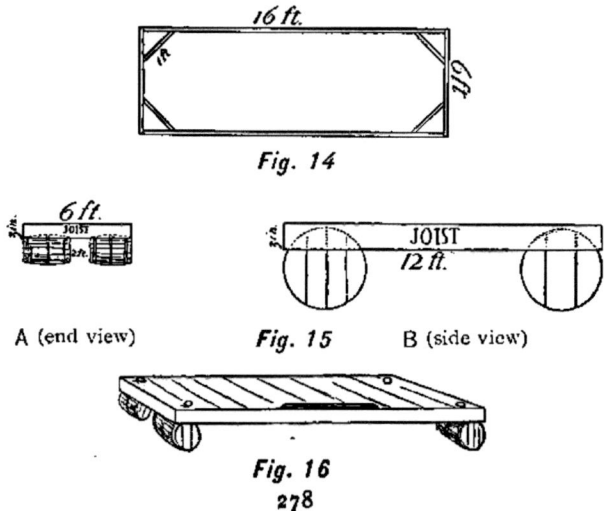

Fig. 14

A (end view)   Fig. 15   B (side view)

Fig. 16

we lifted this hollow rectangle onto them so that it rested on their sides as in Fig. 15. Cutting the four-foot joists into four one-foot pieces, we utilized them as corner braces.

Next we fastened the barrels to the frame, and, after painting them with a coat of thick paint to fill the cracks, we launched the craft. Then we covered the frame with the boards, laying them crosswise. A ring-bolt in each corner and a roller in the middle, and an old hose-pipe tacked around the edges, completed the float as shown in Fig. 16.

This we found was a most excellent float, and, above all, it was light, could be hauled out on the bank easily, or stored during the winter.

As it rose and fell with the tide there was no trouble in launching the boats at any time, whereas with a dock the pleasures of launching at low-water are too well known to be described.

Below is a table of expenditures:

Barrels, at 25 cents each		$1.00
Joists " $20 per M		.55
Boards " 30 "		3.00
Nails " 4 cents a pound.		.20
Paint " 20 cents a can		.20
Rings " 20 cents each		.80
	Total	$5.75

While the prices of these articles, particularly the lumber, have risen somewhat, the cost of this float will remain extremely small.

Chapter XVII

MARLINE-SPIKE SEAMANSHIP

ROPES may be joined to one another either by knotting or by splicing. If the rope belongs to the running rigging (such as halyards, sheets, etc.) of the vessel, it will be necessary to put a splice in it, as a knot would refuse to render (pass) through the swallow (opening) in the block. There are three kinds of splices in general use—namely, the long, the short, and the eye-splice. When joining running rigging a long splice is always employed, as it does not increase the diameter of the rope, and when neatly made cannot easily be detected. The short splice is very bulging, but it can be made quickly and is employed in all cases where the rope does not pass through blocks. The eye-splice is used for making a permanent loop in the end of a rope, such, for instance, as is seen in the hawsers by which steamboats are temporarily made fast to a dock, the loop or eye being thrown over the spile on the pier. Let us first consider the making of the latter splice.

Splices

THE EYE-SPLICE (Fig. 1).—Open the end of the rope and lay the strands 1, 2, 3 upon the standing part as shown in

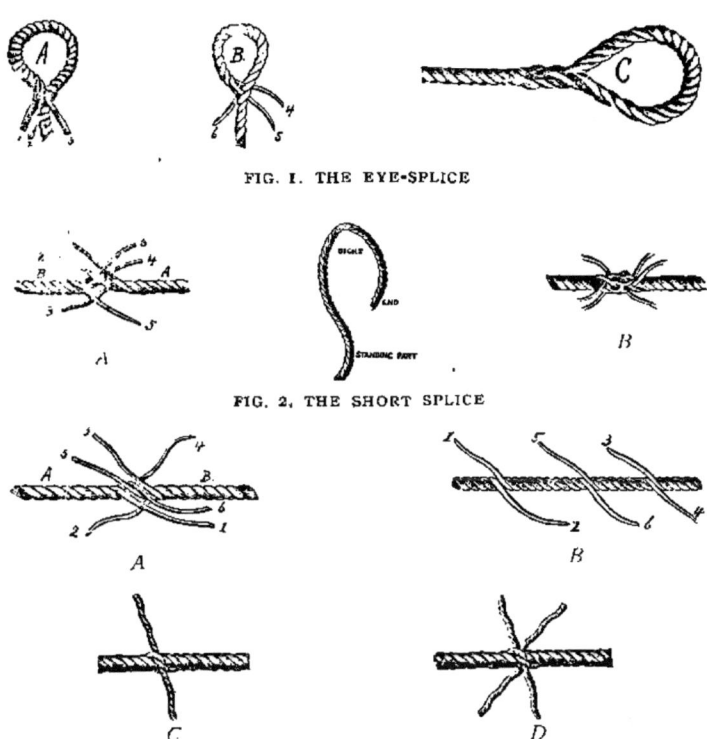

FIG. I. THE EYE-SPLICE

FIG. 2. THE SHORT SPLICE

FIG. 3. THE LONG SPLICE

A in Fig. 1; now push strand 4 through the rope as shown in B; next thrust strand 5 over the part through which the former was passed, and last push the strand 6 through on the opposite side. Repeat this once, then cut off the remaining ends, and the splice will appear as in C.

THE SHORT SPLICE (Fig. 2).—Hold the rope B (Fig. 2 A)

in the left hand; pass the strand 4 over 1, and having thrust
it through under 3, pull it taut; take strand 5 and pass it
over 2 and under 1; pass strand 6 over the first strand next
to it and under the second. Shift the rope around and treat
the other side in the same way, and the result will be as
shown in Fig. 2 B. This single tucking of the ends is not
sufficient for strength, so repeat the operation once, then cut
off the ends of the strands.

THE LONG SPLICE (Fig. 3).—Unlay (untwist) the two ends
to be joined some two or three feet, and place the ends together in the same manner as explained for the short splice. Now
take the strand 1 and unlay it as far back as A, and in the
groove left in the rope wind the strand 2; unlay the strand 3
and in its place lay-up (wind) the strand 4. At this stage
the rope will represent the appearance of Fig. 3 B. The
middle strands, 5 and 6, will now be knotted with a simple
overhand knot Fig. 3 C, care being observed that the knot
is formed to follow the lay (form) of the rope. Next divide
these two strands equally as shown in Fig. 3 D, and tuck
them into the rope on the same principle as explained for
the short and eye splice. The remaining strands will be
treated in the same manner, after which stretch the rope
well and cut off the ends.

Knots

REEF KNOT (Fig. 4).—This commonly used knot is also
known as a flat knot and square knot, and is one of the
most valuable of the many employed. As its name implies,
it is used to tie the reef points of a sail, the stops (short

lengths of rope) used to secure the jib to the bowsprit when the sail is lowered, etc. Should a person find it necessary in order to affect an escape from a burning building to fashion a line by tearing sheets into lengths and tying them together, this knot should be employed, for it will not slip and the bulge where the strips are tied will afford good hold for the hands. In order to make the knot, simply tie an overhand knot, then pass the ends so that they shall take the same lay (form) as the crossed parts beneath. Should the ends be passed (crossed) wrong, an Old Granny knot (Fig. 5) will be the result, and this knot will capsize (pull out of shape) and slip as soon as a strain is put upon it.

BOWLINE KNOT (Fig. 6).—Take the end (1) of the rope in the right hand and the standing part (2) in the left hand; lay the end over the standing part and turn the left wrist so that the standing part forms a loop (4) enclosing the end; now lead the end back of the standing part and above the loop and bring the end down through the loop again as shown. A bowline of this kind, sometimes called a single bowline, is employed in a variety of ways. Seamen sit in the bight (3) of this shape to be hoisted aloft under certain circumstances, and two towing hawsers are often made fast to each other by two bowlines, the bight of one being passed through the bight of the other.

BOWLINE ON A BIGHT (Fig. 7).—Double the rope, and take the double end (1) in the right hand, the standing part (2) of the rope in left hand; lay the end over the standing part, and by turning the left wrist form a loop (3), having the end inside; now pull up enough of the end (1) to dip under the bight (4), bringing the end towards the right and dipping it under the bight, then passing it up to the left over the loop and hauling taut. This knot is employed in the same way as explained for the single bowline, and it may also be stated that it affords much amusement as a puzzle, for if the standing part (2) is held and the knot presented to be untied, only those familiar with the way in which it is made will be apt to discover the secret of dipping the end (1) back and undoing the knot by handling it in a reverse manner to that described for its manufacture.

RUNNING BOWLINE (Fig. 8).—The only difference between this knot and the one described under the head of "Bowline" is that the end (1) of the rope is taken around the standing part (2), and then a single bowline (3) is tied on its own part. As will be understood by reference to the diagram, this forms a slipknot or lasso, and in fact it is employed for the same purposes as the latter. When a shark is hooked by sailors the great fish is hauled up until his head is out of water, then a running bowline is made around the hook-line and allowed to fall down over the fins, when it is hauled taut and the strain taken off the hook and line, so that the danger of the fish escaping may be greatly lessened, for the line is apt to break from the thrashing of the creature or the hook pull out.

WALL KNOT (Fig. 9).—Unlay the end of the rope and whip (tie) it where shown, and form a bight of strand 1, and hold it down at the side represented by 2, pass the end of 3 around 1, and the end of 4 around 3 and through the bight of 1, then the knot will appear as shown in Fig. 10; now haul the parts taut and the knot will be formed.

CROWNED WALL KNOT (Fig. 11).—Over the top of the

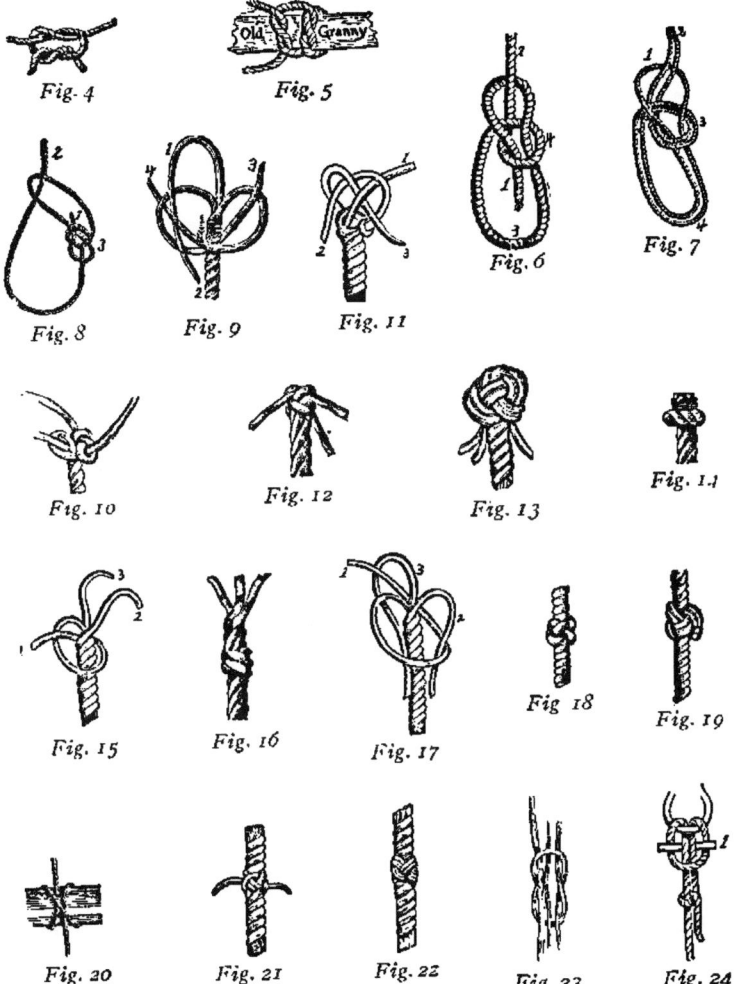

Fig. 4

Fig. 5

Fig. 6

Fig. 7

Fig. 8

Fig. 9

Fig. 11

Fig. 10

Fig. 12

Fig. 13

Fig. 14

Fig. 15

Fig. 16

Fig. 17

Fig 18

Fig. 19

Fig. 20

Fig. 21

Fig. 22

Fig. 23

Fig. 24

KNOTS

knot lay the strand 1, then lay strand 2 over 1, and strand 3 over 2, and pass it through the bight of 1; now haul taut the parts and the knot will take the shape shown in Fig. 12.

DOUBLE WALL AND DOUBLE CROWN KNOT (Fig. 13).—This is made by allowing the strands to follow their respective parts round, first walling, then crowning, as shown in the diagram. This formation is also used as a Stopper Knot and a Man Rope Knot, although a proper Stopper Knot is shown in Fig. 14. It is a very beautiful knot when nicely made, and as a fancy knot is common on yachts and naval vessels.

MATTHEW WALKER KNOT (Fig 15).—As its name implies, this knot is named after the man who invented it. It is exceedingly simple and easy to make, and is in common use on board of all vessels. Unlay the strands for a short distance, and pass the end 1 around the rope and through its own bight; next the strand 2 underneath and through the bight of 1, also its own bight; last the strand 3 underneath and through the bights of 1 and 2. When hauled taut the knot will appear as in Fig. 16.

DIAMOND KNOT (Fig. 17).—Unlay the strands as for a Matthew Walker Knot, and form three bights and then take strand 1 over 2 and through the bight of 3; take strand 2 over 3 and through the bight of 1; take strand 3 over 1 and through the bight of 2, then haul the parts taut, and lay up (arrange) the strands of the rope again, and the knot will then appear as in Fig. 18. What is known as a Double Diamond Knot (Fig. 19) may be made by leading the strands through two single bights, having the ends come out at the top of the knot, then leading the last strand through two double bights; last lay the strands up as previously explained, and the knot will show as in Fig. 19.

TURK'S HEAD KNOT (Fig. 20).—This is purely an ornamental knot, and is used to beautify yoke lines for a rowing boat, man ropes, ridge ropes, gangway ropes, etc. The material used in the construction of this knot is regulated according to the character of the article to be decorated, ranging from twine to signal halyard stuff (line). To make this knot, form a clove hitch, and bring the bight of 1 (Fig. 21) under the bight of 2, then take the end up through it, make another cross with the bights, and take the end down. Fig. 22 represents a Turk's Head of two lays, but it may have any number of lays, it being necessary only to follow the lead around according to the formation desired.

ROPE YARN KNOT (Fig. 23).—It is to be explained that a rope yarn is simply one of the several parts which make a strand of rope. When a strand is untwisted, its parts become rope yarns. These yarns are used for a number of purposes, such as for rough seizings, etc. When a considerable length of rope yarn is required, it is necessary to knot it smoothly, and this is effected in the following manner: Split in halves the two ends of the rope yarns, and crotch and tie the two opposite ends, then jam the tie and cut off the remaining ends.

LARK'S HEAD KNOT (Fig. 24).—This knot is used on the same principle as explained for the Slippery Hitch; when it is desired to undo it quickly, simply pull out the wooden toggle 1. The making of the knot will be fully understood by consulting the diagram.

Ropes are temporarily fastened to one another, or to a

spar, hook, ring-bolt, etc., by bends and by hitches. These are all more or less simple, and a little practice and patience is all that is necessary for the young reader to become expert in their manufacture. Let us first consider the bends in general use.

Bends

COMMON BEND (Fig. 25).—This is also known as a single bend, and is used for making one rope fast to another in a hurry. Make a bight with one rope, and hold it in the left hand; pass the end of the other rope 1 through the bight 2, then back round the two parts 3, over the rope 4, under the rope 5, and over the short end of the loop. If the end 1 is taken around once more and through the bight again, as shown in Fig. 26, the bend will stand a greater strain and be less liable to jam. The bend shown in Fig. 26 is known as a double bend.

CARRICK BEND (Fig. 27).—This, like the common bend, is used for bending hawsers together, but is a trifle more difficult to make. Make a bight with the end of one rope; pass the end of the other rope through the bight and over the standing part of the first rope where marked 1, then under the end 2, and again through the bight and over the standing part 3.

FISHERMAN'S BEND (Fig. 28).—First pass the rope twice round the spar or ring, which act is understood by sailors as "taking two round turns," next take a half hitch round the standing part, then thrust the end under the two turns, and last half hitch the end round the standing part A. When hauled taut the bend will appear as shown in Fig. 29.

SHEET BEND (Fig. 30).—Pass the end 1 through the eye; take two turns round, observing in each case that the end passes under the standing part 2. The greater the strain,

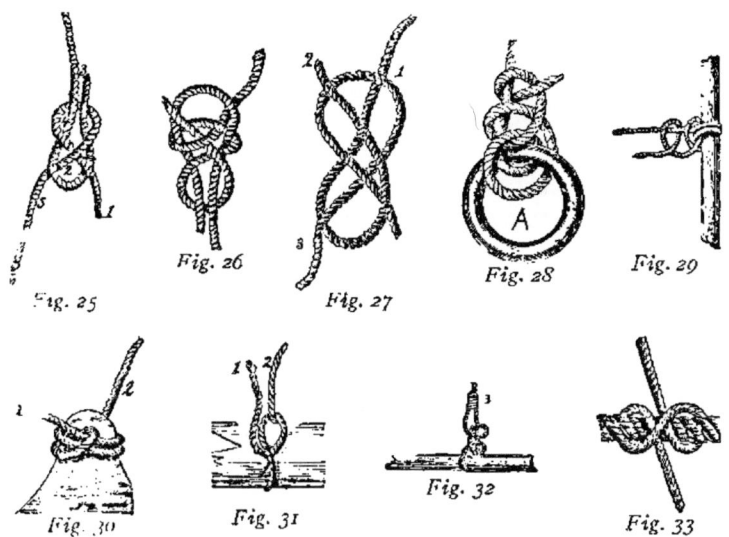

Fig. 25

Fig. 26

Fig. 27

Fig. 28

Fig. 29

Fig. 30

Fig. 31

Fig. 32

Fig. 33

the more the standing part binds the two turns, and insures them from slipping.

Hitches

TWO HALF HITCHES (Fig. 31).—This is an exceedingly simple way of fastening a rope, and it has the double advantage of being proof against jamming. Take a turn around the object to which it is desired to fasten; bring the end 1 on top of the standing part 2, then pass it under and bring it up through the bight; repeat this process, haul **taut,** and the result will show as in Fig. 32. In case the hitch is to be subjected to a great strain, lash the end of the rope to the standing part where marked 3 in Fig. 32.

CLOVE HITCH (Fig. 33).—This is another very useful hitch, but is only employed when the strain upon it is temporary. It is in general use for bending a heaving-line (small rope) to a hawser so that a coil of the former may be thrown from a vessel to the dock and, after it is caught, the hawser pulled ashore.

SLIPPERY HITCH (Fig. 34).—This hitch is simply a turn around a spar or other object or through an eye, the end carried across the standing part, and a loop put through the bight, the end 1 being allowed to hang out. When it is desired to separate the hitch, pull out the loop by hauling on the end 1.

BLACKWALL HITCH (Fig. 35).—This is used in hoisting. Simply take a turn around the back of the hook, crossing the parts of the rope in front as shown. When a strain is put on the standing part of the rope, the underneath part is jammed and slipping prevented.

TIMBER HITCH (Fig. 36).—A hitch employed in towing spars and logs, as it will not slip. Pass the end 1 of the rope around the spar and lead it up and around the standing part 2, then pass two or three turns with the end around its own part as shown in the illustration.

ROLLING HITCH (Fig. 37).—A very good method of clapping (fastening) a tail-block. Take a hitch with the tail 1; take another hitch over the first; pass the end under the standing part 2, and twist the remainder of the tail round the rope, following the lay. A tail-block, being portable, is convenient to make fast anywhere about decks or the rig-ging, and a rope being rove through this block, a purchase, called a "whip," is created.

MAGNUS HITCH (Fig. 38).—Some people confuse this hitch with the rolling hitch just described, but a comparison of the two will explain the difference between them. With the end of the rope 1 pass two turns over the spar; carry the end in front of the standing part 2; pass it again under

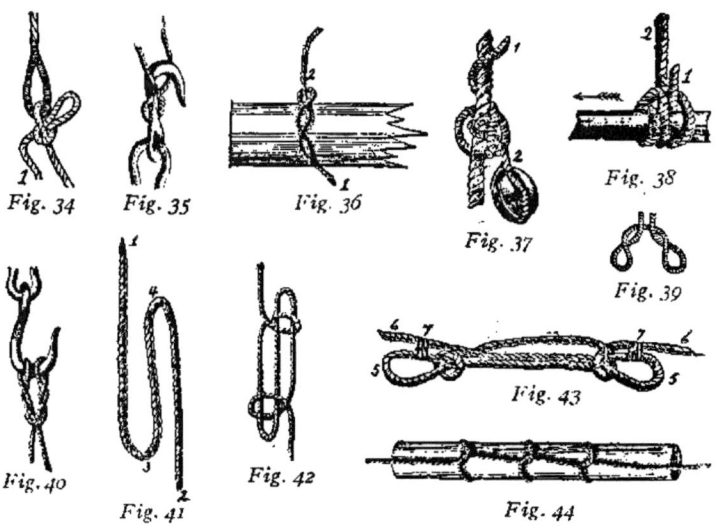

Fig. 34   Fig. 35   Fig. 36   Fig. 37   Fig. 38   Fig. 39   Fig. 40   Fig. 41   Fig. 42   Fig. 43   Fig. 44

the spar and bring it up through the bight. The value of this hitch is its insurance against slipping in the direction represented by the arrow.

CATSPAW HITCH (Fig. 39).—Like the Blackwall Hitch, this one is used for making a rope fast to a hook for hoisting purposes. Seize the bight of the rope in your two hands, and by turning the wrists form the two loops, then hang these loops on the hook as in Fig. 40.

SHEEPSHANK HITCH (Fig. 41).—A quick way of shortening a rope without cutting it is to convert a portion of it into a shape known as a sheepshank. Gather up the spare rope and lay it in parallel lines as shown. These parallel lines may be represented by any number, according to the quantity of spare rope and the length of the sheepshank. In the accompanying diagrams we show the smallest sheepshank that can be made, consisting of three parallel lines. After forming the rope as shown in Fig. 41, take a half hitch with the standing part 1 round the bight 4, and repeat this at the other extremity with the standing part 2 and the bight 3. The result will be as shown in Fig. 42. If it is desired to make this hitch doubly secure, put a seizing (fastening) 7 on the loops 5 and standing parts 6 (Fig. 43).

MARLING HITCH (Fig. 44).—Employed to make a running binding which can be put on and removed quickly.

Part IV

IN THE WOODS

Chapter XVIII

CAMPING in the mountains, fields, and forests is one of the most delightful features of life in the summer-time. But a good deal of the fun depends upon doing things the right way.

To experienced campers many of the following ideas and descriptions may be familiar, but among them there may be some suggestions that will be found of value.

The tent is the all-important thing, and to make one large enough for two or three boys is not a difficult matter. What the boy does not know on his first camping expedition, necessity will teach him, and much satisfaction may be had in constructing bunks and tables and the other varied paraphernalia of camp life.

A Tent of Medium Size

Fig. 1 shows a serviceable and roomy tent and fly of medium size, which measures eight feet wide, ten feet long, and seven feet high to the peak or ridge. The side drops or aprons are thirty inches high, and against them on both sides of the tent cots may rest on the ground as shown in the illustration.

295

The fly is ten feet wide and fifteen feet long, and is an extra covering for the tent in case of a hard rain-storm; while in clear weather and with another ridge-pole and upright, it can be used to lengthen the tent by extending it out beyond the front, where it is to be held fast with stakes and stanchion-ropes.

The plan shown in Fig. 2 gives the dimensions of canvas, and when the final sewing is done the edges C C at both ends of the tent are brought together and securely overcast with stout waxed cord.

The only openings are at front and back, and they can be closed by means of tabs and button-holes at one side, and large bone buttons made fast to the other edge in a corresponding position to the tabs.

Where the iron pins of the uprights project through the canvas, make a circular patch at least six inches in diameter with two or three thicknesses of the canvas, and sew it fast both at the hole and around the outer edge. This will strengthen the canvas at the most vital point, and prevent it from tearing if a heavy wind should strain the tent.

Twilled cotton sail-cloth is the proper material of which to make the tent, but if this cannot be had, then a stout quality of unbleached muslin will answer very well for clear weather; but in wet weather it will not shed the water so well as the twilled duck. The seams can be sewed on a machine, but they will be much stronger if sewed by hand with white cotton cord well waxed. All the edges of the cloth should be bound with rope about the size and strength of clothes-line, so that any attachments made to the edges

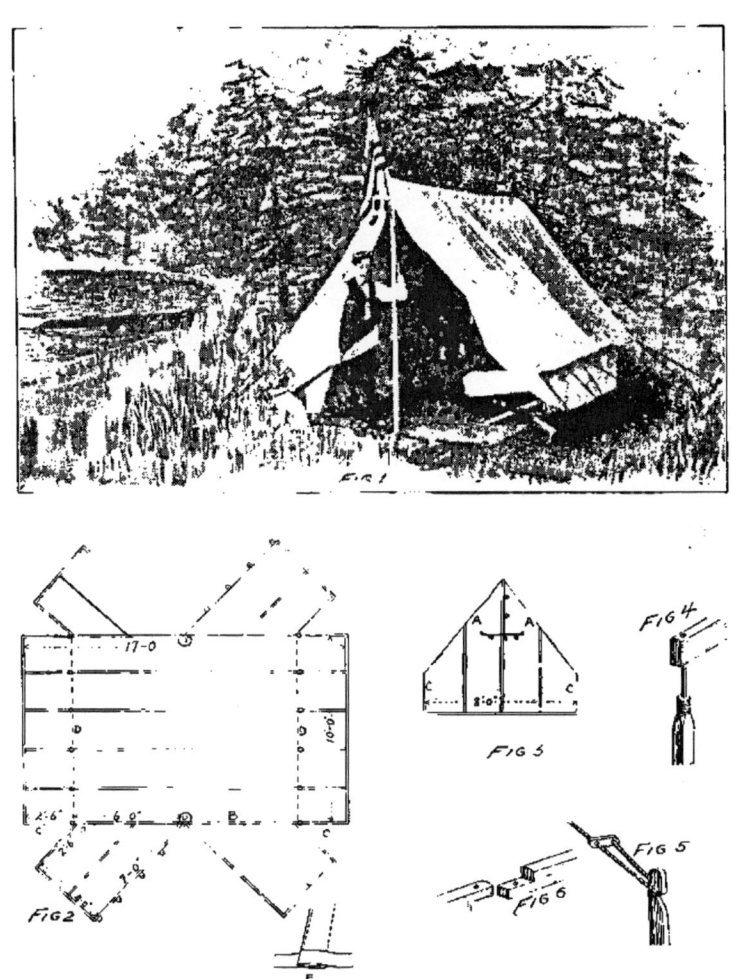

FIG 1

17-0

10-0

D

2-6" 6-0" B

C

FIG 2

E

A A

C C

2-0"

FIG 3

FIG 4

FIG 6

FIG 5

A TENT OF MEDIUM SIZE

will be borne by the rope instead of all the strain coming on the canvas.

On the dotted lines D D in the plan, which indicates the inner edges of the aprons, one-inch harness-rings are to be sewed on the straps, through which to reave the guy and stanchion ropes. There should be four straps to this tent, making five strips of canvas two feet wide; and these strengthening straps are three-quarters of an inch in width, and made by lapping the canvas over and sewing it along both edges as shown in the little diagram marked E below the plan in Fig. 2.

If a closed end is preferred instead of the flaps at the rear of the tent, a back, in one piece, as shown in Fig. 3, can be made and sewed all around the edges, bringing the edges A A against the edge B, and joining the vertical edges C C to the ends of the side aprons on the main sheet.

For ventilation, a flap opening may be made at the top of this end as you can see in Fig. 3; and with tabs and buttons this can be closed when necessary, or tied back with strings, either to the inside or outside of the tent, where they should be caught to small harness-rings sewed to the canvas.

The fly is bound with rope all around the outer edge, from which ropes extend out from each end, so that in hot weather, if the sun plays on the tent, it may be kept cool by raising the outer ends of the fly and propping them up with poles at the four corners, and perhaps one extra one at the middle of each side. (See the illustration for the canopy over the table and seats, Fig. 10).

The ridge-pole to hold up this tent is of pine or spruce,

ten feet long, one inch and a half thick, and four inches wide. The uprights are two inches square, with the sharp corners planed off, making them octagonal in shape, and they should be from seven to nine feet in length. The upper ends of the uprights are bound with cord or an iron band to prevent them from splitting when the iron pin is driven in place. They are to be bored to receive a half-inch pin, so that eight inches of it will project above the top of the upright as shown in Fig. 4. Five-eighth-inch holes are bored in the ridge-pole one inch and a half from each end, and through these the pins in the uprights will pass.

The stanchion-ropes are caught around the heads of long pegs or stakes, twenty-four inches long, two inches wide, and one inch in thickness, with a notch cut three inches from the top as shown in Fig. 5. Cleats four inches long, two inches wide, and seven-eighths of an inch thick are provided with two holes through which the stanchion-ropes pass, and they are used to draw the ropes taut, as shown in Fig. 5, where the strain on the long rope pulls the short end down and chocks the rope.

The stakes are to be driven into the ground so that but five or six inches of them project. The lower they are the better purchase they get in the ground and the more securely the tent is anchored.

The extra ridge-pole for the fly can be cut at one end so that it will lap in a corresponding manner on the front end of the tent ridge-pole as shown in Fig. 6. For long tents, where it is necessary to have the sticks in short lengths, for convenience in carrying them, the ridge-pole can be in two or three pieces, lapped together at the ends as shown in the figure drawing, so that the pin in the upright will complete the union.

When erecting the tent, dig two holes for the uprights to rest in, and embed them so that seven feet of pole will be above the ground, on which the ridge-pole will rest, and in turn the canvas covering. The stakes are driven three feet out on either side of the aprons so that the stanchion-ropes will line with the pitch of the tent.

A Large Camping-tent

For a company of boys numbering from four to eight a large camping-tent is shown in Fig. 7.

If it is made twenty feet long, ten feet wide, and eight feet high to the ridge-pole, it will accommodate six cots and two hammocks swung from the ridge-pole.

A plan by which to cut the cloth and make the tent is shown in Fig. 8, and in Fig. 9 the plan for the back is given. If an open back be preferred, the flaps shown at the bottom of Fig. 8 may be duplicated at the rear of the tent.

This tent, when erected, is twenty feet long and eight feet high from the ground to the ridge-pole, with the aprons at the sides three feet high instead of thirty inches as in the smaller tent. Three uprights two inches and a half square support the ridge-pole, which for convenience of transportation may be in two pieces and lapped at the middle as shown in Fig. 6.

This tent is made in the same manner as described for the smaller one, and a fly twenty-two feet long and eighteen feet

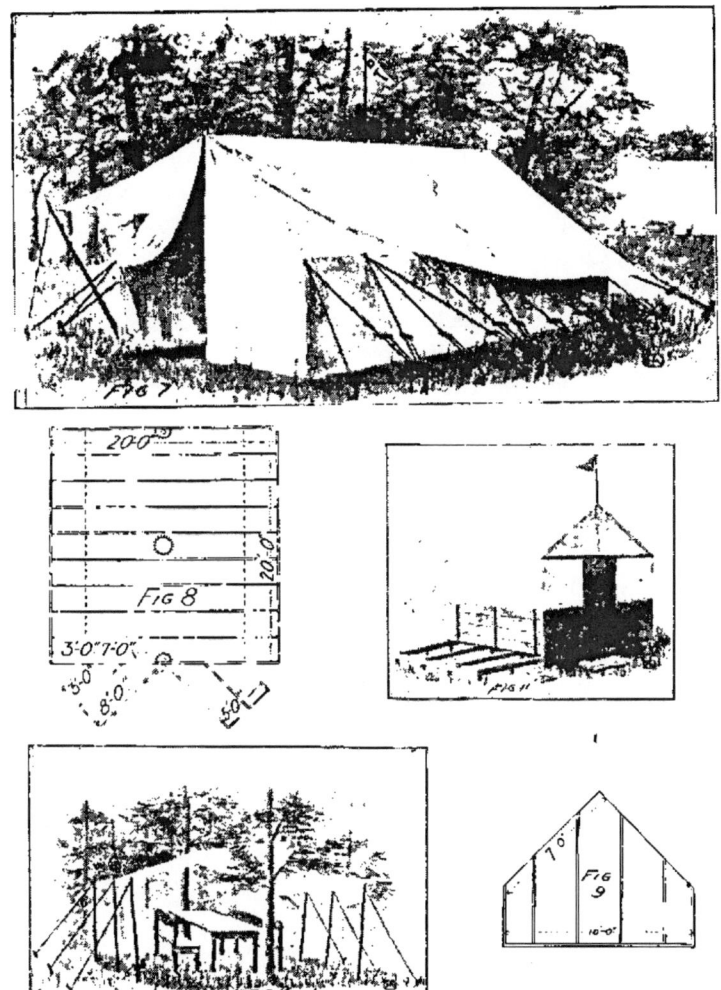

TENTS AND CANOPIES

wide is supported over the tent where, in clear weather, it can be propped up at the outer edges as shown at the left side of the illustration. The fly is drawn back at the right side to show how the guy and stanchion ropes are attached to the stakes, so as to prevent the wind from blowing the tent backward and forward as well as from side to side.

A flag-pole four feet high may be erected on the middle upright by leaving the pin at the top longer, so that it will extend up and into a hole bored in the lower end of the flag-pole. The lower end of the pole must be bound with cord or wire to prevent splitting. A small pulley at the top, and a set of halyards, will make it possible to raise a club flag or pennant.

All around the lower edge of the tent one-inch galvanized rings should be sewed fast about twelve inches apart. Through these the apron and ends may be tied fast to short stakes or wooden pins driven in the ground. This will be quite necessary in the event of a storm or strong wind, as otherwise the lower part of the tent will blow up and flap around in a disagreeable manner.

When erecting a tent of this size, care should be taken to anchor it securely and brace it well with the stanchion and guy ropes, for its size offers considerable resistance to a strong wind. A little care and forethought will sometimes avert a catastrophe with a tent, and when erecting one do not trust anything to luck, but snug your tent and keep ropes taut.

If it is possible to get some boards and a few joist, it would be well to make a flooring, if you are to stay in one place for any length of time.

Always select a level, dry place for the tent, and if possible erect it on ground that is slightly higher than that around it so as to drain the surface-water away.

Flies and Canopies

Every camping-tent should have a fly—that is, an extra canvas roof—for no matter how good the canvas of which it is made, it will become thoroughly soaked in a heavy rain; but if protected by a fly the latter will lead the water off and receive the greater part of the wetting. Such a fly is shown clearly in the illustration of the large camping-tent. Fig. 7.

The fly should always be a trifle wider than the tent is long, and in length it should be long enough to cover the roof of the tent and extend a foot or eighteen inches beyond the sides, where it rests on the stanchion-ropes and is lashed fast to pegs in the ground. The overhang, or extension, leads the water out beyond the apron of the tent and prevents the ground from becoming wet close to the tent.

Another use for this overhang is to prevent the rain driving against the aprons of the tent and wetting them close to the cots. In fair weather, when it is possible to dine outside the tent, the fly can be used as a canopy, if drawn over a ridge-pole and held up at the ends by means of poles and stanchion-ropes.

A canopy of this kind is shown in Fig. 10, where it is erected over a table and seats. It is always well, indeed, to have two flies to a tent, so that one can be used for a canopy or an auxiliary tent, under which a fire can be built and meals cooked and eaten when it is raining.

For a small camp a fly or canopy, twelve feet wide and eighteen feet long, will prove very useful in many ways; but for a larger camp it should measure fifteen by twenty-five feet. Under one of this size a party of ten or twelve people can be comfortably seated, with plenty of room all around.

Flies or canopies should be bound with rope all around the edges, and at distances from twelve to eighteen inches apart three-quarter-inch galvanized rings should be made fast. Through these stanchion-ropes may be reared wherever it is necessary to attach the sheet to branches or poles set in the ground.

A House-tent

One of the latest features in the modern camp is the house-tent, in which the lower part is floored and boarded half-way up, while the balance of the sides and the roof are of canvas. This style of camp-tent has become very popular in California and through the Southwest, where at least six months of each year are spent out-of-doors. For the boys who are about to build a permanent camp for several years' use, a house-tent such as shown in Figs. 11 and 12 will prove very satisfactory, and more desirable than the plain pitched tent.

Fig. 11 shows the house-tent closed in stormy weather or at night, while in Fig. 12 the house is open for fair-weather living. One wooden side is let down to form a piazza, and the canvas side above it is propped out with poles so as to act as a canopy or sunshade.

The frame is twelve feet long, eight feet wide, and nine feet high from the roof to the peak. The wood sides are three feet and six inches above the floor, and out beyond the sides of the house the joist may extend to support one or both of the wooden sides, which can be let down by means of hinges along the bottom. When the sides are lowered

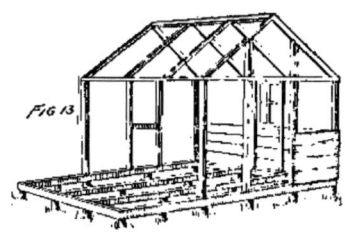

they act as piazzas and nearly double the floor space of the house-tent; while the canvas sides, when propped out with long, slim poles, add equally to the roof area in the way of sunshades.

In Fig. 13 a clear idea is given for the framing, which is of spruce planed on the four sides. The uprights and rafters are of two-by-three-inch stock, while for the under timbers two-by-four or preferably two-by-six rough stock can be used. The joist or flooring beams rest on the ends of posts embedded two feet in the ground, to which they are spiked with long, steel-wire nails. The flooring, of four-inch matched boards, is laid on the space within the four corner uprights, and the same or wider boards may be employed for the sheathing.

305

If both sides are to let down, a window can be set only at the back of this house-tent; but if only one side lets down the window may be arranged at the enclosed side between uprights the same as the rear window is placed.

The triangular end-pieces of canvas are attached to the frame with copper or tinned tacks, so that they will not rust, and the roof and both sides are of one piece made by sewing together lengths of canvas or twilled sheeting. At the front and back it is drawn over the edges of the end rails, forming the roof, and tacked to hold it in place.

At the front, on either side of the doorway, the canvas may be arranged to roll up in clear weather. The rolls are held to the upper frame-bar with cord or straps as shown in Fig. 12.

The front door is thirty inches wide and is made from boards and battens, and provided with a knob lock by means of which it can be opened from either side.

The side that lets down to form the piazza is battened on the outside, as may be seen in Fig. 11 where the house is closed. When the side is down the battens drop in between the extended floor joist or beams.

Folding-cots can be used in this house, or bunks may be built in against the side and end—two at the side and one at the end under the window. When the drop-side is up and fastened for the night, another cot can be placed at that side, while from corner to corner a hammock may be swung.

When camp is broken up in the fall the canvas is to be removed from the framework and kept for next season, but the frame may be left standing. It would be better to remove the door and sashes and slide them under the floor, for they would offer too much resistance to the wind if left standing in place, and might break or cause the framework of the house to rack and become rickety during the winter storms and high winds.

A coat or two of paint on the wood-work will improve its appearance greatly and preserve the wood, if the house is to be used for a number of seasons.

The New Tent

One great drawback to the pitched or army tent is that in wet weather, when one has to stay in-doors, it is not a comfortable abode unless you sit down or keep close to the ground, for there is little or no head room.

In the illustration of the new tent with French roof (Fig. 14) you can readily see the great advantage of this new method of construction, for it affords a great deal of head room.

Two uprights, three ridge-poles, and four angle-bars will be required for the frame, and some long, slim poles with crotched ends can be cut to prop the guy-ropes out from the tent as shown in the illustration. For a party of three or four boys this tent should measure seven feet and six inches high, six feet and six inches broad at the top, eight feet at the bottom, and ten or twelve feet deep. The sides and top are in one piece, twenty-one feet long and ten or twelve feet wide. The rear end is made in one piece and sewed fast to the edges of the sides and top.

At the front two flaps are sewed to the top and sides.

They each measure seven feet and six inches long at the inner edge, four feet across the bottom, three feet and five inches at the top, and seven feet long at the outer edge. They are cut as shown in Fig. 15 A, and when the tent is set up the canvas will appear as shown in Fig. 15 B.

The frame is composed of two uprights two inches square and nine feet long, eighteen inches of which is set into the ground. There are three ridge-poles two inches in diameter and ten feet long; and four brace-bars two inches square, four feet and three inches long, bevelled at the lower ends to fit against the upright post as shown at Fig. 16 A. An iron pin (Fig. 16 D) is driven in the top of each upright and at the outer ends of the brace-bars over which the ridge-poles fit, they having been provided with holes for the purpose. Angle-irons are screwed fast to the bevelled ends of the brace-bars, and a collar of iron is made and screwed to the uprights so that the tongue end of the angle-irons will fit in them as shown at Fig. 16 B. Stout screw-eyes and wire hold the braces in position at the top, as shown at Fig. 16 C, and so prevent the outer ridge-poles from straining the canvas.

One of the best anchorages for the guy-ropes of a tent is made with the lock-stake and deadeye cleat shown at Fig. 17 A. A stake with a notch to hold the rope is driven into the ground, and another notched stake is driven in close to the head, so that when in far enough the notch in the latter will hold the head of the former as shown at Fig. 17 B. The deadeye cleat is cut from hard-wood seven-eighths of an inch thick, and is two inches wide, six inches long, and provided with two holes three inches apart. At one end a

FIG 14

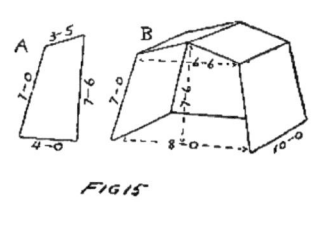

FIG 15

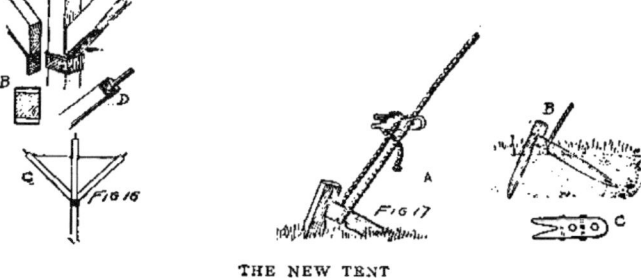

THE NEW TENT

jaw is cut, so that a rope may be caught in it as shown in Fig. 17 A. Steel-wire nails are passed through the holes indicated by the dotted lines in Fig. 17 C, and riveted at the point ends to strengthen the deadeyes.

The manner in which it is used is shown at Fig. 17 A, and if the holes are made the same size as the diameter of the rope, the harder you pull on the tent end of the rope, the more securely the deadeye cleat holds, and the loose end of the rope caught first in the jaw can be given a turn or two around the cleat to make it fast.

The double-peg anchorage is better than a single one, and with this new rope-fastener it will be an easy matter to stay a tent to withstand any wind-storm.

Canvas Cots and Hammocks

Cots are very necessary parts of the camping outfit, and may be made either of canvas and poles or of boughs and leaves. The canvas cot is, of course, much more comfortable than the one of boughs, but sometimes it is not possible to transport them, and then the bough bed must be resorted to.

A simple canvas cot is easily made from two pine or spruce sticks seven feet long, two inches in diameter, and free from knots or sappy places. A piece of light canvas or twilled cotton duck fifty-four inches wide and seventy-two inches long is sewed together so as to form a cylindrical case thirty-six inches wide and seventy-two inches long. Lay it flat and crease it along the edges, then run two or three lines of stitching along both sides four inches in from the edges. This forms the sleeve through which the poles are to be passed.

Crotched sticks are to be embedded in the ground to support the ends of the poles as shown in Fig. 18. These are to extend a foot or eighteen inches above the ground, and should be three inches in diameter and quite strong, so as to avoid breakage and a possible fall.

If a folding-cot with portable ends is desired, it can be made to appear as shown in Fig. 19 by constructing two folding ends, a middle pole, and four iron brace-hooks.

To make the cot twenty-six inches wide, procure the can-

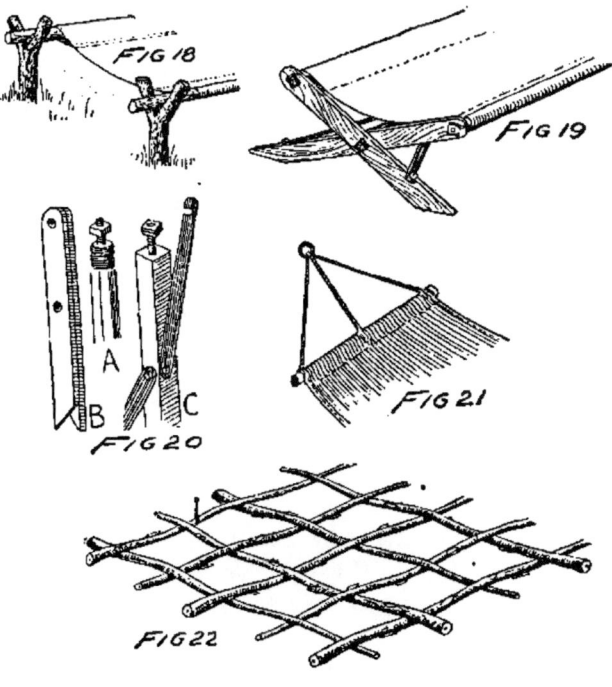

FIG 18

FIG 19

A

B C

FIG 20

FIG 21

FIG 22

vas and poles as directed for the first cot. Bind the ends of the poles with wire or have a blacksmith band them with iron ferrules, then bore the ends and drive threaded pins in, having nuts at the ends as shown at Fig. 20 A. From maple or oak two inches wide and an inch thick cut four legs thirty-two inches long, and bore holes at one end and midway between ends, as shown in Fig. 20 B, to receive the bolt ends in the poles. Bevel off the lower ends of the sticks and place them in opposite directions, so that when opened, in the form of an X, the ends will lie flat on the ground as shown in Fig. 19. From pine or spruce cut a stick two inches square, and provide the ends with bolts and nuts as shown in Fig. 20 C. This is for the under brace, and extends from end to end where the bolt passes through both legs, and is attached with a nut and washer.

From iron an inch wide and less than a quarter of an inch in thickness have a blacksmith cut four hook-braces eighteen inches long with a hole at one end and a notch at the other. With round-headed screws attach two of the braces near each end of the pole, as shown in Fig. 20 C, so that when the cot is set up the notches will hook over screws driven in the upper edge of each leg near the bottom as shown in Fig. 19. These will steady the cot, and prevent it from rocking from end to end as it would do if not braced.

A hammock that can be swung between the uprights of a tent is made of canvas thirty inches wide and seventy-two inches long. It is lapped over at the ends and sewed with several lines of stitching, so as to receive a two-inch bar to which the three ropes are made fast as shown in Fig. 21.

The end ropes should be twenty-four inches long and the middle one eighteen. From the bars at each end they are brought together and bound to rings which slip over hooks made fast to the tent uprights, or they can be lashed fast to the uprights. Any number of these hammocks may be made and easily carried, as they roll up snugly and occupy very little room in a bedding-kit. They are much easier to handle than a woven or braided hammock, the strands of which are forever catching in everything and anything with which they come into contact.

When making a cot of boughs the most satisfactory and comfortable affair is the basket-woven or lattice mattress of small, pliable saplings trimmed and interwoven as shown in Fig. 22. The long pieces should be alternated so that the large end of one stick will be next the small end of another, and thus distribute the strain evenly over the lattice. This arrangement applies also to the shorter or cross-pieces, and when finished the mattress is laid on a pair of poles supported with crotched sticks, as shown in Fig. 18, but without the canvas.

Over this lattice short twigs with clusters of leaves are spread, to make a soft mattress, and on these in turn a blanket or two can be spread and tied down at the corners, so that the leaves may not become dislodged.

Tables and Benches

Every boy should know how to make a table from some fence boards, a rail or two, and stakes for the legs. The table shown in Fig. 23 is made from three boards about eight inches wide and five feet long battened together at the ends and across the under side of the middle.

A rail is nailed across two tree-trunks thirty-two inches from the ground, to which one end of the boards are attached. Two stakes three inches thick are driven in the ground four feet from the trees, and across the upper ends of them a rail is nailed fast to support the other ends of the boards.

A larger table is shown in Fig. 24, and like the smaller one it is built against two trees. The boards, three or four in number, should be from six to eight feet long. They are nailed fast to four or five inch rails attached to the tree-trunks and to stout posts embedded in the ground. The middle of the table is supported by a batten, or rail, which is nailed fast to the top of a post embedded under the centre of the table.

Chairs made for camp life from rustic wood and pieces of board need not be so well constructed that any great amount of time should be expended on them, but they should be strong and serviceable.

A simple chair that any boy can make from branches or small tree-trunks, two or three inches in diameter, is shown in Fig. 25. The seat is eighteen inches high, sixteen inches square, and the back posts are thirty-six inches high. Two pieces of wood, eighteen inches long, are cut as shown at Fig. 26 A, and two more, thirty-six inches long, are cut as shown at B. The laps are cut out with saw and chisel so as to receive the seat-rails, the braces, and the back board, which are made fast with steel-wire nails as shown at C. The seat is made of ordinary boards nailed to the top edges

314

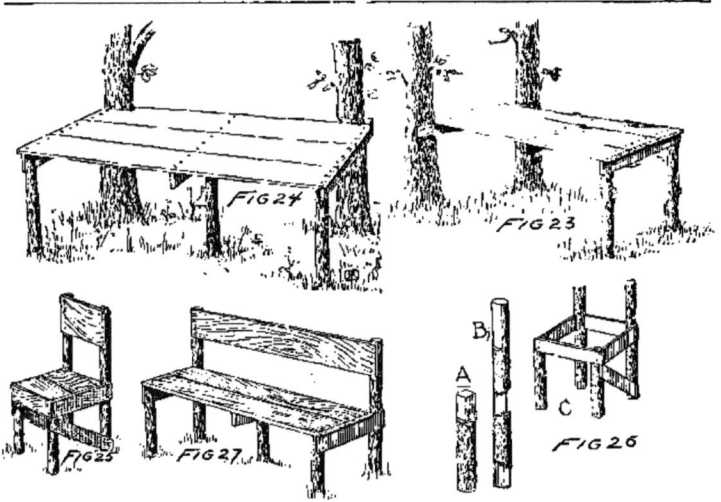

of the rails all around, and if the edge is smoothed off there will be less liability to tear one's garments.

In the illustration of a canopy (Fig. 10, page 301), a table and benches are shown. The table is thirty inches wide and five feet long, and it can be built either detached or fast to the ground. If the corner-posts are embedded a foot or eighteen inches in the ground it will make the table firmer and less liable to rack than if built loose or detached.

Two benches running the length of the tables are made in a similar manner to the chairs, but if the corner-posts or legs are to be embedded in the ground the side braces will not be necessary. The seat should be eighteen inches high, sixteen inches wide, and from five to eight feet long, as occasion requires, and with a middle brace it will appear as shown in Fig. 27.

Camping Equipment

In fitting out for a camping expedition it is always best to make a memorandum of the things you will need some time before you start, for so surely as you do not do this there will be some important things forgotten. The stuff that will fill an ordinary clothes-basket should be enough for a company of four boys, but for a greater number the supply must be increased accordingly.

In this list there must be included a kettle, two pans, tin or enamelled dishes, a frying-pan or two, a broiler, a wooden pail for water, and smaller tin pails; a lantern, candles, matches in tin boxes, hatchet or axe, blankets, knives and forks, spoons, and a few other culinary accessories. The dry groceries will have to be taken from home, unless they can be purchased near the camp or from some farm-house. From the latter it is generally possible to obtain butter, milk, eggs, a chicken or two, and other food that you may stand in need of if hunting or fishing fail you.

In Fig. 28, showing a corner of the tent, a portable table is supporting some of the things it would be well to have in camp, and while a boy may think that he knows what is wanted, it would be well for him to take his mother's or older sister's advice on the subject.

Lockers and Mess-kits

Lock-boxes with handles, in which to store dry groceries and foods, and mess-kits for the kitchen and dining ware, are among the most important parts of the camping outfit.

They may be made from ordinary well-constructed boxes, and provided with hinged lids, a hasp and padlock, and handles at either end by means of which they may be carried easily.

The lock-box shown in Fig. 29 A is eighteen inches wide, twenty-four inches long, and twelve inches deep, and with two thin boards four compartments are made as shown in Fig. 29 A. A lid is made of three boards and two battens, and securely attached to the box with strap hinges.

A hasp and padlock as well as two handles can be purchased at a hardware store and screwed fast to the chest.

A mess-kit may be made of a box with both lid and bottom nailed on securely. It is then sawed around three inches from one side, dividing it so that quite a little of the wood is fast to both sides. With hinges these are fastened together like a Gladstone bag, and on the inside, pockets and straps can be arranged to accommodate cooking-utensils and food-stuffs. Fig. 29 B shows this kit, and with a trunk-strap and a rope it can be easily carried from place to place.

For knives, forks, spoons, kettle-lids, and other small paraphernalia of the camping outfit a nest of pockets may be made from denim or unbleached muslin, like the one shown hanging on the wall in Fig. 28. The pockets are commodious and will accommodate many little things, and the nest can be folded over and tied at the corners with stout cord. A nest of this description should be three feet long, thirty inches high, and with three lines of pockets as shown in the illustration. The sewing should be done by hand with heavy linen or carpet thread, so that the stitching will not break.

317

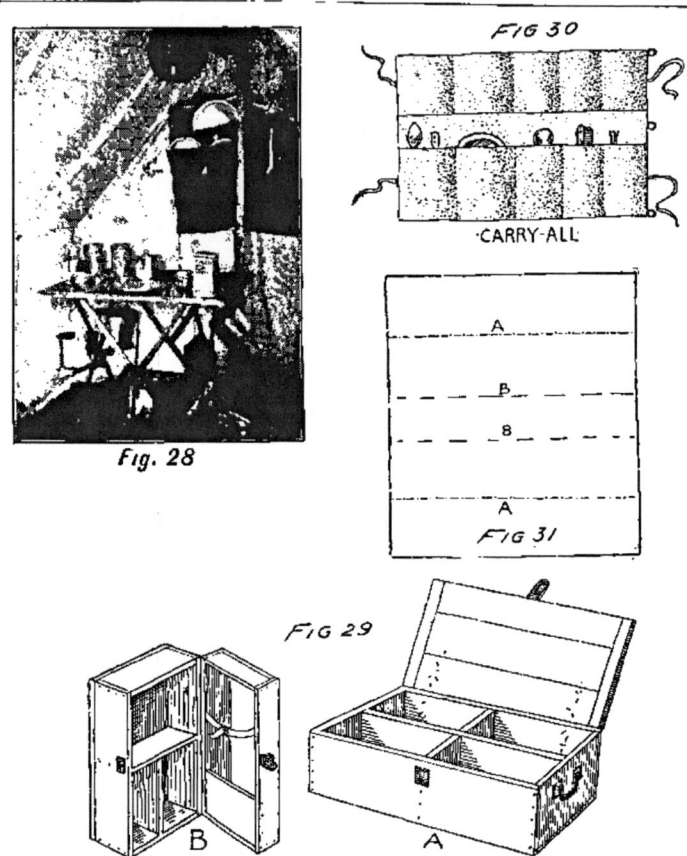

Fig. 28

FIG 30

·CARRY-ALL·

FIG 31

FIG 29

B

A

A carry-all (Fig. 30) is made of denim or light sail-cloth, and will be found the most convenient sort of a catch-all, for it may be folded over and rolled up, then bound with a shawl-strap to carry it easily.

A piece of denim a yard wide and forty-two inches long is folded at the dotted lines A A as shown in the plan (Fig. 31). The edges will then reach the lines B B. Sew the flaps at the two ends and divide the long pockets into smaller ones as shown in Fig. 30. Knives, forks, spoons, and a variety of small things can be kept in this nest of pockets, and when in camp it may be hung from one end by rings, so that the pockets occupy a horizontal position and the contents can be easily gotten at.

A Stone Stove and Camp-fires

The old-time tripod and kettle over an open fire of brush and logs is an unhandy means of cooking, for a sudden gust of wind will blow the smoke and sparks in all directions and dissipate the heat as well.

The up-to-date campers will make a stone stove similar to the one shown in Fig. 32. This holds the fire within the stone enclosure, and retains the greater part of the heat, which in the open fire is blowing to the four winds and giving very little benefit to the pot.

Flat stones should be used in the construction of this stove, and if it is possible to get some clay from the bed of a brook it can be used in place of cement for sealing the joints. This of course will make the fire burn better, as the only draught will then enter at the bottom, or doorway, through which the sticks are fed to the fire.

These doorways or draught-holes should be made on two or three sides of the stove, and when one is in use the others may be closed or left open, according to the strength of the wind and the direction from which it is blowing.

The pot should be hung on the ridge-pole so that it touches the top of the stove and holds in the heat. Fish may be fried in a pan or broiled much better than over an open fire, and water can be boiled quicker and coffee made easier.

This stove can be made either round or square, and if bricks are available for use they will be better than stones as the joints are closer and they are not so ungainly to handle. Over the stove a ridge-pole or bar should be supported on a yoked stick at one end and a twin-stick tripod at the other. The yoked or crotched stick is embedded in the ground, or it can be the sawed-off stump of a small tree. The lower ends of the twin sticks should be let into the ground for a foot or eighteen inches, so that the ridge-bar can be removed without its supports falling over.

Always build a fire or a stove in the shade, for it will not burn so well if the sun plays on it. In rainy weather a canopy over this stone stove will keep it dry and cause it to burn better than if exposed to the elements.

Here are some other ideas for camp-fires proper. Let us suppose that the party is provided with the necessary utensils for camp-cooking—a camp-kettle, coffee-pot, frying-pan, saucepan, and some sort of baking-pan. These should prove sufficient, unless the party intends having quite elaborate menus. If it is intended to remain at the camp only while cooking one or two meals, make your fire in this manner: Cut two green poles about five or six inches thick and about two feet long. In these cut notches about a foot apart. Level the ground where you intend to build your fire, and lay these poles down with the notches up and about three feet apart. Now cut two or three poles about four feet long and lay them in these notches. Gather a good

Fig. 33

FIG 32

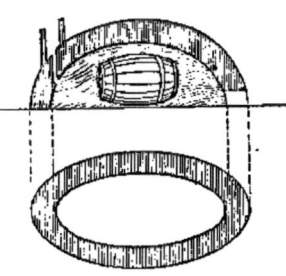

Fig. 34

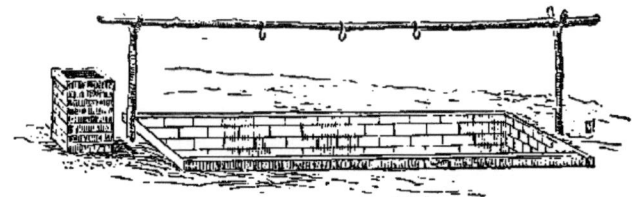

Fig. 35

supply of dry wood, grass, bark, or chips, and make your fire on the ground between the poles. The air will circulate under and through the fire, and the poles will prove just right to set your cooking-utensils on. Do not pile on wood by the armful. Add a little at a time, and you will find you can cook rapidly and well, and not burn your face and hands while attending to your cooking.

If it is intended to remain several meals at the camp it will pay to put up a crane. This is built in this manner: Cut two green posts two or more inches thick and three feet long, having forks at one end. Drive these into the ground at each end of your fire. Cut another green pole the same diameter and long enough to reach between the forks. Flatten the ends so that they will set snug in the forks.

The poles should be driven into the ground so that when the bail of the kettle is slipped on the crane the bottom of the kettle will just clear the fire.

If the camp is to be of a permanent nature, or it is expected to remain there for some days or weeks, it will be well to arrange for a better kitchen that will not be affected by the winds, the *bête noire* of camp-cooking. Dig a trench (cutting the sides square) as long as the distance between your uprights, and about eighteen inches wide and a foot deep. Make your fire in this hole, on the ground, and you will find that the wind will not worry you one-half as much as before (Fig. 33). If you wish to take the trouble, and the material is handy, the plan in Fig. 35 is a most excellent one to follow. Wall up the sides of the trench with brick, add a little chimney at one end, and get several iron "S" hooks from which to suspend your kettles. This will save the lifting of the crane every time you wish to handle the kettles suspended over the fire. By this method you will economize on fuel and save heat.

The plan used in the army for camp-cooking and described below is the best for all-around work. To make this kitchen takes more time and a little more labor, but in the end the laborers will be well paid for their work. It is particularly adapted for clayey soil. Dig a hole about three feet square and two feet in depth, generally in the slope of a hill. On one side run a shaft laterally, about one foot square and six feet in length, and one foot from the surface of the ground. At the extreme end sink a shaft vertically and form a chimney, and at equidistances pierce holes of sufficient diameter to prevent the kettles from slipping through. By this mode the kettles can be placed over the fire to boil, or on the side to simmer, with less difficulty than by any other means. Fig. 36 A and B.

I want to tell the young camper how to bake his own bread in camp, so if he camps far from a store or house where he can buy his bread he will not have to eat crackers, or those indigestion-producers, flapjacks, that the youthful camper knows how to make, or thinks he does. I have eaten many a one in my young days before putting on the "army blue," but their weight in gold would not induce me to eat some that I swallowed as a boy and thought "fine" We will assume that before going into camp your dear mother has taught you how to mix a batch of dough or a pan of biscuit. We will now make an oven in which to bake the bread or biscuit. A bank from four to six feet is the best for the purpose. Dig down the bank to a vertical face, and at the base excavate a hole, say three to four feet horizontally, care being taken to keep the entrance as small as possible. Hollow out the sides of the excavation and arch the roof,

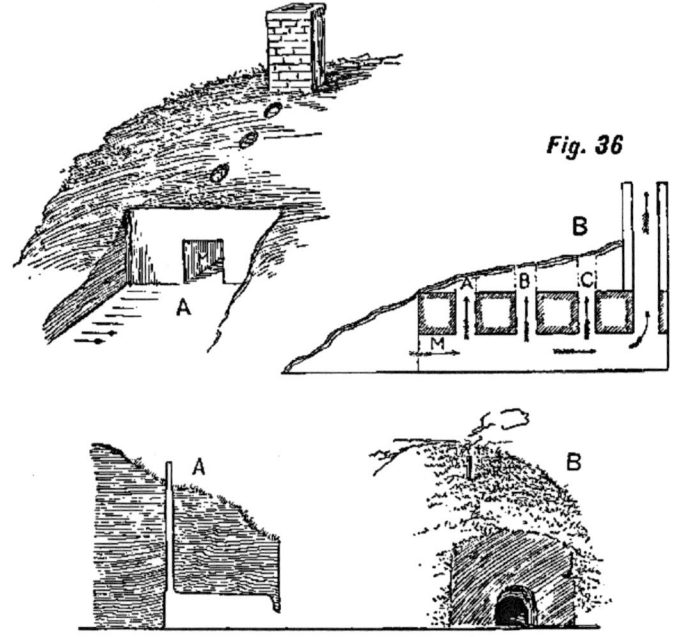

Fig. 36

Fig. 37

till the floor of the oven is about two feet wide and the arch about sixteen inches at the centre. Fig. 37 A and B.

Now carefully "tap" the back end for the chimney, and insert a piece of stove-pipe if handy. A hole from four to six inches will give a good draught. Wet the inside of the

324

oven, and smooth over the walls so that the mud presents a hard finish, and leave to dry for a day. When you are ready to bake, build a good fire in the oven, and when it is well heated remove the fire, scrape out all ashes, and place the pans of dough inside. Close up the entrance with a board, and cover with mud so as to keep in all the heat. With proper care this oven will last several weeks.

A bank may not be handy in which to build an oven of the kind described above; if such proves the case, it is not a difficult matter to construct a good oven on the level ground by following the method below. If a flour-barrel is handy, use it; if not, make use of willow twigs stuck in the ground and bent over so as to form a mould. Over the barrel or willow mould plaster a stiff mortar made of mud, commencing at the base. Lay it on about six inches thick. Allow it to dry for a day or two, and when nearly dry cut out a door at one end and the flue at the other. A small mud chimney will increase the draught if a piece of stove-pipe is not at hand. If a barrel has been used as the mould it may be burned out without danger to the oven. Carefully remove all dirt, and keep up a fire for half a day before attempting to bake. Fig. 34. (See page 321.)

Camp-cooking

Even the finest of camps is a dreary place unless the commissary department is well organized. "Uncle Harry," who is an old and experienced camper-out, gives some useful suggestions to his nephews, and other boys will doubtless appreciate his lectures on things culinary.

"Let us suppose," begins Uncle Harry, "that you have gotten the camp into ship-shape order, and after your hard day's work are ravenously hungry and very impatient for supper, or rather dinner, for the last meal of the day in camp is always the most important one. We will appoint Aleck as cook, and while he is busy over the fire neither of the others shall interfere with him or his duties, for no axiom is more true than that 'too many cooks spoil the broth.'

"Ben and Bob must see that the cook is well supplied with water and has plenty of small-split firewood close at hand. Then Bob will set the table, while Ben goes a-fishing and catches half a dozen trout or other small fry from the lake. In the mean time Aleck has pared and washed a dozen potatoes. These are placed in a kettle nearly full of water, and hung over the fire half an hour before supper-time. He will keep them boiling furiously until he can run a sliver of wood easily through the largest one. Then the water must be drained from them, and, still in the kettle, they must be set aside, but near enough to the fire to keep hot until wanted.

"Ben's fish all weigh less than a pound, and so are too small to do anything with but fry. After they are cleaned, Aleck rolls them in corn-meal and lays them carefully in the frying-pan, which is already on the stove, and in which a small quantity of cotton-seed oil is sizzling merrily. If you should have no oil, pork fat will do nearly as well, only have it boiling hot before placing the fish in it.

"Aleck has heard of half a dozen methods of making coffee, and hesitates before deciding which to try. He has been told to put his coffee in cold water and let it come to a boil, and that the coffee must not see the water until it is boiling; he has heard that coffee must never be boiled, and that the only way to extract its strength is to boil it; and so in thinking it all over he is much perplexed. Finally he remembers a method which his old uncle who is in the army has mentioned to him, and decides to try it."

"Oh, Uncle Harry, you are not a bit old," interrupts Aleck.

"In preparing coffee by his old uncle's method," continues Captain Archer, only noticing the interruption with a smile, "Aleck fills the coffee-pot with water, and sets it on the broiler wires, which he has laid across from one log to the other of the stove. While it is coming to a boil he measures out his coffee at the rate of a heaping table-spoonful for each cup to be made, puts it into his tin cup, pours in all the hot water it will hold, and sets it in a warm place on the stove. As soon as the water in the coffee-pot boils, he pours off some, so as to leave the pot about three-quarters full, and empties in his cupful of soaked coffee. Setting the pot back, he allows its contents to again come to a boil, and then lifts it from the fire. He pours out a tin cupful of the coffee, and pours it slowly back into the pot, throwing away the residue of grounds that remain in the cup. For about a minute, or while the rest of the dinner is being served, the coffee-pot stands in a warm place near the fire, and then its contents are ready for drinking.

"If either of you had wanted tea, Aleck would have put in the pot a teaspoonful of tea leaves for each cup to be made, poured boiling water over it, let it stand in a warm place two or three minutes, and it would have been ready for you.

"Here you have a plain, easily cooked dinner of fried fish, boiled potatoes, and coffee, to which you can add from your supplies bread and butter, or crackers, pickles, condensed milk, salt, pepper, and sugar. I think you will find it enough for a first experiment.

"For breakfast next morning you will have coffee, fried potatoes and breakfast bacon, and griddle-cakes."

"Oh, Uncle Harry, I can't make griddle-cakes," exclaimed Aleck.

"I think you can, if I tell you how, and you try hard. At any rate, you had better try, for they enter largely into the composition of camp meals. To make the simplest flour griddle-cakes, put into a pan a quart of your prepared flour, a teaspoonful of salt, a handful of corn-meal, a table-spoonful of brown sugar, two eggs, if you have them, and mix with cold water into a batter. Stir thoroughly until no lumps are left, and then fry on a hot griddle. In frying use as little grease as possible. More griddle-cakes are spoiled by the use of too much grease in frying than in any other way. A bit of pork rind or an oiled rag rubbed over the griddle is sufficient. Take turns in frying the cakes, so that two of you can be eating them as fast as they are done. They are only fit to eat when hot from the griddle.

"The cold boiled potatoes left from dinner the night before may be cut up and fried with half a dozen slices of breakfast bacon, and when all is ready you will have a breakfast to which I think three hungry boys will do ample justice.

"When you become tired of fish, catch frogs. They are considered delicacies on first-class tables, and add a pleasant variety to a woodman's fare. Catch them with a light rod,

328

short line, and small hook baited with a bit of scarlet flannel, or at night by use of a jack-light. Stupefied by its glare, they will let you pick them up. Kill your frog by a tap on the head, cut off his thighs and hind-legs, skin them, roll them in Indian-meal, and fry brown in hot oil or pork fat.

"You will also probably have an opportunity of adding squirrels to your bill of fare. When you have got your squirrel, chop off his head, feet, and tail, cut the skin crosswise of the back, and strip it off in two parts, fore and aft; also cut the body crosswise into two parts. Throw them into a kettle, and let the hind-quarters parboil until tender. Then fry them, until of a rich brown, in oil or pork fat, hissing hot. Use the fore-quarters for a stew.

"To make a stew use almost any kind of flesh or fowl. The chief thing to be remembered in making a stew is to stew it enough. An old camp jingle runs thus:

"'A stew that's too little stewed
Is understood to be no good.'

"Let your meat boil for more than an hour, or until it begins to fall from the bones. Add potatoes, pared and quartered, an onion sliced, salt, pepper, and a thickening made of flour and melted butter, to be stirred in gradually.

"In making a meat soup provide plenty of meat, and do not be afraid to let it boil. It is hard to boil it too much, and three hours is not too long. When nearly done, scrape a potato into the soup for thickening, and season with salt and pepper.

"To cook rice, let a cupful soak overnight. In the morning pour off the water in which it has soaked, place it in a kettle of cold water, and boil it slowly, without stirring, until the kernels are soft. Remember to salt it. Rice is good with condensed milk, sugar, butter, or syrup. It is good to add to your soups and stews, and it is particularly good when added to the batter from which you make your griddle-cakes.

"To make mush stir corn-meal into boiling water; season with salt. Eat hot with syrup. Save what is left over, and fry it next morning. The same rule applies to hominy.

"These are the rudiments of camp-cookery. Not an extended bill of fare, but I think you will find it appetizing and nourishing."

And the boys agreed with him.

The Care of a Gun

Aside from the pride and satisfaction which every sportsman should take in keeping his favorite weapon bright and free from spots, inside and out, it pays to keep a gun clean. The residue left in the barrel after firing contains acids, which will soon eat "pits" or spots in the metal, and when once started, it is almost impossible to prevent them increasing in size and number. When badly pitted, the recoil is increased by the roughness in the barrel. A gun can be cleaned by the following directions: The cleaning-rod should have at least three tools — a wool swab, a wire scratch-brush, and a wiper to run rags through. Have plenty of water at hand—warm if you have it, if not cold will do nicely. Put a swab on the rod, and some water in a tin basin or wooden pail. By placing one end of the

330

barrel in the water, you can pump it up and down the barrel with the swab. When it is discolored take fresh water, squeeze out the swab in it, and repeat the operation, until the water comes from the barrel as clean as it went in. If the gun has stood overnight, or longer, since using, it is best to put on the scratch-brush after the first swabbing, and a few passes with this will remove any hardened powder or leading. The next step is to fill the wiper with woollen or cotton rags, and dry the barrel thoroughly. When one set becomes wet take another, until they come from the barrel perfectly dry. Then stand the barrel on end on a heated stove, changing it from end to end, taking care that it does not become overheated. By the time it is well warmed up, the hot air from the stove will have dried out every particle of moisture left in the barrel. If no stove is at hand, the last set of drying rags used must be plied vigorously up and down the barrel until it becomes quite warm from the friction. Drying is the most important part of cleaning, and if the least particle of moisture is left in the barrel it will be a rust spot the next time the gun is taken from its case. The gun may now be oiled, inside and out, with sewing-machine oil or gun-grease, which can be had in any gun store. The woollen rags used for greasing soak up a great deal of oil, and should be dropped into the gun-cover for future use.

In regard to the safe handling of guns, almost all rules centre in that of always carrying the gun in such a way that if it should be accidentally discharged it would do no harm. If this rule is borne in mind, and strictly obeyed in the beginning, it becomes a habit and is followed intuitively. The gun may be carried safely on either shoulder, or in the hollow

331

of either arm, with a sharp upward slant. When momentarily expecting a bird to rise, and obliged to have the gun cocked, it should be carried across the breast with a sharp upward slope to the left. This is the only way the gun should be carried cocked. A breech-loader is so easily unloaded that there is no excuse for getting into a wagon or boat, or going around a house, without unloading. Never hand a loaded gun to any one who asks to look at it. Whenever you pick up any kind of a gun to examine it, always open it to see if it is loaded, and the habit will grow so that you will do this almost without knowing it. It seems needless to say never pull a gun towards you by the muzzle through a fence or out of a boat or wagon, yet the violation of this rule is the cause of more accidents than anything else. Never climb a fence with your gun cocked.

In learning the art of shooting on the wing—and this is the only way in which a shot-gun should be used—the following suggestions may be of some help, but no amount of printed directions can teach you to shoot. Practice is the best teacher. Nine out of ten young sportsmen shoot too quickly. A game bird rises with a startling whir of the wing (and sometimes when least expected), which gives the idea that he is making much greater speed than he really is. Beginners are apt to become excited, and throw up the gun anywhere in that direction, and blaze away with no definite aim. For this reason it is best to begin with blackbirds, rice-birds, and rails.

In almost every shot it is necessary to hold ahead of the bird, to allow for the time it takes to explode the cartridge and throw the shot to the bird. Even in this short space of time a cross-flying bird would be safely out of the shot circle if you aimed right at him. If a bird flies straight away from you, neither rising nor dropping, you should aim right at it. If flying straight across, you should hold well ahead of it. If quartering, still hold ahead, but less.

Many will ask how far to hold ahead, and this is a difficult question to answer accurately, as we have no means of knowing just how far ahead we do hold. One might say six feet and another six inches. What might appear to be an inch at the muzzle of the gun might really be a foot in front of a bird forty yards away. It must be learned by experience, and when accustomed to it the aim will be taken almost instantly, governed by the direction of flight, the speed of the bird, and the distance from the shooter.

It is best to ask permission of the owner to shoot over his land. You will seldom be refused, and will frequently be given permission to shoot over land which is posted "No Shooting." The land-owners know that it is the lawless hoodlums who do them damage.

Every true sportsman strictly obeys the game laws, and it is to his advantage to do so, although in many States the laws are practically a dead letter. Shooting out of season has nearly killed the game in many localities, when it would still be abundant if the game laws had been observed.

Chapter XIX

TRAPS AND TRAPPING

Snares and Deadfalls

THE ways of trapping are as various as the ingenuity of savage or civilized man can devise. I like best the traps that one can make. They seem to give the animal a fairer show; they develop our own constructive faculties; and the nearer we can get to the savage way the more fun it always is. Steel traps have a place that wooden traps can never fill; but give me something that I can make with my own hands, with the simplest tools, out of whatever materials the spot affords where the animal lives.

Of all the animals in this country there is none that affords less harmful sport than the rabbit—more properly hare—of which there are several species. Its wonderful powers of increase enable it to hold its own, as far too many of our best and most valuable animals do not. Further· more, rabbits are very easily trapped.

Every one knows its little trail, as broad as one's hand, through the bushes or broom-hedge, or its footprints as it hops over the clear snow. Here, where the path goes under a fence-rail, it has stopped to gnaw. The rabbit follows this path in season and out, though in the far North, where the snows keep piling and piling up, its little road may change with each successive snowfall. Trappers there put out a large number of snares, setting them right in the middle of these paths. In Fig. 1, No. 20 soft brass or copper wire is used—a piece say twenty inches long being bent into an oval or round noose some four inches through, the end being twisted around a convenient limb or root, or stick thrust into the snow over the path, and the space on each side bushed in with evergreen twigs, so that the rabbit will be sure to pass through the noose. Snares are easily taken up and set somewhere else after each snowfall. The best way is to rig the noose to a spring-pole (Fig. 2). The spring-pole that I have seen the Indian trappers make is simply a pole lashed to the side of a convenient sapling, the heavy end being high in the air, while the short end is caught under a stake with a crotch or little limb sticking out, driven into the ground at the side of the path. A "twitch-up" is a sapling bent down, but this generally needs to be held down in another way. On each side of the path a stake is firmly driven into the ground. About seven inches from the ground, and on the sides which face, a deep notch is cut into each stake, and a stick flattened at each end is placed across, like the letter H. The sapling is bent down, a strong cord fastened to the end, and tied around the middle of the cross-piece. The noose dangles below, clearing the ground by two inches (Fig. 3). If the pole is strong enough it lifts the game into the air out of reach of predatory animals. All stakes bearing strain of pulling must be firmly driven into the ground, or in wet weather they will pull out.

Rabbits, as gardeners know, are fond of carrots and other

vegetables, as well as apples.   There are many ways of rigging a snare with bait.   The trap is arranged so the rabbit puts its head through a noose, and springs the trap as it touches the bait.   One of the best traps I know of this kind

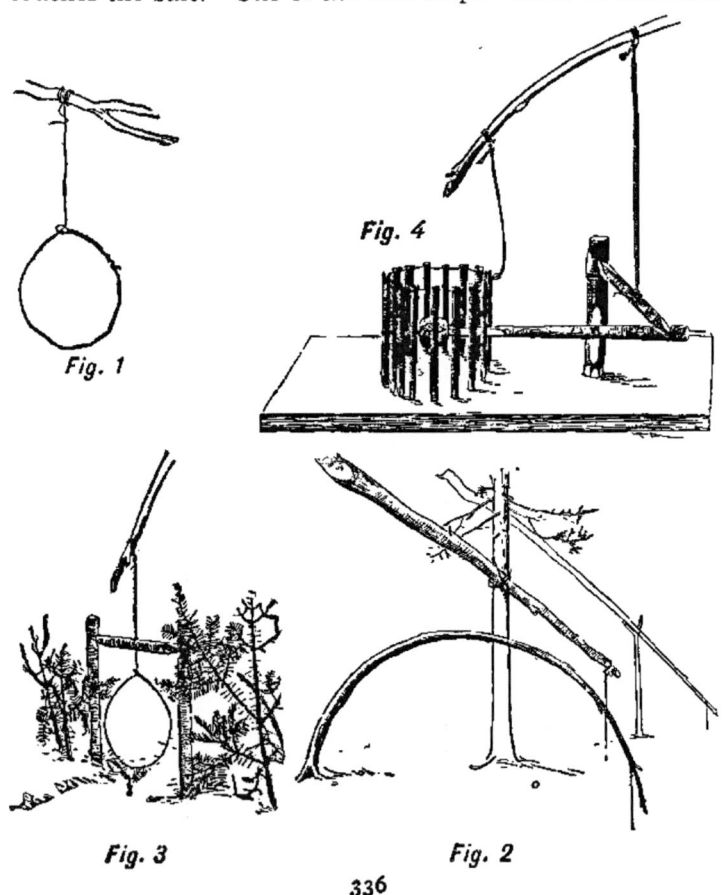

Fig. 4

Fig. 1

Fig. 3   Fig. 2

is called, in northern Vermont, a "French twitch-up" (Fig. 4). This trap can be made at home, and carried and set wherever needed. It is made as follows: Take a board about twenty inches long and ten inches wide. Measure off eight inches from one end, and with a pair of dividers describe a circle five inches in diameter. Around this circle bore holes three-eighths of an inch in diameter an inch apart, through the board, and drive in pegs five inches high. Five inches from the other end bore a larger hole, and set up a square peg (or a round one with flat side) seven inches high. Procure a half-inch stick long enough to reach from the centre of the circle of pegs to the upright and three inches beyond it. Screw this stick fast to the upright at a point two inches from the board—loosely, so it will work up and down, sharpening the end inside the pen, and cutting a notch on the upper side at the other end as shown in Fig. 4. Cut another notch near the top of the upright post, and fit into the two notches a half-inch stick with chisel-shaped ends. This arrangement resembles very closely the figure 4. A strong cord from the middle of this short stick leads to the spring-pole at a point about a foot from the end.

A noose of fine, soft wire or plaited horse-hair is fastened to the end of the spring-pole, and laid evenly around on the tops of the circle of pegs, which must be of an equal height. An apple or a carrot is speared upon the sharp end of the bait-stick. The rabbit smells the bait, puts its head over the fence and through the noose to take a nibble. When it touches the bait-stick, up goes the noose, and it is caught. But the snare on top of the little fence is likely to fall or be rubbed off, so a deep, sharp notch must be made into the top of every peg into which the noose fits. This is undoubtedly a Yankee improvement on a very old device. Formerly there was no pen and the noose was laid on the ground.

One of the very best traps for rabbits is a kind used in the South (Fig. 5). How often on a frosty morning would one's heart thump as one came into view and looked to see if the trigger was up and the door was down!

It is made of rough boards twenty to twenty-four inches long, one being an inch shorter, and all at least six inches wide, nailed into a long box. The rear being closed up with a board, and the top being an inch shorter, there is room for a door which slides up and down. Two thin strips are nailed upright to the front of the side-pieces, to keep the door from falling outward; small cleats inside complete a channel, in which the door slides easily up and down. Then with an auger or bit two holes are bored into the top five-eighths to one inch in diameter, one hole being nine inches from the front, the other nine inches to the rear of the first. Into the one next the door a stake is set up about ten inches high, with a crotch at the top. Then a stick eight inches long and as thick as a lead-pencil is cut; five inches from one end a cut is made half-way through, and a deep notch taken out the short end. This is dropped, notch upward, into the other hole. A stiff stick eighteen inches long is then cut, a string tied to each end, and then balanced in the crotch. The door is raised five inches, and one string tied to a nail in the top. The other string is tied to the upper end of the trigger, the notch of which is caught on the under side of the top board. The trap thus set is placed at right angles to the path, not directly in it. Foolish Bunny comes along. A good hole is

338

something a rabbit is ever on the lookout for. Here is a new one; he will look into it and see what it is like. It is not necessary to put even a carrot or an apple inside. He crowds in, butts his head against the trigger at the end, up it goes,

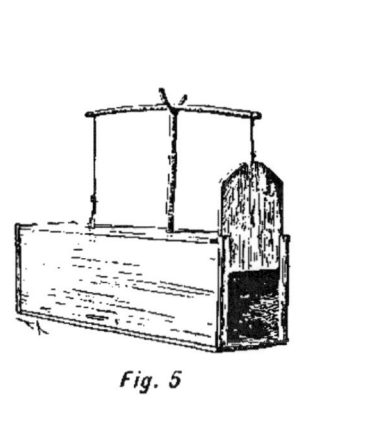

Fig. 5

Fig. 6

down drops the door behind, and he is fast. The trigger must be set under the front edge of the hole, otherwise the rabbit will not be able to push it from him.

Instead of a box, a section of a hollow log, called in the South a "gum," may be used, two stakes being driven in front to hold the door. Fig. 6.

The muskrat is an abundant animal about ponds, ditches, and the banks of sluggish streams. It is easily trapped. They remind one of little beavers, and if their fur was not so very common it would be more highly prized, for it is really soft and fine. If one can find their runway (a path eight or nine inches wide along which they travel from place to place) one can always capture them by the same kind of trap that an Indian sets for beaver and otter, as well as for musquash. He calls it the "*kilheg'n.*" Fig. 7.

Drive two stakes two feet or more high and at least an inch thick into the ground three inches apart at one side of the path. Opposite these two sticks drive in two more, and lay a stick across between them, pushing it down nearly level with the path for a bed-piece. Then get a pole of any length whatever, lay the butt end across the path on top of the bed, hewing the sides flat, if necessary. See that it rests evenly on the bed, and keep the other end in place with a stake driven on each side. This pole is called the "fall."

Lash each pair of stakes together at their tops with rope or tough bark or withe, to prevent spreading, and lay a stiff stick across. Cut a half-inch straight stick and lay it on top of the bed, lashing one end loosely to the stake, leaving the other end free to rise and fall. This is the trigger. Now for the "crooked stick." It is a stick as long as from the bed to the cross-piece, and has a sudden bend at the upper end. Often one can find a small sapling an inch through with just the right bend at the end. Notch it as shown in Fig. 8. Tie a stout cord or withe around the fall, raise the same nine or ten inches, lay the crooked stick over the cross-piece, and tie the withe fast. Then bend the other end of the crooked stick towards the ground, and catch the top of it behind the trigger, which is raised just enough (two inches) for the

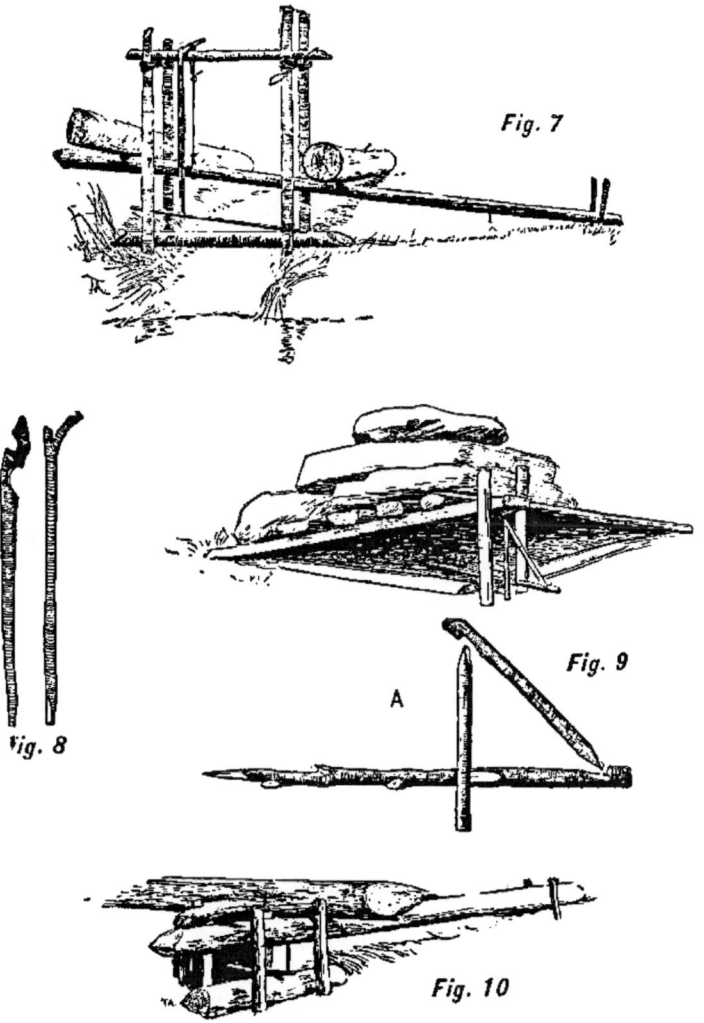

Fig. 7

Fig. 8

Fig. 9

A

Fig. 10

SOME USEFUL TRAPS

purpose. When the rat comes along it steps on the trigger, freeing the crooked stick, whereupon the fall drops and pins the creature there. Heavy weights should be piled upon the fall alongside the path, and the sides should be brushed in to keep the animal from going around. No bait is required for this trap.

Alongside of their pond on a level spot contrive another trap (Fig. 9) in the following manner:

Take a flat stick, about two inches wide, lay it on the ground, and close to one end drive an upright stake on each side. Let them stand some six inches high. Then, beginning close to the two stakes, lay a two-foot stick at right angles, its end resting on the first one. Alongside of this lay another stick a little shorter, continuing thus, and making each successive stick shorter, until the end of the sticks is reached, thus forming a three-cornered platform, which is then weighted with heavy stones. Construct a figure 4 (Fig. 9 A) out of sticks as thick as one's finger, making the bait-stick eighteen or twenty inches long. Set the figure 4 under the platform at the very end of the stick, the bait-stick passing between the upright stakes. Bait with a carrot, a parsnip, apple, etc., and a rat should be there in the morning.

If the trap does not lie flat on the ground place sticks under it. This same trap, baited with a fowl's head or a bird or meat, is also useful as a skunk-trap, being placed in the woods near their burrows.

The mink is another common animal, and it is found by almost every brook-side. It is a great traveller, following the stream, feeding upon fish, and picking up a bird or mouse whenever opportunity affords. For a trap I take two round poles six to eight feet long, and about three inches thick at the butt. On a level spot, never more than a few feet away from the water, I drive a stake firmly into the ground, and lay the two poles, butts together, one on top of the other, against the stake, and drive two more stakes on the other side about six inches apart. Sometimes when the ground is soft two stakes (Fig. 10) should be driven in front instead of one. A stick a foot long will serve equally well for the bed-piece. Then a pen or house is built of stakes, or long chips, or stones, or pieces of board in the form of a V or ⊓, about nine inches tall, eight inches deep, and six inches wide. Then two sticks are prepared—one three inches long and half an inch thick, called the "standard" (Fig. 12), the other eight inches long, and of the same thickness, called the bait-stick, one end being sharpened, the other flattened. The bait, the head of a fowl or fish, is tied to the sharp point of the bait-stick. The fall is raised, the standard set sideways on the flat end on the bait-stick, and the fall lowered, until it rests on top of the standard, the bait-stick being inside the house. As the sticks are arranged, the mink, entering over the bed and under the fall, will have to give quite a pull before dislodging the standard on which the fall rests. So take a peg, cut a notch into it near the top deep enough to secure the bait-stick, and drive it into the ground inside the pen and close to one side. Now the standard can be set much nearer the outer end of the bait-stick, and the moment the bait is tugged at, the bait-stick flies from under the notched peg, and down comes the fall. The bed may be hewn to an edge on top, and the parts of the trap should work without a hitch. A stone, or board, or sheet of bark, or a handful of evergreen boughs should be laid over the house, not only to keep the animal out, but also the rain and snow from the triggers which may freeze up and stick fast. Two pegs driven into the ground at the end of the fall will hold it in place, and, like every deadfall, it should be heavily weighted with logs as shown in Figs. 10 and 11.

There are many different ways of building traps with this simple bait-stick and standard—a combination in general use in the fur countries. Some are made large for fishers, and set on logs and high stumps for sable or marten. In Canada, where the snow is very deep, I have seen long lines of sable-traps on stumps seven feet from the ground, the other end of the fall resting on another stump of the same height. In such cases a tree is cut for the purpose, and by a skilful way of chopping, the stake in front of the trap is left standing as part of the stump, and the chips are sharpened and driven into the top of the stump for the house.

Again, a hollow is chopped into a tree, a stake driven in front, and the bait-stick thrust inside.

There are many other deadfalls in use. Among the most deadly is what may be called the "wigwam." It is thus constructed: With a hatchet or an axe break some small sticks, and driving them into the ground in the shape of a crescent build the bait-pen or house. Bring them together at the top as in Fig. 13. Next cut a green stick about four inches in diameter and about eight feet long. Lay in front of the pen, directly up against it. Peg it firmly there by driving wooden pins against it at the ends. So much done.

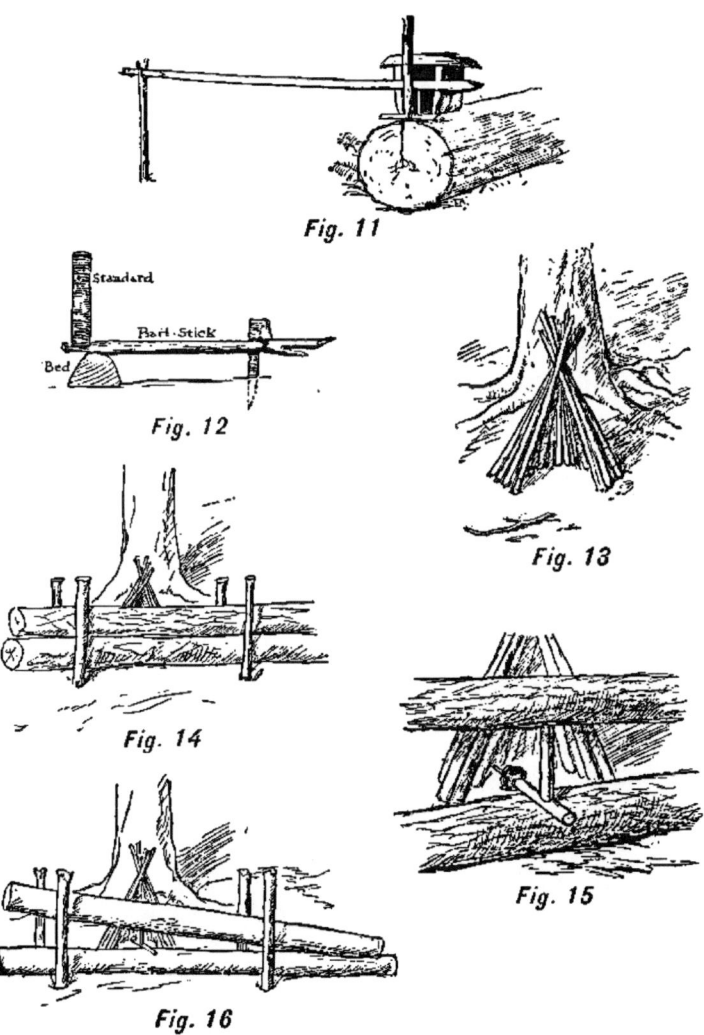

Fig. 11

Standard

Bait-Stick

Bed

Fig. 12

Fig. 13

Fig. 14

Fig. 15

Fig. 16

DEADFALLS

Now get another stick of the same length and lay it on top of the first pole. Fix it in position by driving pins against it as in Fig. 14. When this is finished take two small, round sticks or twigs, cut one about five inches in length, and the other near ten inches, or the depth of the bait-pen. Raise the top log and lay the longer of the little round twigs on it, with the end on which the bait is to be placed on the inside. The ends of the little twig must be round. Set it on end, with the upper end resting on the upper log and the lower end resting on the first little stick as in Fig. 15.

When an animal comes to get the bait he has to put his fore-legs into the pen, and the minute he touches the bait the upper log falls, catching him in the centre of the back. Skunks can be easily caught this way without the least smell. Spikes may be driven through the upper log for large game. Fig. 16 is a variation of the same idea.

Woodchucks or ground-hogs will be attracted to a trap by baiting with their favorite food; but they soon go into winter quarters, from which they do not emerge until spring. There are special traps for other animals and birds. Good judgment, knowledge of the appearance and the food and habits of the bird or animal are necessary to success in trapping, as well as an eye quick to recognize the signs of the game, particularly their runways.

Traps in cold countries need not be visited oftener than once a week, but if they are near home most boys like to go to them every day. Skinning can best be done at home. The curing of skins is a matter of great importance if the fur is to be sold, for dealers will only pay for good fur properly prepared. It must be "prime"—that is, from November to the middle of April (water fur a fortnight later) the inside of the skin will be white and the fur thick and glossy; at other times it becomes dark and thin and the fur poor. Muskrats,

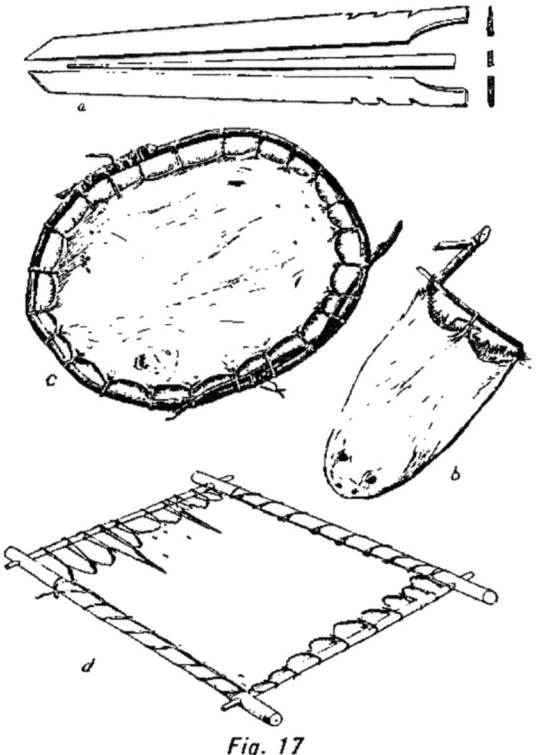

Fig. 17

mink, sable, foxes, weasel, opossum, and skunk require to be *cased*—that is, without any cut down the middle. Wolf, badger, raccoon, bear, beaver must be *open*. The manner

347

of preparing *cased* fur is to make a cut around the ankles, then a slit down the back of the leg to the tail, the skin to be peeled off the legs and the root of the tail to be put into the end of a split stick and the core pulled right out. Then the skin is pulled off over the head. In the case of certain animals, like the mink and muskrat, there is a scent-bag near the tail which is liable to get cut, with unpleasant consequences, so the best trappers prefer to remove the hide by commencing at the lips and peeling it off through the opening of the mouth, making no other cut in the skin save at the legs, when the skin is opened by a cut from leg to tail as at the start. The muskrat may be stretched on a pliant stick three feet long, bent into a bow, and the skin, fur inward, pulled over it. The legs are slitted and caught over notches in the side, and one end of the stick is bent squarely across and fastened either into the split top of the other or into a notch, and the loose middles of the skin tied up to the cross-piece. Fig. 17 *b*.

For mink, etc., never use a single board—it may tear the skin—but make a double stretcher (Fig. 17 *a*). Take a half-inch board of pine or cedar, two feet long and three inches wide, and taper it to two inches at one end and shave the outside almost to an edge. The board is then split in half with a saw; where no saw is at hand the two pieces are whittled out separately. The stretchers are now put into the skin, and the legs pulled out as far as they will go and tacked in place, or a slit made in each and the leg hooked over a notch in the edge of the stretcher. Then a wedge two feet long, an inch wide, and tapering to a point is inserted between the stretcher, and driven down until the skin is as tight as a drum-head. The middles are then tacked fast, and a square-pointed stick inserted into the tail. If the boards threaten to collapse, two short sticks with ends lashed together pushed over them will keep them flat. The tail-piece (Fig. 18) shows a mink-skin properly stretched. A fox-stretcher will be exactly twice the dimensions of the mink-stretcher; others in proportion. The raccoon, bear, etc., is skinned by a cut from chin to tail, cuts being made up the legs at right angles to the cut, and stretched upon a square frame (Fig. 17 d) by means of a lacing of cord or tough bark. Formerly all open skins were stretched on the hoop-stretcher (Fig. 17 c), but now only the beaver is treated that way.

Skins must never be dried in the sun nor by a hot fire. Nor should any preservatives whatever be applied, not even salt, until ready for tanning. All fat should be removed. taking care for knife-cuts.

Fig. 18

Chapter XX

TREE HUTS AND BRUSH-HOUSES

THE most delightful season in the woods, throughout the northern and middle parts of the United States, is during the summer months, and in the South right up to Christmas; while in other parts of the country, through southern Texas and California, the woods are attractive all through the year.

Brush-houses, sylvan retreats, and tree huts of various kinds are made by boys all over the country, and some very unique and original ones are often constructed from simple and inexpensive materials. Everything from the back-yard "lean-to" and the tent of sheets to the tree huts that are inaccessible when the rope-ladder is drawn up may be made by boys who are at all handy with tools, and a well-built tree hut is an ideal place in which to spend one's vacation days.

The following ideas and suggestions may be of service, and they have all been tested in practical experience.

A Low Twin-tree Hut

A very serviceable twin-tree hut is shown in Fig. 1, and it can easily be constructed, at a small cost, from ordinary boards and timbers. If it is built high up in the trees it is doubly secure from invasion, for the ladder can be drawn up when the owners are at home and it will be a difficult matter for outsiders to enter.

To properly build this hut select a location between two trees six to eight feet apart. The trees should have comparatively straight trunks at least fifteen inches in diameter, and no cavities at the base nor indications of decay.

With an axe clear off the brush and small branches for twenty feet up from the ground at the inside of the trunks, or where the hut is to be located. From a lumber-yard obtain four or five pieces of spruce or other timber two inches thick, eight inches wide, and sixteen feet long. Saw off and nail two of these pieces to the trunks of the trees eight feet above the ground, first cutting away some of the bark and wood of the trunk to afford a flat surface for the timbers to lie against on each side. Six-inch steel-wire nails will be required for these anchorages, and under the timbers and lying flat against the tree-trunks bracket-blocks two-by-eight inches and fifteen inches long are securely spiked to lend additional support to the cross-timbers.

Cut two timbers six feet long and two others the length of the distance between tree-trunks. In the six-foot pieces cut notches at the under side as shown in Fig. 2 C C. Into these the ends of bracket-timbers D D will fit. Cut the ends of the timbers forming the square frame so that they will dovetail as shown in Fig. 3. Spike the six-foot timbers to the tree-trunks so that they will rest on the first two timbers that were nailed to the trees, and from the two-by-eight-inch wood cut four brackets D D, and spike them

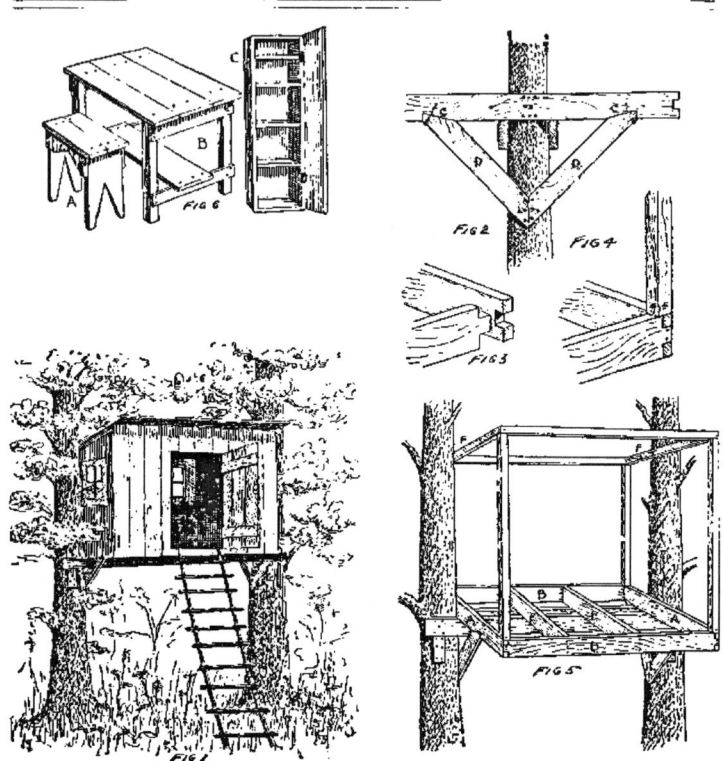

fast under each cross-timber so each tree will appear as shown in Fig. 2. Place the remaining two timbers in position so that the ends will fit into those fastened to the trees, and nail them fast as shown in Fig. 4.

In Fig. 5 the first timbers can be seen spiked to the tree-trunks, where they are supported by the fifteen-inch blocks nailed fast below them. The cross-timbers are shown at

A A, and the last ones, forming the frame that are let into dove-tailed joints at the ends, are shown at B B. Cut two more timbers E E, and lay them across the supporting timbers, nailed to the tree, so they will fit inside the front and back timbers B B, where they are to be well secured with long nails. The floor frame will then be complete.

From two-by-three-inch spruce construct a frame seven feet high at the front, six feet at the back, and spike the side timbers F F, forming the top, to the inside of the tree-trunks as shown in Fig. 5. The bottom of the uprights are to be mounted on the corners of the floor frame as shown in Fig. 4, where four long nails will hold them securely in place.

Cut two timbers and arrange them in an upright position at the front thirty inches apart, where the door will come, then half-way between the floor and top of the framework run a timber all around except between the door timbers. This will add a strengthening rib to which the sheathing boards can be nailed, and will also make one more anchorage to the tree-trunks. The side-rails should be spiked to the tree-trunks in a corresponding manner to that of the top or roof-strips. From a lumber-yard obtain some four, six, or ten inch matched boards, planed on both sides, and use them for the floor and sheathing.

The roof may be made from the same kind of boards, and over them a thickness or two of tarred paper is to be laid and fastened down at the edges and seams with small metal washers and nails that can be had where the paper is purchased. This will make the roof water-tight, for a season at least; and if it is given one or two coats of paint it will preserve the paper so that it may last for several years.

Two or three windows twenty-four inches square may be placed in the back and sides of the hut above the middle rib; and a door of boards held together with battens, as shown in the illustration, is to be made and hung with long, stout strap-hinges. A knob lock or a hasp and padlock will keep the door closed when the hut is unoccupied. When in use a wooden button will hold the door shut from the inside.

A ladder of hickory poles and cross-sticks should be made twenty inches wide and provided with loops at the top that will fit over large nails driven in the door-sill, so as to keep it from slipping when it bends under the weight of a boy.

Where the rungs join the side-rails of the ladder the union is made by lashing the cross-sticks fast with tarred rigging or stout cotton line. If a flexible ladder is preferred ropes may be used in place of the side-rails to which the rungs are lashed fast. When the owners are at home the ladder can be drawn up and hung on nails driven in the front edge of the roof. If a rope-ladder is used it can be drawn in and rolled up.

Inside of the hut, at either end, a seat eighteen inches wide should be built in about sixteen inches up from the floor. These seats can be used as bunks if desired. Some narrow shelving should be arranged over the windows and fastened there with brackets, on which small things may be kept.

A small table may be made from some ends of the sheathing boards and two-by-three-inch spruce sticks; and boxes may be used for seats, or small benches can easily be knocked together as shown in Fig. 6 A. Under the table a ledge

A HIGH TWIN-TREE HUT

twelve inches wide is to be attached to the lower cross-rails that connect the legs as shown at Fig. 6 B.

A wall-nest may be made from a shoe-case in which four or five shelves are arranged as shown in Fig. 6 C. A door made from the box-cover is attached with hinges, and a catch or hasp will keep it closed.

A High Twin-tree Hut

Twelve or fifteen feet above the ground, and built in between the trunks of two stout trees, a high tree hut is shown in Fig. 7. Larger and more substantial trees must be selected to build this hut in than the ones for the low hut, and as a rope-ladder will probably be used a landing-deck or piazza should be built at the front of the hut.

While this hut is built between two trees it is also built against them, as the trunk of each tree can be partially enclosed in the hut. The under cross-timbers that support the floor frame are to be attached to the trees the same as described for the low tree hut, and on these the other timbers are laid and fastened as shown in Fig. 8. The main timbers extend beyond the outside of the trunks, and the supporting and floor timbers enclose each trunk. At the front the frame is carried forward two feet more than at the back, allowing this much for the width of the deck. The uprights are arranged somewhat differently also, as they are bound at the top to scantlings that butt into the trunks. Fig. 8 A A.

Instead of a flat roof like the low hut, this one is to have a pitched roof, the supporting timbers of which are attached to the ridge-poles B B, which are fastened to the tree-trunks in the same manner as the under cross-timbers. This construction is clearly shown in Fig. 8, where the location of each upright and cross-piece is indicated.

A rail is run along the front and one end of the deck, and is fastened at the top of four uprights of two-by-three-inch spruce, the lower ends of which are securely nailed to the front stringers as the illustration shows.

In place of the supporting brackets D D that are let into the timber C at Fig. 2, longer brackets or props are caught under the floor timbers and braced at the lower end against the trunks, where an additional anchorage or support is made by a stout block which is securely spiked to the trunk underneath each bracket end as shown in Fig. 8 C C. The frame is then enclosed as described for the low hut, and windows and a door are mounted as shown.

A long, stiff ladder may be used to climb up, but a more interesting ladder can be made of rope and hickory rungs. By means of a thin rope attached to the bottom rung the ladder can be hauled up to the deck so that it is out of the reach of other boys; and being fastened at the top, no one can remove it or pull it away as they could a stiff ladder.

A rope-ladder is made of stout clothes-line and hickory rungs lashed together securely with strong line as shown in Fig. 9. The rungs are of straight hickory with or without the bark on, one inch and a quarter thick and twenty-four inches long. Near the end of each rung a notch is cut on both sides for the rope to lie in, as shown at the upper end of Fig. 9, and each union is to be very securely bound with the line so as to prevent slipping.

The ladder is hung on stout wooden pegs driven into the deck through holes one inch and a half in diameter. An extra rope is to be carried from the top rung up over the pegs and down again, where a wrap is taken over one or two

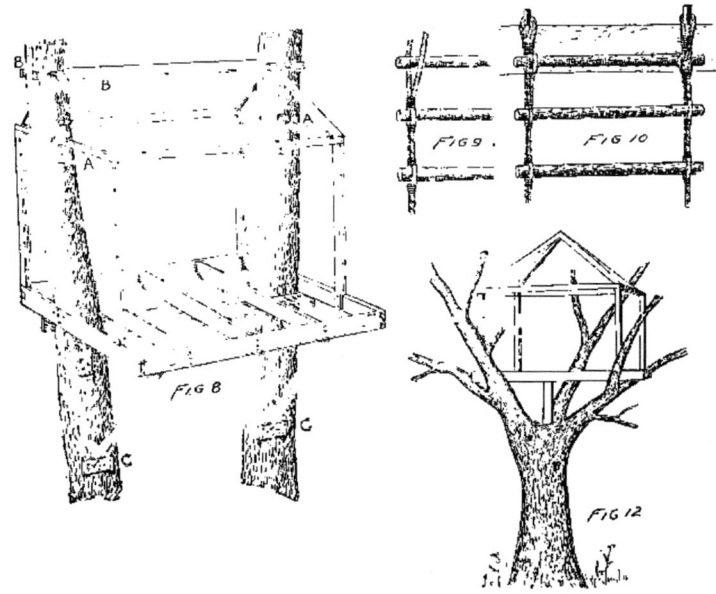

FIG 9.

FIG 10

FIG 8

FIG 12

rungs; then it is lashed fast to the other ropes with the stout line as shown in Fig. 10.

Bunks and furniture can be made for the interior, and any other convenient accessories to the comfort and pleasure of the boy owners may be added as need arises.

A Single-tree Hut

In the spreading branches of a large oak-tree a very snug roost can be made high above the ground as shown in Fig. 11 (frontispiece).

This single-tree hut is twenty-five feet above the ground, and below it is a landing from which the rope-ladder is dropped. From this landing to the piazza or deck of the hut a stiff ladder is made fast both at top and bottom, and an opening in the floor of the deck will allow room to climb up on the deck.

As very few trees are alike it would be difficult to give a plan for the floor timbers among the out-spreading branches; but from the plans shown for the twin-tree hut some idea of the construction can be had for single-tree huts.

The main tree-trunk will, of course, have to project up through the hut, and the location in the tree should be selected so that out-spreading branches will form a support to the lower edges of the floor frame as may be seen in Fig. 12, the plan of a low tree hut.

A peaked, a mansard, or a flat roof can be placed on the hut, depending on the main trunk to give it support; and if the space in the tree will permit, a deck across the front and both sides will be found useful. The floor timbers should be well braced to the main trunk of the tree with long and short bracket-pieces or props. These will help greatly in making the hut steady in the tree, and where the lower ends are attached to the trunk large spikes should be well driven in. Cleats or blocks can be nailed fast under the

359

ends also, as they will help to support and strengthen the anchorage.

Water and food can be kept cool by suspending them in a shady place. Water in a porous jug or earthen pitcher will keep very cold if hung in the tree branches where the air can freely circulate around it. Keep fire away from the tree huts, and do not light any matches nor burn candles, for if once a fire is started nothing will save your hut. It is too high to reach with a bucket, and, located as it is, a perfect draught will fan a small flame into a raging fire in no time.

A Low Single-tree Hut

It is not always best to build a hut in high trees, nor is it possible to do so in every case, because there may not be any high, large trees at hand strong enough to support a hut. For younger boys a low tree hut is preferable, so that if a possible misstep should result in a fall it would be less harmful than from a high tree. An apple or maple tree often affords a good support for a low tree hut, and if the trunk is substantially heavy a house similar to the one shown in Fig. 12 (page 358) can easily be constructed. The tree should be large enough to bear the weight of the house without straining it, particularly in a storm or high wind.

The general construction of the frame is shown in Fig. 12. The frame should be of two-by-three-inch spruce and the flooring beams can be of two-by-four-inch spruce or other timber. One or two windows and a door may be arranged in the hut, and tar-paper tacked on the roof will make it water-proof.

Access to the hut can be had by means of a ladder made from two-by-three-inch spruce rails with hickory rungs, or two-by-one-inch hard-wood sticks securely nailed to the rails.

A Brush-house

In nearly every part of the country where there is low ground one may generally find a high growth of plant life having a long stalk, with the greatest number of leaves at or near the top. Artichokes, cat-tail reeds, wild sunflower, and the stronger species of flag have stalks and reeds sufficiently strong from which to make the sides and roof of a hut or small house such as Fig. 13 depicts.

This growth is often ten feet high, and will have a straight and uniform reed at least seven or eight feet up from the ground before the thick top foliage reduces it in size. This last should be cut away and the smaller under branches and leaves trimmed off, leaving a comparatively straight shaft from six to eight feet long. This will be limber enough to be woven basket-fashion, and quite stiff enough to hold the thatching of meadow-grass or cat-tail reeds.

To build a brush-house like the one shown in the illustration, four sticks are to be set in the ground about six feet apart, forming a square. These should be eight feet long and sunk two feet into the ground, the upper ends being bound together with rails two inches wide and an inch thick.

A pitch can be given to the roof by cutting off the rear posts six inches and leaving six inches more of the front posts out of the ground, thereby allowing a pitch of one foot

A BRUSH-HOUSE

to the six-foot length of roof. This slant is not necessary, however, and the roof may be flat if it is easier to make.

From the reeds a basket framework with eight-inch meshes is to be woven, as the boys are doing in Fig. 14. Three of these frames are to be made for the sides and rear of the hut, and at the front, above the doorway, a smaller one is to be made to cover the space between the front posts.

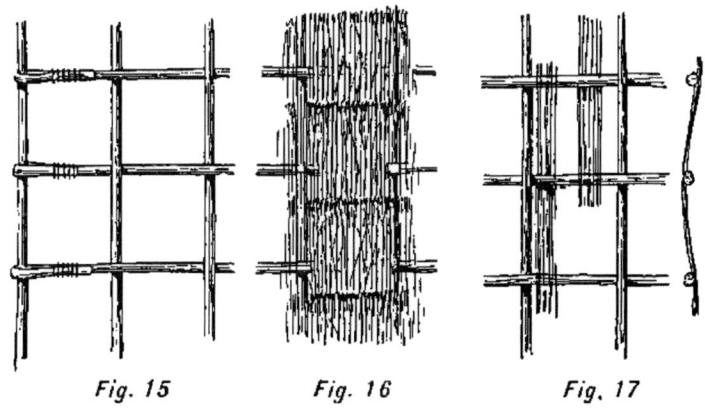

Fig. 15   Fig. 16   Fig. 17

The ends of the cross-reeds are to be bent around the end upright reeds as shown in Fig. 15, where they can be bound with string or tied with grass. The window openings in the side frames are made by cutting out a section of one or two uprights and turning the cross-reeds back and tying them. At the doorway two upright sticks are driven into the ground and a rail nailed across their upper ends.

To this wooden frame the front reeds may be attached, and the skeleton hut or house is then ready to be thatched

363

with long, dry grass or dried cat-tail reeds. The thatching is done by interweaving long grasses or reeds between the cross-reeds in a vertical position as shown in Fig. 16. The thatching material should be from eighteen to twenty-four inches long so that it can be interwoven between three cross-reeds as shown in Fig. 17, where a few strands of grasses are placed in position to give an idea of how to weave the grass.

Timothy or straw can be used to good advantage for thatching material, and if it is employed it should be woven with the heads up and not too close together, as the air should get through the thatching to keep the occupants of the hut cool. Of course a house may be made larger or smaller than the one described, but the principle of good construction is the same. Never depend on the four sides to hold together without the corner-posts, as the first good

wind that happened along would blow it flat, and perhaps beyond the possibility of repair.

The edges of each side are lashed fast to the corner-posts with grass or string, and when the roof is made it should be lashed fast to the top of the sides and front with long reeds or grass.

The roof is woven the same as the sides but is thatched closer; and about four inches of the roof should extend over the sides, front, and rear.

A Brush "Lean-to"

The general lines of a miniature barn are shown in the illustration of a brush "lean-to" (Fig. 18). This is con-

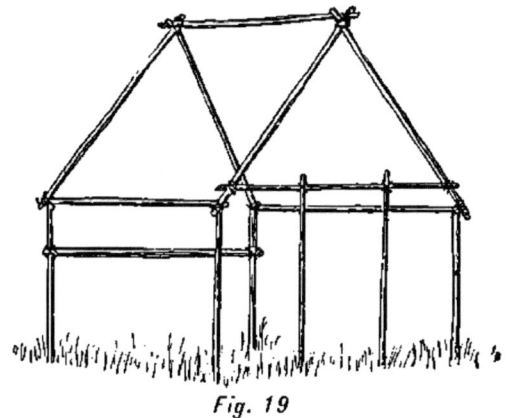

Fig. 19

structed in nearly the same manner as the brush-house, and thatched with grass or reeds as shown in Figs. 16 and 17.

The corner-posts are three feet high, the ridge-pole seven feet and six inches above the ground, and the hut may be from five to eight feet square or made oblong, as a matter of choice.

A frame of scantling should be made for this lean-to the same as if a wooden structure were to be built, and it must be nailed together well to stand the strain of the wind blowing hard against it. In general construction the frame should appear like Fig. 19; and to the sticks the edges of the thatched framework of reeds is to be lashed fast with grass, either before or after the thatching is done.

A brush-house or any hut built on or near the ground is not so cool to stay in as one in the trees, but it is, of course, much easier to construct, as the boy builders do not have to move about so carefully when at work, and their materials can be picked up quickly.

Brush huts and houses can be built on the plains where trees are scarce, but in a country rich in woods and forests the boys prefer the tree huts, not only for their cool location, but on account of the romance involved in the climbing up to an inaccessible eyrie.

Chapter XXI

WALKING-STICKS

How to Grow Them for Pleasure and Profit

HERE are some suggestions for an entirely new and fascinating out-of-doors occupation.

It has become a habit with me when walking in the woods to keep a sharp lookout for stocks for walking-sticks, so that in the course of many years I have got together quite a unique collection. To these a number have been added through exchanges with friends.

This hobby has borne other fruit than the mere gathering together of curious sticks. For have I not learned the scientific and common names of most of our trees and shrubs, their habits, and their values, their uses in the arts and sciences, their medicinal qualities! So you see, my young reader, what unthinking people would call a useless and eccentric occupation (this gathering of old sticks) has in reality proved to be an innocent and instructive pastime, and I propose to continue to ride this walking-stick hobby just as diligently as I used to ride grandpa's walking-cane to " Banbury Cross " when a child.

My first interesting cane capture consisted of a very curiously shaped natural stick as shown in Fig. 1. It was of a young hickory sapling at whose roots grew a bitter-sweet vine, which, being of an ambitious turn of mind, had taken many turns around the sapling in its eagerness to climb up in the world. The sapling in the mean time extended its bark well over the leader of the tough and clinging bitter-sweet till but little of it was to be seen. At last the sapling, feeling unusually vigorous, burst asunder the clinging bitter-sweet vine, the result being a very unique walking-stick, and a good illustration of the "survival of the fittest."

The dead bitter-sweet vine was withdrawn from the hickory, and from its root a handle was carved and bent. On many occasions I have twisted vines of bitter-sweet and the fox-grape around saplings of oak, hickory, and chestnut, and have obtained very satisfactory results.

Where a vine is situated some distance from the sapling selected for a cane, the vine can be "piped" (laid under the ground) up to the sapling, and then twisted around it and securely fastened at the top with wire, from three to four feet above its root. If the sapling is so situated that it obtains a bountiful supply of food and sunlight, a unique cane of natural growth will be the result.

Having taken a hint from nature in the case of the bitter-sweet vine and the hickory sapling, I extended my experiments in many directions. Taking three cuttings (slips) of basket-willow, I planted them close together as shown in Fig. 2. After they had taken root and begun to push out branches, I reduced the number of branches to one for each cutting, always retaining the most vigorous branch.

As the three willow-trees increased in height the side branches were constantly cut off. This treatment forced the growth of the willows upward, so that when they had attained a height of five feet I bound them together with a living cat-brier vine, which was planted at their base, and in course of time obtained a light walking-stick of novel pattern as shown in Fig. 3. Another very interesting experiment was grafting three willow stocks together so that they formed a union, and became as it were one tree. This was done by carefully cutting away two slices from three young willows so as to form an obtuse angle as shown in Fig. 4.

The angles so formed were carefully and accurately fitted together as shown in the section Fig. 5. To hold the willows closely together, and to exclude all air, I wrapped them tightly with strips of unbleached cotton-sheeting. As soon as they showed signs of life at their tops by sending out young branches, I felt certain that a union of their barks would form at the points indicated by the arrows in Fig. 5. But it was not till several trials had been made that I was successful in this novel experiment of combining three willow saplings.

It very often occurs that after a tree has been cut down a number of canes or suckers will start up from the stump. These suckers make excellent walking-sticks when properly cured and peeled. For a lady's riding-whip I know of nothing better than three willow withes plaited together. This plaiting must be done when the willow withes are young, and when attached to the parent tree, on which they are allowed to remain for a year after having been plaited together. By this time they will have grown firmly together in consequence of the bark conforming to the bent strands of the plait.

The following kinds of native woods are used for walking-sticks:

HOLLY.—Sticks of this wood are found growing out from the sides of older growths, and shooting up in nearly a straight line. Occasionally they may be cut with a crutch-piece across the growing end, or with a crook or knob. These are the most valuable. They may be found on a well-grown sapling in the deep woods. This should be

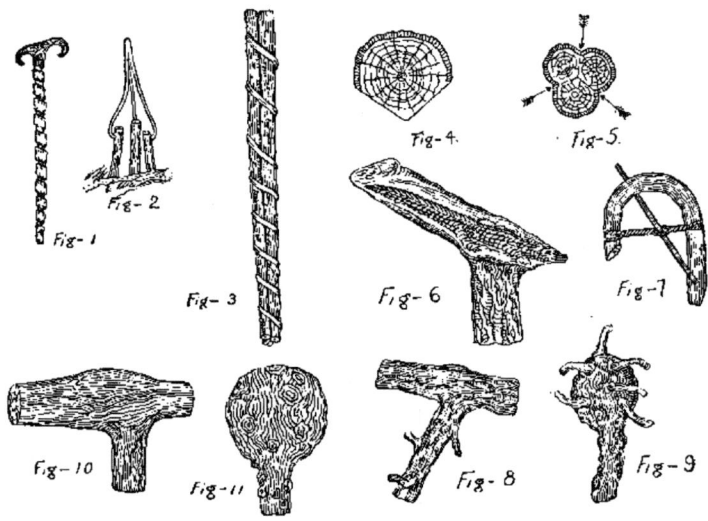

pulled or dug up for the sake of its roots. Saplings and hedge-sticks may often be found from three to four feet long, and from three-eighths to a quarter of an inch in diameter. These are not suitable for walking-sticks, but they make excellent whip-handles. The holly makes tough, supple, and moderately heavy walking-sticks, and its close-grained

370

wood admits of much skill in carving the knob formed by the root and its rootlets.

ASH.—Respectable sticks of this wood may sometimes be cut out of a hedge or pulled from the side of an old stump. Ash sticks must also be roughly trimmed and well seasoned before they are barked and polished. The root knobs admit of excellent grotesque carving.

OAK.—This of all sticks is the most reliable, and stout oaken cudgels are esteemed by most persons as affording the best props for failing legs, as well as the best weapons of self-defence against quarrelsome dogs, ruffians, and tramps. Straight sticks of sapling oak are not always easily obtained, but copse-wood sticks pulled from the trunks of trees form excellent substitutes. These should be selected for walking-sticks that taper from one inch below the knob or crutch to one inch at the ferrule end. Oak sticks split in drying when the bark has been stripped off or the knobs and branches cut too close, or when the sticks are dried too rapidly in a very dry place. They are then rendered useless for walking-sticks and cudgels.

ELM.—From the roots of elm-trees saplings often shoot up to a height of some ten feet; these furnish good walking-sticks of fancy styles, the rough bark serving the purpose of ornamentation when the sticks are dried, stained, varnished, and polished.

Among fruit trees the cherry, apple, and pear furnish some very nice, fancy walking-sticks, being supple and of moderate strength.

When sticks are half dried—that is, when the bark is shrunken, has lost its sappy greenness, and refuses to peel freely—they may be trimmed, straightened, or bent, as required. The wood and also the form of the knobs and roots will admit of much taste being displayed in grotesque and fancy carving.

I know of a young man in Florida, not yet twenty-one years of age, who is paying his way through college by collecting and curing sticks of the wild orange, on the handles of which he carves during his leisure time and vacations full-length figures of alligators as shown in Fig. 6. I have examined several of these sticks, and the entire work seems to be done with small chisels and a parting or V-tool. These sticks are in constant demand with visitors and tourists in Florida, and have become known as "orange-wood 'gator canes." This fact may be suggestive to some of our ingenious farmer boys who are struggling to obtain a college course.

Walking-sticks can be gathered at all seasons. The sticks should be laid aside in a moderately dry and cool place, and should not be worked or the bark taken off till they are half dry. They are then most supple, and may be bent or straightened without injury. When laying by sticks to dry, the knots and spurs should not be trimmed close; it is best to trim them only roughly, leaving the spurs of branches and roots on the stick fully an inch long.

To straighten or bend the sticks, they should be steamed until they are supple, or buried in hot, wet sand until they become soft; they must then, while still hot, be given the form they are intended to keep, and kept in this form until they are cold. Straight sticks are tied firmly together in small bundles, and wound with a coil of rope from end to end; they are then suspended to a beam by their knob ends, and a heavy weight is attached to the ferrule ends. Crooks may be turned by soaking the end in boiling water for half an hour, then bending it to the desired form, and retaining it in its position by means of a tourniquet (as shown in Fig. 7) until the stick is cold.

The bark may then be taken off with a sharp knife, but care must be taken not to split or chip the wood. Knots may be trimmed at the same time, and the root knobs turned into grotesque shapes. There are no rules that can be given to guide one when carving the roots into handles, since their forms are governed by the outlines of the roots, these often being very suggestive of themselves. The group of heads shown in Figs. 8, 9, 10, and 11 will illustrate what I mean. Figs. 8 and 9 show the rough stick, Figs. 10 and 11 the finished heads.

One or two points should receive considerable attention when designing the handles. If the stick is to be a fancy one to be carried and swung in the hand, the roots can be carved into grotesque or fancy forms. But if for use, the handle should be round and smooth, so as to fit comfortably in the hand. The head of a dog, or a swan or goose, forms an appropriate design for a stick that is to be held on the arm when lighting a match, or when wishing to have both hands free. The crutch and hook are also comfortable forms.

Wooden handles are given touches of rich brown by applying a red-hot iron to the parts to be colored.

All sticks with the rough bark left on should be neatly trimmed naked around the neck of the handle, and the whole lightly gone over with fine sand or emery paper. The cane should then receive several dressings of boiled linseed-oil and be left to dry. When dry, a coat of shellac varnish is applied. Oak canes look best when carefully barked in hot water, the loose bark being removed by rubbing with coarse canvas, and the cane then dried, dressed with boiled linseed-oil, again dried, then polished, and varnished with shellac or furniture varnish, and again polished.

Dogwood and Osage orange sticks can be stained black by brushing them over with a hot and strong decoction of logwood and nut gall. When this is thoroughly dried, brush them over with vinegar in which a few rusty nails have been steeped for two or three days. Some persons use ink for a black stain, others introduce "drop black" in the varnish; a brown or mahogany stain may be obtained by adding some "dragon's-blood" to the varnish. The lower ends of the sticks should be guarded from excessive wear by a neat brass ferrule; these are cheaper to purchase at a hardware store than to make, though I have often used brass thimbles and tailors' steel thimbles as a substitute. These can be fastened by means of hot shellac, or with a brass pin driven into a hole in the thimble and passing through the wood of the stick.

For fastening carved or rustic heads or handles on sticks hot glue or thick shellac varnish is used. A good-sized hole is first bored into the handle and a hole of similar size in the stick; a dowel is driven into the hole in the stick (using plenty of glue), after which the handle is driven on to the dowel-pin. Handles may be made of horn, which can be softened for bending by boiling in oil (not kerosene) or hot

374

fat. Hard-woods that will take a polish, and vegetable ivory, which is very easy and pleasant to carve, are good materials to use for handles. For small sticks, bone will be found an easy material to shape into handles.

All the manufacturers of walking-sticks and umbrella and parasol handles state that the demand for native woods suitable for canes and sticks is constant all the year round, and that the sticks may be gathered at all seasons of the year and sent to market, both straight and crooked sticks being salable, also roots for handles.

With this we reach the end of our out-door handy book, which we trust may become the daily and invaluable companion of all healthy, active American boys. The in-door handy book, the book of electricity, and the book of mechanics for boys, which are to follow, will form, we believe, the distinctive American boy's library of practical handy books.

INDEX

377

THE END

CPSIA information can be obtained at www.ICGtesting.com
Printed in the USA
LVOW12s1920290415

436596LV00001B/34/P